CAMBRIDGE LIBRARY COLLECTION

Books of enduring scholarly value

History

The books reissued in this series include accounts of historical events and movements by eye-witnesses and contemporaries, as well as landmark studies that assembled significant source materials or developed new historiographical methods. The series includes work in social, political and military history on a wide range of periods and regions, giving modern scholars ready access to influential publications of the past.

A Monograph on Trade and Manufactures in Northern India

William Hoey (1849–1919) was a magistrate in Lucknow, India when this book was published by the American Missionary Press in 1880. At the time, Lucknow was the seventh largest city in the British Empire, and it was the capital of the province that had most recently come under British rule. Hoey's monograph captures the details of trade in the city and surrounding regions at this time of change. Part 1 outlines the prominent features of trade in the area and includes tables of imports and exports. Part 2 focuses on Lucknow specifically, and contains the author's discussion of the impact of British rule on the city. The third part is a detailed A-Z of every trade, including information on production, prices and profit, and the work concludes with an extensive glossary of Indian terms. The level of detail in this work makes it an invaluable historical document.

Cambridge University Press has long been a pioneer in the reissuing of out-of-print titles from its own backlist, producing digital reprints of books that are still sought after by scholars and students but could not be reprinted economically using traditional technology. The Cambridge Library Collection extends this activity to a wider range of books which are still of importance to researchers and professionals, either for the source material they contain, or as landmarks in the history of their academic discipline.

Drawing from the world-renowned collections in the Cambridge University Library, and guided by the advice of experts in each subject area, Cambridge University Press is using state-of-the-art scanning machines in its own Printing House to capture the content of each book selected for inclusion. The files are processed to give a consistently clear, crisp image, and the books finished to the high quality standard for which the Press is recognised around the world. The latest print-on-demand technology ensures that the books will remain available indefinitely, and that orders for single or multiple copies can quickly be supplied.

The Cambridge Library Collection will bring back to life books of enduring scholarly value (including out-of-copyright works originally issued by other publishers) across a wide range of disciplines in the humanities and social sciences and in science and technology.

A Monograph on Trade and Manufactures in Northern India

William Hoey

CAMBRIDGE UNIVERSITY PRESS

Cambridge, New York, Melbourne, Madrid, Cape Town,
Singapore, São Paolo, Delhi, Tokyo, Mexico City

Published in the United States of America by Cambridge University Press, New York

www.cambridge.org
Information on this title: www.cambridge.org/9781108036603

© in this compilation Cambridge University Press 2011

This edition first published 1880
This digitally printed version 2011

ISBN 978-1-108-03660-3 Paperback

To

MAJOR FENDALL CURRIE,

Deputy Commissioner of Lucknow,

THIS WORK IS INSCRIBED,
AS A MARK OF HIGH ESTEEM FOR HIM
AS A PUBLIC OFFICER AND PERSONAL FRIEND,
BY
The AUTHOR.

A MONOGRAPH

ON

TRADE AND MANUFACTURES

IN

Northern India.

BY

WILLIAM HOEY, C.S.,

OFFICIATING CITY MAGISTRATE, AND ON SPECIAL DUTY AS LICENSE TAX OFFICER
IN THE CITY OF LUCKNOW, IN 1879-80.

LUCKNOW.

PRINTED AND PUBLISHED AT THE AMERICAN METHODIST MISSION PRESS.

1880.

INTRODUCTION.

In December 1878 I was transferred from Unao to Lucknow, and specially deputed to revise the assessments of License Tax in Lucknow City, made under Act II of 1878. I commenced operations in January 1879. I had not been stationed in Lucknow previously, and I knew nothing of the City; so, although I had been engaged for the last three months of 1878 in a camping tour for a similar purpose in the Unao District, I may be said to have been breaking quite new ground when I entered on this special duty; the more so, too, because the features of rural and city trade differ widely. I soon found that the only safe method of assessing a License Tax was to study the trade and manufactures, the arts and dealings, of the people with whom my duty brought me into contact. I therefore adopted a system of local inquiry, personal visitation, and note-taking. I took up sample cases of all trades, dealings, and manufactures, noted the processes of manufacture, principles of dealing, and trade-practices, and endeavoured to form an approximate notion of the probable profits of each business. These notes will be found thrown into a cyclopœdic form in Part III of this book.

I had originally intended to send up these notes to the Local Government in the form of a Report, but I thought at the same time that there might be other officers in a position where my notes would be of assistance to them in the assessment of License Tax, and that there is matter in the notes of interest to commercial men and others outside official circles; I, therefore, but still with much diffidence, determined to publish these notes in the present form.

Lucknow is the seventh largest city in the British Empire. Its population, estimated in the Census of 1870 at 273,126, probably passes 300,000, and its area is not much less than 30 square miles. It is the capital of the province most recently added to British India. It is still in a transition state, bearing the memories of a past rule, and feeling the pressure of a new regime; late a close preserve in economic isolation, and suddenly opened to the shock of free trade. It is a densely populated city, in which meet the extremes of struggling poverty and wasted wealth; where all English manufactures that can push Indian out of the market are forcing their way, and where new industries are raising their heads ; while all productive arts and trades that are beyond the influence of European competition are to be seen in a more or less flourishing state. It is therefore a focus of intense interest to the student of social and economic problems : and, for this reason, I have given a review of the trade of Lucknow City in Part II.

The first part of this book is an attempt to shew the prominent features of the trade of Northern India. I have avoided all detail, wishing only to shew in broad relief the interdependence of the North-West Provinces, Panjab, and Oudh—economically one though territorially divided fields—with the foreign territories round them on the north, west, and south, and with Bengal on the east. This subject is invested with special interest, because no part of India can compare with the Upper Provinces in the number of the extern territories and the variety of the races with which they trade; and political relations are bringing us year by year into closer contact with the countries beyond the north and west of India.

I have nothing more to add, but to beg that the reader will, in perusing the following pages, remember that this book has arisen out of notes made for official purposes, and has been written under the pressure of very heavy duties.

LUCKNOW :
27th August, 1880.   }   W. HOEY.

Corrigenda.

Page 25 line 9 from the bottom, for *which were* read *which had been.*
„ 26 „ 4 „ top „ *secuuity.* „ *security.*
„ 29 „ 26 „ „ „ *report* „ *work.*
„ 30 „ 16 „ „ „ *miles via* „ *miles : viá.*
„ 47 „ 14 „ bottom, „ *from their* „ *from this.*
„ 53 „ 17 „ top dele *oculist and*
„ 53 „ 31 „ „ for *oculist* „ *optician.*
„ 53 „ 38 „ „ „ *neutal* „ *neutral.*
„ 55 „ 12 „ „ „ *Part II* „ *Part III.*
„ 56 „ 17 „ „ „ *sán glass* „ *sán. Glass.*
„ 58 „ 5 „ „ „ *addah gar* „ *addah gári.*
„ 58 „ 42 „ „ „ *Rs. 9-12-8* „ *Rs. 912-8-0.*
„ 60 „ 2 „ „ „ *they rent* „ *they pay rent.*
„ 62 „ 14 „ bottom, „ *eqxceed* „ *exceed.*
„ 64 „ 8 „ „ „ *for same* „ *for the same*
„ 64 „ 5 „ „ „ *tákhu* „ *sákhu,*
„ 66 „ 26 „ top „ *axsis* „ *axis.*
„ 68 „ 32 „ „ „ *class* „ *classes*
„ 69 „ 19 „ „ „ *ryrup* „ *syrup.*
„ 70 „ 29 „ „ „ *retai* „ *retail.*
„ 75 „ 20 „ „ „ *chik 10 yards* „ *chik 2 yards.*
„ 82 „ 8 „ „ „ *chapekhána* „ *chhápekhána.*
„ 88 „ 19 „ „ „ *hútas* „ *bútas.*
„ 90 „ 18 „ „ „ *bakarmandi* „ *Bakarmandi.*
„ 92 „ 16 „ „ „ *58-0-0* „ *48-0-0.*
„ 101 „ 6, 9, 13 & 18 „ „ *gudar* „ *gudarfarosh.*
„ 110 „ 30 „ „ „ *done by placing* „ *by overlaying the silver with it before placing.*
„ 133 „ 20 „ „ „ *Khogirhoz* „ *Khogirdoz.*
„ 133 last line „ *pansori* „ *Pansári.*
„ 151 line 33 „ „ „ *diamond pencil* „ *diamond or a pencil.*
„ 169 „ 38 „ „ „ *nila sumair* „ *nila surmai.*
„ 179 „ 26 „ „ „ *shirfraosh* „ *shirfarosh.*
„ 182 „ 24 „ „ „ *laui* „ *lauki.*

PART I.

THE TRADE OF NORTHERN INDIA WITH OTHER STATES AND PROVINCES.

THE term 'Northern India' is an expression adopted, in Act II, 1878, by the Legislative Council of India, to denote 'the Upper Provinces,' as they were styled some twenty years ago—*i e.*, the North-West Provinces, the Punjab, and Oudh: and, accepting the term merely for the convenience of designation, and not for any propriety which it possesses, the following note will be devoted to a rapid sketch of the trade of the country denoted.

There is no need to describe in detail the physical features of Northern India. A line drawn north and south in continuation of the Doab Canal between Delhi and Saharanpur divides the country into two large tracts. To the north-west of this line lies the Punjab proper, sloping to the south and drained by the Indus and its five tributary rivers, the Jhilam, Chinab, Ravi, Beas, and Satlaj, which give it its name. To the east and south-east lie the hill provinces of Kumaon and Gurhwál, the provinces of Delhi and Allahabad, the quondam kingdom of Oudh, and the eastern districts of the N.-W. Provinces; all sloping to the south-east and drained by the Ganges and five tributary rivers, the Rapti and the Ghágra, the Sai and the Gumti on the north, and the Jamna on the south of the Ganges. The joint area of these two vast tracts is 192,600 square miles, or nearly one-seventh of the whole area of India; and the population is approximately 53,600,000.

Thirty years ago the Panjab had been but recently annexed to British territory, and was practically little known to our countrymen. Oudh was still a nominally independent kingdom—an ally of the East India Company. The North-West Provinces, including the old Subah of Delhi, were under British rule. Seven years later came the Mutiny, which convulsed these provinces and threatened the extinction of English rule in Northern India. It found the seat of war without a railroad and almost without telegraphic communication. There was a line of rail from Calcutta to Ráníganj, and one from Bombay to Tannah; but these were out of the territorial limits of the *war* of 1857, and of little use in transport. Troops moved slowly up the Ganges by boat and along the Grand Trunk Road and its feeding lines, but were retarded by the delay in transport of ammunition and baggage. Every facility for the movement of troops and supplies was wanting. This picture of the helplessness of our military situation of 1857 is, *mutatis mutandis*, a fair picture of the backward state of commercial intercourse. The communications between Upper India and Calcutta and Bombay were tedious and dangerous, both by road and river. Bombay was almost unknown to residents of Northern India, and Calcutta was still dimly known as the capital of 'The Company,' for as yet natives in the mufassil had not realized that that greatest anomaly in Government which the world has seen, had ceased to be, and had given place to Government by the Crown. The province of Oudh was practially closed to the trading enterprise of foreigners, and communications between the Panjab and Delhi were as they had been when the former State was an independent kingdom.

The Mutiny of 1857 is the turning point in the history of commercial progress in Northern India. That grave commotion revealed to the Government of India its inherent weakness. When an infinitesimal number of Europeans is expected to control an infinitely greater number of foreigners not in any way attached to the rule of the minority, it is absolutely necessary that the small force of Europeans should be practically omnipresent, which means, in the case of India, where there is a multifariousness of interest and of religion and nationality in the subject race, tending to prevent combination, that the European force should be able to communicate freely, and combine and present itself in strength at any notice in the shortest possible time. This was felt when the Mutiny broke out; and when that convulsion subsided, there followed a movement of railway construction and road improvement. There is now unbroken communication between Calcutta (through Patna, Banáras, Allahabad, Agra, Delhi, Mírath, Saharanpur, Amballa, Ludhiana, and Lahaur) and a point fifteen miles beyond Jhilam, within some one hundred miles of Peshawar and the Khaibar Pass, the gate of India. A line runs from Karáchí, the extreme west point of British India, a place absolutely unknown to traders in Northern India in 1857, up to Lahore : and on its way sends out a branch across the frontier pushing into the Khelát territory. Delhi, Agra, and Allahabad communicate with Baroda and Bombay by railways which open up the states of Rajputana and Central India : while Oudh, which was ten years ago virgin to the track of the steam engine, is now cut across with a line from Cawnpore to Banáras and is further cut by a loop line from Lucknow to Alígarh on the great East Indian line.

Thus has railway communication extended since the eventful days of 1857, and, though probably this is much owing to military motives, the results have been of infinite benefit to the commerce of Northern and, in fact, of all India. The cotton of Rajputana and Bundelkhand and Rewah now passes easily into Lower Bengal and to the port of Calcutta, and a brisk trade in oilseeds, dyes hides, and skins, is done between India and the great port. A much greater instance of the benefit which extended railway communication has conferred on India in general, and not merely on the northern portion, is to be found in the events of the last ten years in the facility afforded for the transport of grain from Northern India to Lower Bengal and to Madras and Bombay in the years of famine. One item alone shows the importance of railway transport in times of famine. Between October 1st 1878 and February 1st 1879 there were exported from Cawnpore station alone to the Bombay side not less than 4,90,000 maunds of juár and bájrá. Too much importance cannot be attached to the effect which the late famine in Madras has had on the minds of the traders of Northern India. They have learned to look to foreign markets and to hold correspondence with traders in other trade-centres :and for this purpose they avail themselves of telegraphic communication. This expansion of the commercial horizon is a precursor of higher trading views.

The establishment of railway communication has had an appreciable effect on river traffic. A specific instance of this will be found in Part II, when the trade of Lucknow is examined in detail. The only extensive river-borne traffic now remaining in Northern India is on the Indus, by which export is made from the Panjab to Karáchi, and on the Ghágra and Ganges, by which goods pass into Bengal, and through Patna, down to Calcutta, from places where conveyance by rail is not convenient.

The chief mart on the Ghágra is Nawabganj. It is the great central trade depôt of the north-east of Oudh, as Lucknow is of the north-west, and the chief articles of commerce are grain, hides, and oilseeds. It is north of the river and is not connected with Faizábád (on the O. & R. Railway line) by permanent bridge or steam ferry, the only means which would serve to draw traffic into Faizabad to the O. & R. Railway Company's line. There is also a break in railway communication at the Ganges at Banáras. Hence the force of situation makes the river Ghágra the route of export to and exchange with Lower Bengal. The chief place to which consignments are made by the Ghágra route is Patna, which lies on the Ganges at a point some distance lower than the confluence of the two rivers.

The following chief items of import and export by the river Ghágra to Bengal will show how great the traffic on this river must be and, if it be economically worth while to take it up by rail, some one may be found to push the enterprise :—

	1877-78.		1878-79.	
	IMPORTS.	EXPORTS.	IMPORTS.	EXPORTS.
Cotten, raw, ...	...	2,918	140	971
Cotten manufactures, ...	...	515	...	30
Drugs, ...	...	1,140	60	952
Dyes, ...	...	796	356	136
Fibrous products, ...	..	125	20	40
Fruits and nuts, ...	520	2,383	3,022	72
Wheat, ...	11,384	4,46,379	2,544	1,20,464
Gram and pulse, ...	21,990	441,349	4,588	34,097
Other Spring crops, ...	94,246	1,41,563	19,576	17,448
Rice, husked, ...	48,245	17,658	29,902	9,854
Do. unhusked, ...	20,893	15,225	31,413	1,751
Other grain crops,... ...	86,095	27,241	10,452	4,780
Hides, skins and horns, ...	400	44,884	...	21,231
Metals, ...	1,010	123	5,195	1,180
Ghi, ...	...	12,322	...	8,562
Other provisions, ...	993	...	135	...
Salt, ...	75,735	175	62,746	...
Saltpetre & other saline substances,	7,285	8,074	7,432	5,182
Linseed, ...	561	14,52,874	3,028	11,67,952
Mustard and Rye, ...	2,825	8,06,498	36	592,103
Til, ...	...	6,069	...	25,495
Other oil seeds, ...	200	1,88,241	...	2,77,675
Spices, ...	94	1,692	145	606
Sugar, refined, ...	950	3,24,614	549	95,913
Do. unrefined, ...	70	3,07,025	...	1,45,987
Tobacco, ...	1,095	...	38,311	16
Timber, ...	...	900	...	4,985
Firewood, ...	...	20,257	...	26,990
Wool and woollen goods, ...	...	...	...	2,906

THE foregoing table gives a summary view of the traffic on the Ghágra for two years. The districts trading by this route are Gorakhpur and Basti in the North-Western Provinces, Gondah and Bahraich in Oudh, and also the kingdom of Naipal through these districts. Considering the great importance of Naipal as an exporter to India of drugs, dyes, fibres, grain, spices, oil-seeds, and timber and firewood, and an importer from India of cotton and cotton manufactures, sugar and tea, the construction of a light railway from a point on the base of the Tarai, on the road into Naipalganj, through Bahraich and Gondah, to Nawabganj seems an enterprise worthy to be entertained. The line might be continued through Basti and Gorakhpur districts to Patna, or a steam ferry be established between Nawabganj and Faizabad. The latter would be more advisable if the bridge were built at Banáras to join railway communication over the Ganges. There is little doubt that this project would, if carried out, open Naipal to India and the resulting advantages would be mutual.

The Ganges and its canal must always remain a commercial route : and so probably must the Indus. The latter river presents a feature which it enjoys in common with the Ganges. It leads to a great seaport, Karáchi, as the Ganges does to Calcutta : but while the Ganges and Ghágra are availed of for return traffic, the Indus is not so used to the same extent. It seems that the current of the great river of the Punjab is so much against the return of heavily laden vessels, and the facility of communication by rail with Calcutta for the import of foreign goods so great, as to render the latter route preferable to the former for import, while the Indus remains the chief channel of export.

The trade of Northern India is with three classes of territory. The first is foreign countries. These are, going from extreme south-west to north-east, Sewestan, Kabul, Tirah, Bajaur, Kashmir, Ladakh, Chinese Tibet, Little Tibet (lying to the north of the British hillstates of Kumaun and Garhwal) and Naipal, which runs along the north of Oudh and the districts of Gorakhpur and Basti. Next come the independent or tributary states within India. These are, beginning again in the west, Baháwalpur, and the many states of Rajputana and Central India, between Baháwalpur on the west and Bundelkhund and Rewa on the east. The third class of territory is under British rule, the Central Provinces, the Presidency of Bombay, and the Bengal Presidency, including Behar. All trade with foreign territory other than the countries enumerated is through the ports of Bombay, Calcutta, and Karáchi.

The Governments of the Panjab, and the North-West Provinces and Oudh, have adopted an elaborate system for the registration of traffic between the territories administered by them and all external territories. Thus it may be said that there is a cordon of registering posts drawn round the whole frontier of Northern India. There is also a line of similar posts along the boundary which divides the Punjab from the North-West Provinces. The officers in charge of these registering posts submit periodical traffic returns and from them these governments compile annual reports of the trade between Punjab and other states and provinces around it, and between the North-West Provinces and Oudh and states and provinces around them. To obtain a concise view of the present state of trade, I have taken the reports of the two governments for the year 1877-78, and have compiled from the statistics therein given a compressed schedule of net imports to and net exports from Northern India during 1877-78. As it is especially my desire to show how far each of the territories included in the schedule is dependent on Northern India and *vice versa*, I have in every case inserted only the net amount of import or export as the case may be. Interchange of equal amounts of any given commodity is purely an accident of territorial contact and may be disregarded. Thus, looking at the column of imports under the head of Ladakh it will be found that Ladakh sends into Northern India horses, ponies, and mules, sheep and goats, borax, intoxicating drugs other than opium, charas, fruits, nuts, salt, other saline substances, raw silk, raw wool and manufactured woollen goods. In return she takes from India a trifle of raw cotton, Indian twist and yarn, European and Indian piece goods, drugs not intoxicating, dyeing materials, indigo, manjit, safflower, a small amount of fibrous products, some grain, gums, skins, metals, oils, provisions, spices, sugar, tea and tobacco. A similar reference will show the interdependence of all foreign states and of other Provinces of British India with Northern India. With reference to the column headed Sindh it is to be observed that this consists for the most part of traffic on the river Indus, and that this is chiefly export traffic to the port of Karachi by a steam flotilla and country boats. The column which deals with the Great India Peninsula Railway and Port and Presidency of Bombay shows, as far as possible to determine, all the net imports and exports between the provinces of Northern India and the Bombay Presidency and all countries trading with India through the port of Bombay. As regards the heading 'Behar, Bengal and port of Calcutta,' there has been considerable difficulty in comparing and assimilating the statistics of the Panjab government and those of the North-Western Provinces, and Oudh; but an effort has been made to arrive at a combined total. This column on the export side includes all net exports from Oudh and the North-Western Provinces to Behar and Bengal and to the port of Calcutta, by road, by rail, and by the rivers Ghágra and Ganges. Similarly the column of import includes all net imports to North-West Provinces and Oudh from Behar, Bengal and Calcutta. To each of these columns have been added the figures for the Panjab. The trade between the Panjab and Behar, Bengal, and Calcutta, has been estimated in the following way. The traffic registered by the North-Western Provinces Government as passing into the Panjab consists only of goods which have been produced within the the North-Western Provinces or which have been already registered as imports in the North-Western Provinces. The Panjab Government includes under import from the North-Western Provinces, all goods imported from the North-West frontier, irrespective of place from which or to which consigned. All goods imported into the Panjab from Bengal, Behar and Calcutta must pass through the North-Western Provinces. The exports shown in the North-Western Provinces returns as made to the Panjab have therefore been deducted from what the Panjab Returns show as imported and the excess has been taken as import from places further east than the North-West and Oudh and have been added into the column 17. A similar calculation has been made as to exports. There is no doubt that a total approximately correct has thus been arrived at.

The columns Nos. 18 headed 'Total of net imports' and 'Total of net exports' show the totals of the net amounts imported into and exported from Northern India, but these columns would give no key to the several amounts of imports re-exported and consumed locally, or to the amounts of exports which are merely held in transit or which are produced locally in Northern India. I have therefore added another column (19) which shows in the Table of Imports the amount under each head of imported goods which is locally absorbed in Northern India and shows in the Table of Exports the amount out of the total exports which was under each head produced locally. The advantages of this are obvious. Take wheat and other grains. It will be seen that Northern India exports wheat, gram and pulse, and other spring crops, while it imports largely rice and other rain crops, but it does not exclusively import or exclusively export any of these. It draws on other territories to supplement its own locally-produced supplies: and, as a rule the import of rain crops is needed to supplement the local supply for local consumption and the import of spring crops goes to augment the local stock remaining after excessive export of a bonâ fide surplus spring crop. Grain near the frontier and readiest for export may be treated as being pushed on and part of it replaced by imports from the countries beyond the frontiers farthest from the ports. The following table will show this.

		Net weight exported.	Exported but replaced by import.	Total. exported.
Wheat,	...	55,65,874	7,30,660	62,96,534
Gram and pulse,	...	24,48,928	4,55,054	29,03,982
Other Spring crops,	...	7,50,801	91,509	8,42,310
		Net weight imported.	Exported but replaced by import.	Total Imported.
Rice,	...	22,80,353	1,48,621	24,26,974
Other rain crops,	...	13,68,248	4,04,063	17,72,311

This is the net result in the case of rabi crops of two factors, excess local production and foreign demand, and similarly in the case of kharif crops of deficient local production and demand for a foreign supply.

The most prominent articles of net export from Northern India are raw cotton, Indian piece-goods, indigo, spring crops (already noted), hides, skins and horns, dye lac, shellac, ghi, saltpere, oilseeds, other seeds, sugar (refined and unrefined), Indian tea, tobacco, and wool (raw and manufactured).

The year 1877-78 was a year exceptionally poor in cotton-production. The Panjab suffered severely by this, the outturn of cultivation being in that year about $\frac{1}{3}$ of the average: and for this an allowance of at least 50,000 maunds may be safely made in the column of total of net exports. Indian cotton piece-goods are in excess and become an article of export because of the abundance of the raw material in parts of Northern India, chiefly in the Panjab, and the special demand created by Kabul and by places drawing supplies from the Panjab through Sindh.

Indigo is chiefly produced in the N.-W. Provinces and is exported to Lower Bengal. The seed of the plant is also largely exported because it has been found that better plants are grown in Bengal from seed raised in Upper India than elsewhere. Indeed it is in a great measure owing to this that the indigo plantations in the North-West can hold their own.

Hides, skins, and horns are almost entirely an article of export and go in great part to Europe from the port of Calcutta. It may seem strange that although Northern India adds these animal products to its articles of commerce, it makes no effort to utilize the bones of animals for purposes of manure. Yet it is so. Some years ago a Company was formed in Calcutta for the manufacture of bone manure, but the undertaking failed. It seems that the place for manufacture was not well chosen. It was too remote from the field where the materials for manufacture are most abundant and the cost of carriage to Calcutta adds too much to the cost of production of the artificial manure to enable the producer at Calcutta to place it in the market at a price within the power of the cultivator to pay. A bone-manufactory would have a better chance of success at Cawnpore or Lucknow than at Calcutta.

Lac shows a net export of dye-lac (2,274 maunds) and shell-lac (40,159 maunds) but also shows a corresponding import of 82,073 maunds, stick lac and other kinds, derived from Bundelkhand, Rewah, and Bengal. This is explained by the existence in the North-West Provinces of the great centre of lac manufacture, the town or city of Mirzapur. This is an old seat of this manufacture which needs no description here.

Oilseeds are a staple article of export from Northern India : but the richest soil for their production is that drained by the river Ghágrá. A reference to pages 3 and 4 will show that the Ghágra carried to Bengal 24,43,682 maunds of the whole exports, 42,65,042 maunds, under this head. The following table shows the contributions and direction of export of all oilseeds.

	CONTRIBUTED.			EXPORTED.			
	By Northern India.	By other territories.	Total.	Towards Calcutta.	Towards Bombay.	Elsewhere.	Total.
Linseed	17,55,240	1,44,966	19,00,206	17,98,097	1,02,099	10	19,00,206
Mustard & Rape,	16,01,866	64,316	16,66,182	12,82,219	3,83,470	493	16,66,182
Til,	3,59,499	49,399	4,08,898	1,61,559	1,99,474	47,865	4,08,898
Other oil seeds,	2,62,646	27,130	2,89,776	2,66,165	9,336	14,275	2,89,776
	39,79,251	2,85,791	42,65,042	35,08,040	6,94,379	62,643	42,65,042

Sugar is necessarily an article of net export under both heads, because Northern India numbers sugar-cane among its staple crops, and because the unrefined product is refined within its limits by Europeans and by many native manufacturers. The cane-juice is boiled, and the water evaporated. The residue which dries in a hard lump is *gur*. This is sometimes crystallized by the aid of carbonate of soda and lime, and becomes *shakkar*. If the boiled cane-juice be not completely evaporated, it is called *ráb*, and this is subjected to pressure. The uncrystallisable molasses which exude are drained into a vat, and called *shira*. This is used to distil spirits and to prepare tobacco for smoking. The *ráb*, from which *shira* is squeezed out, is covered up in baskets and covered with a weed called *siwár*, and damped. A further deposit of *shira* falls through at the bottom, and a cake of sugar, in the form called *chini* or *khand*, forms on the surface. *Khand* is further refined by boiling with milk and water, and straining into an earthen pot. Inside this pot are placed strings or thin slips of bambu* on which the sugar crystallises. This is called *misri*. What remains in the earthen vessel is reboiled, and yields a coarse stuff called *bhura*, from its brown colour. This is also a form of sugar.

Other articles of net export may be passed without further note except tobacco and raw wool. The former is chiefly remarkable for the largeness of the amount exported to Rajputana and the Central Provinces, but the total of net exports is small, owing to the high figure of imports from Bengal, 52,768 maunds. The chief point to be noted regarding wool is that it goes chiefly down the Indus and its tributaries to Sindh. This is natural, as the supply is drawn from the territories north and west of the Panjab.

By far the most prominent articles of net import into Northern India are metals, European piece goods, drugs and medicines, dyeing materials, fibres and fibrous products, grain of the kharíf harvest (already commented on), stick lac (already explained), salt, spices, foreign tea, and wood.

Northern India is almost quite barren of metals. Brass and copper are imported for the most part from Calcutta and Bajaur. Naipal and Bundelkhand contribute a trifle. The rest comes into the Panjab through Sindh. Northern India absorbs over 77 per cent, almost the whole of the imports. Iron shows a net import of 7,09,856 maunds. Railway materials are excluded. More than half of this comes from the port of Calcutta, not quite one-fourth from the western port through Sindh, and Bundelkhand supplies over one-fifth of the total imports. The Central Provinces, Rajputana, Naipal, Sewestan and Bajaur make up the rest by small contributions. About 10,000 maunds of the total imports are re-exported to Kashmir, Kabul and

---

* This has given rise to a Hindi proverb current in Oudh.

Sangat hí gun ho,it, sangat hí gun já,e,
Báns pháus misrí, ekí bháo biká,e

literally 'worth comes by association and by association worth departs : the bambu enclosed in sugar is sold at the same price with it.' The sugar crystallized on little bambu frames, in shape like a basket, called *kújá* (properly Persian, *kúsá*) is familiar to recipients of *dális*. The sugar and bambu are of course sold together.

Rewah. Other exports are trifling. Other metals come almost exclusively from the seaports. It is not a little remarkable that the whole 1,48,511 maunds of iron imported from Bundelkhand come into Northern India by road, and yet Bundelkhand has practically closed all other iron fields round Northern India. This would hardly be so but for the proximity of a line of rail. Forty years ago Naipal was the field from which Oudh drew all its brass and copper, and also much iron. But now that kingdom shows exports of only 411 maunds of brass and copper, and 1,376 maunds of iron. It is true that there are not any very good routes of communication through the hills of Naipal so as to facilitate export of metals to Northern India ; but this alone does not account for the smallness of the import of iron from a field as rich in metal as Naipal is reputed to be. The net import of metal from Naipal in 1878 and 1879 was under 500 maunds. Comparing this with the net import of 1,787 maunds in 1877-78, it may perhaps be concluded that the import is declining, and yet the net demand of Oudh alone for brass, copper, and iron from Indian fields of production is over 18,000 maunds per annum.

Tea naturally shows a net import under the head of foreign tea and a net export under the head of Indian tea. The export of the latter is chiefly to Calcutta, from which port also almost the whole supply of foreign tea is imported. The consumption of foreign tea within Northern India figures at 7,104 maunds out of the total 16,470 import. Of the balance which was in transit, 8,894 maunds went on to Kabul. The demand made for China tea by our Afghan neighbours is steady, and it is a noteworthy fact that they prefer it to Indian tea.

Wood shows a net import of 799,843 maunds under the heading timber, exclusive of logs imported into the Panjab from Kashmir and other foreign territory on the north and west by river; and 3,41,632 maunds under the heading firewood. Timber is contributed largely by Kashmir, Bajaur, Sewestán, Bundelkhand and Bengal, but Naipal shows the enormous figure of 519,232 maunds. The timber in transit was only 13,230 maunds. This went into Rajputana. The amount of firewood absorbed locally was 3,41,633 maunds, 29,538 maunds went into Bengal, Oudh sending 20,257 maunds by the river Ghágra, but this came originally chiefly from Naipal. The Panjab derives its firewood from Kashmir, Bajaur, Kabul, Tirah and Sewestan. The North-West Provinces draw on Rajputana, Bundelkhand and Rewah.

The total import of salt into Northern India was, in 1877-78, 15,02,660 maunds. Of this total 12,01,377 maunds were consumed locally, and the rest was in transit, chiefly to Kashmir, Bajaur, Kabul, Naipál and Rewah. Foreign salt comes chiefly from the salt marshes of Rajputana at Sambhar, Dindwara and Pachbadra. That produced within the boundaries of Northern India is either the rock salt, known in bazars as Lahaurí, coming from the salt mines at Pind Dádan Khán and elsewhere, or the outturn of salt pans in the Panjab at places lying within the districts of Rohtak and Gurgaon. It is to be regretted that it is impossible to determine separately the proportion of each class exported and imported, and locally consumed or held in transit.

The remaining chief heads of net import are drugs and medicines, dyeing materials and spices.* By far the most important contributor under this head is Naipal. Kashmir approaches it in a few items, and Kabul passes it in *manjít*: but in spices Naipal leaves them far behind. It is also very prominent as an exporter to Northern India of fibres, grains, gúms and resins, hides, oilseeds, timber and firewood. By far the largest portion of the trade between Naipal and the plains is done through the Bahraich district in Oudh (the great mart being at Nánpára) and Naipalganj in the Nepalese territory. The next largest share is enjoyed by the districts of Gondah and Bastí. Gorakhpúr receives Tarai produce very largely.

The trade between Northern India and Little Tibet is done through the British Hill Districts of Kumaon and Garhwal, and the traders are almost exclusively Bhotias, who come and go between marts in either territory. The British marts are Barmdeo, Bagesar, Pilibhít, Ramnagar and Almorah, and those on the other side of the frontier are Taklakot, Tara, Missar, Gartok, Milam and Isaparang; but the fact is we know comparatively nothing about the natural resources of the country with which we trade beyond Kumaon and Garhwal.

The trade of Kashmir and of Ladakh overlap each other somewhat, if I may use the expression, and goods going to or from one country are sometimes shown as going to or from the other. This is owing to the choice of route by traders. All trade with Yárkand also passes through these countries, and is included in the columns bearing their names. The import of silk from Kashmir has been increasing of late years, and the import of shawls decreasing. The latter fact is owing to the establishment of shawl-weaving by Kashmiri settlers in various Indian cities. Silk and charas are the most important imports from Yarkand, and wool from Ladakh.

Trade with Kabul cannot, perhaps, be very accurately gauged at present, but so much is known that the import to Northern India of drugs (notably charas and asafœtida,) dyes, fruits and nuts, ghí, spices, tobacco, wool and pashm is increasing; metal and silk are stationary; and the export of piece goods, indigo, and tea are increasing. Much tea passes on from Kabul to Bukhára. Bajaur, Tirah, and Sewestan are remarkable chiefly for their contributions of timber and firewood and fibrous products. Bajaur is a very large exporter under the last head, and Sewestan sends much wool into British territory. Sewestan is the territory west of the Dehraját. Bajaur is the hilly country west of Hazara and north of Peshawar. Tirah is the Afridi country, southwest of Peshawar and north-west of Kohát. They all draw on Northern India for manufactured cotton, salt and sugar; but the insecurity of transport,

---

* A note on drugs imported from Naipal will be found at page 21,

owing to the mountain robbers who demand a black mail, 'badraga,' is a serious drawback to free commercial interchange.

The foregoing notes will, it is hoped, if combined with a study of the following tables, give a general idea of the interdependence of Northern India and the surrounding circle of foreign and tributary states and British provinces. A detailed review of articles of commerce has been avoided, as it would have swelled these pages beyond the limits of a brief note on general trade, which was their original scope, and the subject therefore reserved. To visit a few shops in any bazar, a parchúnwálá's, a pansárí's, an attár's, a gandhi's, a rangrez's, a bazzáz's, and a few others, take an inventory of all articles found for sale, and with a note on each, giving a description of each article, its place of production, mode of preparation and uses, would give any one an intensely interesting insight into native trade and life. The notes on trades and manufactures in Part III are an attempt to explain processes of manufacture and trade practises : but a review of products is subject which yet remains. A list of over three hundred drugs lies before me, and many might be added. Dyes have attracted the attention of many, but enquiry still elicits some new facts, and dyeing materials and dyeing processes will always repay inquiry. Spices in use in the East are little known to Europeans beyond the 'masála' brought to their bungalows by khánsámás, and food grains and vegetable products used for food are reckoned by the crops ordinarily cultivated and sold in ganjes, yet it is surprising how many wild products are at all times used as food-staples by the poor, and are resorted to by a large section of the population in years of drought and high prices. This subject, however, is one as yet, I believe, wholly untouched.

TABLE OF IMPORTS.

NET IMPORTS into Northern India from

(Animals are given in numbers

DESCRIPTIONS.	Kashmir.	Ladakh.	Chinese Tibet.	Bajaur.	Kabul.	Tirah.
	1	2	3	4	5	6
Animals, living 1. Horses, Ponies and Mules,	—	360	1	—	1,018	5
2. Cattle,	322	—		229	69	47
3. Sheep and Goats,	12,810	1,934	72	2,820	583	534
4. Other Kinds,	3,795				77	124
Borax,	—	2,051	3,121	—	...	...
Canes, Rattans, and Bamboos,	...	—	—	—	...	3,255
Cotton, raw,	7,456	—	—	—	...	...
Cotton, manufactured, 1. Twist and Yarn (European,)	—	—	—	—	...	...
2. „ „ (Indian,)	—	—	—	—	...	...
3. Piece Goods (European,)	—	—	—	—	...	...
4. „ „ (Indian,)	—	—	—	—	...	...
Drugs and Medicines, 1. Asafœtida,	—	—	—	—	2,473	...
2. Other sorts not intoxicating,	13,547				5,742	304
3. Pan or Betel Leaves,	—	—	—	—	...	...
4. Intoxicating drugs other than Opium,	—	2	—	—	...	35
a. Ganja,	—	—	—	—	...	...
b. Bhang,	24	—	—	—	...	...
c. Charas,	90	707	69	—	2,180	...
Dyeing Materials, 1. Indigo,	—	—	—	—	...	...
2. Maddar or Manjit,	—	—	—	—	80,136	...
3. Safflower,	43	—	—	—	337	...
4. Turmeric,	—	—	—	—	...	...
5. Al,	—	—	—	—	...	...
6. Other Kinds,	7,142	—	—	1,211	...	135
Fibrous Products, 1. Fibres, raw,	1,534	—	—	18,034	7,316	4,757
2. „ manufactured,	1,940			12,037	9,699	1,605
Fruits, Vegetables, & Nuts, 1. Cocoanuts,	—	—	—	—	...	...
2. Betel Nuts,	—	—	—	—	...	...
3. Potatoes,	—	—	—	—	...	...
4. All other kinds,	6,967	20	—	611	94,946	384
Grains, 1. Wheat,				8,463	...	...
2. Gram and Pulse,				1,415	58	130
3. Other Spring Crops,				—	...	153
4. Rice Husked,	}4094	—	—	4,257	...	
5. „ Unhusked,					...	
6. Other Rain Crops,					...	
Gums and Resins,	36	—	—	—	40	...
Hides and Skins, 1. Hides of Cattle,	204	—	—	59	...	...
2. Skins of Sheep and small animals,	745				...	...
Horns,					...	...
Lac, 1. Dye,	—	—	—	—	...	...
2. Shell,	—	—	—	—	...	...
3. Stick and other kinds,	116	—	—	151	...	...
Metals and Manufactures of Metals, 1. Brass and Copper,	—	—	—	225	...	...
2. Iron,	—	—	—	1,404	...	...
3. Other Metals,	—	—	—		...	...
Oils,	17	—	—	4,024	...	119
Provision, 1. Ghee,	36,786	—	—	8,641	6,983	400
2. Other kinds,	—	—	—	—	...	...
Salt,	—	163	2,661	—	...	...
Saltpetre, 1. Saltpetre,	4	—	—	—	...	...
2. Other saline substances,	—	84	—	—	...	...
Seeds, 1. Oil Seeds — a. Linseed,	12	—	—	—	...	...
b. Mustard and Rape,	20,819	—	—	790	...	...
c. Til or Jingelly,	400	—	—	257	...	136
d. Other Oil Seeds,	596	—	—	7	...	35
2. Other Seeds — a. Indigo Seeds,	36	—	—	—	...	...
b. Other kinds,	2,272	—	—	—	21	...
Silk, 1. Raw,	988	42	—	—	4,107	...
2. Manufactured,	—	—	—	—	134	...
Spices,	—	—	—	—	1,116	...
Stone and Marble,	4,360	—		—	85	...
Sugar, 1. Refined above 7 Rs. per maund,	—	—	—	—	...	...
2. Unrefined below 7 Rs. per maund,	—	—	—	—	...	...
Tea, 1. Indian,	—	—	—	—	...	...
2. Foreign,	—	—	—	—	...	...
Tobacco,	—	—	—	—	8,299	...
Wood, 1. Timber,	69,416	—	—	22,370	...	5,689
2. Firewood,	38,787	—	—	44,013	13,180	88,231
Wool, 1. Raw,	1,054	1,502	7,605	1,008	11,199	262
2. Manufactured Wool and Piece Goods,	2,220	84	—	41	928	...

other States and Provinces, during 1877-78.

all other items in weight)

Sewestan.	Little Tibet.	Naipál.	Sindh.	Baháwalpur.	Rajputána.	Bandelkhand.	Rewah.	C. P.	G. I. P. Ry. and Port and Presidency of Bombay.	Behar, Bengal and Port of Calcutta.	Total of net Imports.	Net import after deducting col. 19 in Table of net Exports.
7	8	9	10	11	12	13	14	15	16	17	18	19
201	125	606	'38	13	...	...	...	1,528	230	...	2,597	...
711	47	...	...	1,833	17,640	...	...	...	...	1 693	24,119	23,312
8,986	2,266	...	43	300	45,753	...	...	...	3	...	76,104	66,471
1,510	41	...	...	18	...	...	...	5	28	...	5,598	552
...	18.546	...	...	...	...	...	...	...	...	...	23,723	16,700
...	...	5	...	...	...	17,448	3,793	1,110	2,167	1,576	37,379	33,167
...	...	574	...	...	27,446	3,267	3,456	46,020	1,210	...	81,399	...
...	...	...	1,426	...	...	...	...	...	1,476	30,329	33,231	28,243
...	...	...	...	...	...	41	...	...	916	11,665	12,622	6,993
...	...	...	26,682	...	...	...	...	...	...	3,19,556	3,46,238	2,89,091
119	...	...	...	84	1,192	323	...	...	22,321	...	23,919	...
2,590	1	13,612	13	...	975	16	...	...	37	...	3,634	3,195
...	...	...	...	...	...	837	9,950	...	...	30,981	77,563	44,096
...	...	697	...	...	644	...	...	418	...	83,371	84,433	84,433
...	...	...	...	...	445	86	24	541	1,126	86	3,042	2,577
...	...	2,407	...	...	507	236	...	1,456	198	253	2,650	2,650
...	...	12	...	24	...	3,033	...	...	...	...	5,464	3,562
...	...	...	...	2,571	2,061	...	...	...	...	...	5,143	4,138
4	...	123	...	...	644	6	...	...	...	...	3,221	...
...	...	...	...	...	1,070	...	...	...	...	...	81,333	76,364
...	...	59	...	...	...	...	...	...	...	5,414	5,794	...
...	...	11	...	...	...	101	3	...	...	17,480	17,643	12,754
...	...	9.992	...	...	3,695	2,405	...	...	12	...	6,113	6,093
55	...	5,842	...	...	...	36,386	710	5,006	...	25,213	85,850	69,135
1,599	...	1,480	...	...	...	...	3,391	...	...	9,951	52,424	44,625
805	...	...	...	...	...	498	16	...	9,391	37,896	75,367	43,300
...	...	...	...	...	...	...	...	...	4,312	17,000	21,312	20,973
666	...	17.965	...	...	...	5,822	3,844	4,84,094	...	17,420	1,48,645	1,05,779
...	...	12,228	...	41,193	...	57,371	1,27,311	2,54,411	...	...	7,30,660	...
...	...	17,704	...	87,768	...	12,662	80,906	1,167	...	...	4,55,054	...
...	...	5,796	...	36	...	157	84,200	...	...	...	91,509	...
163	...	2,00,492	5,468	3,761	...	6,987	1,08,054	5,845	...	16,04,390	24,26,974	22,80,353
...	...	3,36,158	...	...	...	28	6,848	33,693	...	1,06,796	...	...
...	...	60,852	...	2	...	11,809	22,340	2,64.477	...	14,12,831	17,72,311	13,68,248
28	...	7,773	...	...	...	4,794	6,102	1,700	...	...	20,473	16,738
...	3	2,107	...	670	3,439	...	833	170	...	...	7,228	...
...	10	154	...	793	5,622	85	23	...	...	...	6,950	...
...	...	179	...	84	550	...	203	3	...	...	1,762	...
...	...	...	...	...	...	63	2	...	...	...	65	...
...	...	...	...	...	...	55	3,049	233	...	...	3,337	...
...	...	...	...	...	...	8	25,542	17,831	517	37,908	82,073	82,066
...	11	411	2,582	...	...	119	...	...	...	52,006	55,354	42,893
4,173	15	1,376	1,65,375	...	3.608	1,48,511	664	8,002	15,847	3,70,428	7,19,423	7,09,856
...	...	...	11,524	4	...	50	...	...	...	47,973	59,551	52,538
...	...	48	7,149	328	...	827	129	...	...	28,648	41,289	31,638
3,900	...	12,596	...	1,374	...	2,264	12,030	...	...	...	84,974	...
419	...	...	2,840	...	11,159	9,043	620	...	...	47,726	71,807	42,178
...	27,973	...	192	...	13,69,394	...	...	...	...	1,02,277	15,02,660	12,01,377
...	...	155	...	...	7	...	...	...	...	...	166	...
189	...	...	50	13,243	400	351	...	...	...	40,355	54,672	50,284
...	...	6,511	...	...	9,537	8 186	1,17,842	2,878	...	...	1,44,966	...
25	...	20,722	...	11,939	3,714	1.798	4,511	...	...	...	64,319	...
...	...	1,084	...	12,353	...	2,817	22,690	9,662	...	...	49,399	...
...	...	24,972	...	...	...	750	577	193	...	...	27,130	...
...	...	...	5,039	945	649	...	...	1,238	...	...	7,907	...
442	...	58	...	181	...	131	552	4,072	...	...	7,729	...
...	...	...	...	...	...	4	51	...	...	...	5,192	857
...	...	...	...	81	...	5	...	...	...	3,143	3,363	878
...	...	28,363	2.394	...	...	1,121	...	...	2,028	44,421	79,443	69,462
951	...	33	51,560	...	2,16,741	1,304	...	893	...	1,17,305	3,93,232	3,92,402
...	...	...	...	...	...	759	...	...	...	1,720	2,479	...
...	...	...	...	...	...	...	...	...	1	16,401	16,470	7,104
5,257	10	...	58	...	...	...	...	...	...	52,768	70,164	...
48,816	...	5,19,232	3,140	...	...	12,560	1,904	3,702	...	1,29,183	8,13,073	7,99,843
82,620	10	26,898	...	...	21,135	25,547	50,803	2	...	...	3,71,216	3,41,632
3,349	2,049	311	...	1,130	9,511	13	...	...	...	...	88,993	...
44	252	...	...	...	755	65	...	...	...	...	4,478	...

TABLE OF EXPORTS.

NET EXPORTS from Northern India to other

(Animals are given in numbers

DESCRIPTIONS.	Kashmir.	Ladakh.	Chinese Tibet.	Bajaur.	Kabul.	Tirah.
	1	2	3	4	5	6
Animals, living 1. Horses, Ponies and Mules,	118	—	—	—	...	...
2. Cattle,	—	—	—	—	...	...
3. Sheep and Goats,	—	—	—		...	...
4. Other Kinds,	—	—	—		...	...
Borax,	178	—	—	—	60	58
Canes, Rattans, and Bamboos,						
Cotton, raw,	592	2	—	8,008	911	618
Cotton, manufactured, 1. Twist and Yarn (European,)	646	—	—	63	96	...
2. " (Indian,)	505	1	3	93	447	23
3. Piece Goods (European,)	7,508	248	19	657	12,612	17
4. " (Indian,)	4,516	93	43	3,400	27,657	374
Drugs and Medicines, 1. Asafœtida,	—	—	—	—	...	...
2. Other sorts not intoxicating,	—	185	2	127	...	...
3. Pan or Betel Leaves,	—	—	—	—	...	...
4. Intoxicating drugs other than Opium,	105	—	—	—	...	...
a. Ganja,	—	—	—	—		...
b. Bhang,	—	—				
c. Charas,	—	—			...	...
Dyeing Materials, 1. Indigo,	547	42	1	561	10,651	6
2. Maddar or Manjit,	1,076	7	4	222	...	...
3. Safflower,	—	—	—	12	...	...
4. Turmeric,	—	—	—	—	...	...
5. Al,	—	—	—	—		
6. Other Kinds,	—	—	—	—	43	...
Fibrous Products, 1. Fibres, raw,	—	1	—	—	...	...
2. " manufactured,	—	15	—	—	...	...
Fruits, Vegetables, & Nuts, 1. Cocoanuts,	—	—	—	—	...	
2. Betel Nuts,	—	—	—	—		
3. Potatoes and vegetable,	—	—	—	—		
4. All other kinds,	—	—	10	—		
Grains, 1. Wheat,	1,89,005	530	68	—	15,918	357
2. Gram and Pulse,	88,164	—	—	—	—	—
3. Other Spring Crops,	1,749	—	—	9,599	445	—
4. Rice Husked,	—	} 921	91	—	604	1,380
5. " Unhusked,						
6. Other Rain Crops,	5,115	32	—	6,351	346	4,586
Gums and Resins,	—	3	—	1,450	...	...
Hides and Skins, 1. Hides of Cattle,	768	—	3	15	1,435	...
2. Skins of Sheep and small animals,	—	48	—	—	274	2
Horns,	—	—	—	—	15	...
Lac, 1. Dye,	—	—	—	—	...	...
2. Shell,	—	—	—	—	...	...
3. Stick and other kinds,	—	—	—	—	...	...
Metals and Manufactures of Metals, 1. Brass and Copper,	1,611	109	21	—	478	7
2. Iron,	8,898	153	46	—	1,672	24
3. Other Metals,	872	12	—	46	...	...
Oils,	—	21	—	—	40	...
Opium,	—	—	2	—	...	...
Provision, 1. Ghee,	—	—	—	—	...	...
2. Other kinds,	4,855	—	—	4,776	5,374	...
Salt,	1,03,523	—	—	58,276	78,038	4,541
Saltpetre, 1. Saltpetre,	—	—	—	—	—	...
2. Other saline substances,	506	—	—	15	502	...
Seeds, 1. Oil Seeds, a. Linseed,	—	—	—	—	...	...
b. Mustard and Rape,	—	—	—	—	25	...
c. Til or Jingelly,	—	—	—	—	...	...
d. Other Oil Seeds,	—	—	—	—	...	...
2. Other Seeds, a. Indigo Seeds,	—	—	—	—	...	...
b. Other kinds,	—	—	—	—	...	...
Silk, 1. Raw.	—	—	—	4	...	...
2. Manufactured,	4	1	—	—	...	...
Spices,	1,965	21	1	514	...	12
Stone and Marble,						
Sugar, 1. Refined above 7 Rs. per maund,	17,247	428	4	1,002	9,413	157
2. Unrefined below 7 Rs. per maund,	16,847	30	13	4,841	436	273
Tea, 1. Indian,	2,912	209	4	10	3,023	...
2. Foreign,	162	—	—	9	8,894	...
Tobacco,	8,793	21	10	1,190	...	80
Wood, 1. Timber,	—	—	—	—	...	...
2. Firewood,	—	—	—	—	...	...
Wool, 1. Raw,	—	—	—	—	...	...
2. Manufactured Wool and Piece Goods,	—	—	—	—	...	...

States and Provinces during 1877-78.

all other items in weight)

Sewestan.	Little Tilet.	Naipál.	Sindh.	Baháwalpur.	Rajputána.	Bandelkhand.	Rewah.	C. P.	G. I. P. Ry. and Port and Presidency of Bombay	Behar, Bengal and Port of Calcutta.	Total of net Exports.	Net export after deducting col. 19 in Table of Imports.
7	8	9	10	11	12	13	14	15	16	17	18	19
...	...	775	...	...	510	...	...	9	...	3,448	4,155	1,558
...	...	2,401	...	...	...	...	...	...	2	7,232	9,633	...
...	...	2,073	...	...	...	...	...	...	...	2,073	5,046	...
1	...	...	1,580	...	223	3	...	239	2,006	2,675	7,023	...
...	...	169	...	48	3,995	...	...	...	...	...	4,212	...
97	...	1,005	63,265	971	...	...	...	...	...	57,666	1,33,135	51,786
1	2	3	...	624	3,066	13	4	470	...	...	4,988	...
70	3	863	2,735	27	274	...	114	471	...	...	5,629	...
470	199	5,938	...	2,769	20,323	183	2,713	1,725	766	...	57,147	...
4,450	41	16,337	40,533	...	...	...	1,671	5,543	...	16,323	1,20,981	97,062
...	...	4	...	...	...	...	2	204	...	229	439	...
...	...	...	29.921	753	1,208	...	...	620	651	...	33,467	...
...	...	...	360	...	...	...	...	...	...	...	465	...
...	...	...	...	...	1,424	...	...	65	10	403	1,902	...
...	...	...	23	...	...	...	...	612	131	241	1,007	...
5	...	...	5,963	...	...	...	...	2,595	1,103	58,618	80,092	76,871
...	...	...	1,419	1,957	...	...	...	...	...	284	4,969	...
...	...	7	468	...	6,847	15	...	340	80	...	7,769	1,975
...	...	...	...	...	4,628	...	...	196	65	...	4,889	...
...	...	...	...	...	...	...	20	...	...	...	20	...
...	...	...	3,780	9	3,716	...	...	...	9,167	...	16,715	...
...	...	...	...	42	7,491	4	...	224	37	...	7,799	...
...	...	...	7,388	...	4,877	...	...	9,787	...	...	22,067	...
...	...	339	...	...	...	...	...	...	...	...	339	...
...	...	1,783	3,550	5,923	14,252	...	...	3,273	1,557	1,117	2,672	2,672
...	...	...	...	...	...	...	...	...	14,075	...	42,866	...
1,651	2,457	...	13,03,905	...	3,66,964	...	...	...	1,95,488	42,20,191	62,96,534	55,65,874
3,427	708	...	1,67,319	...	5,35,311	...	...	...	3,08,664	18,00,389	29,03,982	24,48,928
88	15,042	...	2,331	...	2,96,354	...	...	...	5,654	5,11,048	8,42,310	7,50,801
...	9,978	...	...	...	70372	...	...	...	62,572	...	1,48,621	...
...	2,703	...	...	...	...	...	...	...	...	...	...	...
71	3,294	...	2,11 007	...	1,38,959	...	...	...	32,302	...	4,04,063	...
...	...	...	157	69	575	...	...	...	1,077	404	3,735	...
...	...	...	2,090	...	...	30	...	...	408	2,85,058	2,89,807	2,82,579
...	...	...	235	...	...	...	...	16	6,356	20,683	27,614	20,664
...	...	...	...	...	...	...	...	...	896	14,782	15,693	13,931
...	...	...	...	...	...	...	...	67	12	2,195	2,274	2,209
...	...	...	71	211	1,092	...	...	...	255	38,530	40,159	36,822
1	...	...	...	755	1,598	...	223	7,259	399	...	12,461	...
...	...	...	...	413	...	...	3,361	...	...	...	9,567	...
...	...	1,294	...	...	1,509	...	...	1,108	2,172	...	7,013	...
651	...	70	...	...	3,332	...	...	586	4,951	...	9,651	...
...	...	...	...	...	...	...	...	...	...	1,28,873	...	...
...	23	...	22,880	...	39,681	...	...	2,240	27,775	25,513	1,18,114	33,140
...	15	5,344	...	1,351	...	...	...	4,791	3,123	...	29,629	...
2,333	...	23,094	...	84	...	7,862	19,337	4,191	4	...	3,01,283	...
..	...	...	1,742	...	...	290	6	4,901	9,873	54,460	71,272	71,106
...	...	137	...	...	...	...	1,591	1,475	162	...	4,388	...
...	10	...	332	...	...	...	...	...	1,01,767	19,01,408	20,03,517	18,58,551
...	11	...	2,37,297	...	...	...	...	457	1,46,173	13,56,718	17,40,676	16,76,357
...	23	...	1,73,236	297	47,842	...	...	...	26,238	1,64,016	4,12,355	3,62,956
...	52	...	1,503	...	14,223	...	...	...	7,833	2,98,584	3,22,195	2,95,065
...	...	...	...	...	...	...	...	...	444	1,52,041	1,52,485	1,44,578
...	...	...	205	...	36,150	...	...	...	9,158	55,487	1,00,950	93,221
22	...	...	609	182	1	...	...	199	1	3,317	4,335	...
...	...	...	974	...	981	...	...	232	353	...	2,485	...
1	25	...	...	570	3,254	...	2,079	757	...	...	9,981	...
...	...	...	...	500	...	...	162	...	168	...	830	...
146	1	407	30,468	7,002	1,34,391	272	737	79,978	52,022	71,128	4,04,802	4,04,802
1,064	1,867	14,945	1,05,058	17,947	3,85,940	...	8,167	1,53,018	68,385	...	7,79,871	7,76,892
...	...	...	357	...	133	...	...	61	529	11,114	18,352	18,352
...	...	...	...	...	301	...	...	...	...	...	9,366	...
146	...	140	3,668	700	33,852	4,284	3,097	26,895	5,645	...	88,375	18,211
...	...	...	...	...	13,085	...	...	...	...	...	13,230	...
...	...	...	46	...	...	...	...	...	...	29,538	29,584	...
...	...	...	1,02,114	...	...	...	4	69	37	2,359	1,04,583	65,590
...	...	302	1,196	...	...	...	35	400	...	4,033	5,966	1,468

APPENDIX TO PART I

THE DRUGS OF NAIPAL ORDINARILY FOUND IN INDIAN BAZARS.

WITH a view to aid in the preparation of an accurate list of drugs which are procured or procurable from Naipal, I have taken the list incorporated in the Trade Report of the Department of Agriculture and Commerce, North-Western Provinces and Oudh, for 1878-79, and collating Butler's list in his work on Southern Oudh, and Powell's list in his volume on Punjab Products, and also consulting Hooker's and other works on travel in the Tibet and Naipal territories, I have made out the following list of Tibet and Naipal drugs ordinarily found in Indian bazars. As the subject is admittedly one of great importance, and its importance has been recognized by the Department of Agriculture and Commerce, I have in several instances given etymological notes, which will serve to illustrate important points in the identification of plants.

The only proper course to ensure a valuable note on drugs is for some officer to take all books of travel which refer to Naipal and the adjacent countries, and works of authority, such as Powell's list and the like, make a careful study and copious notes from them, and then travel along the frontier from bazar to bazar, and obtain all the specimens which he possibly can. In this way a great help to our knowledge of native medicine would be gained : but to supplement it, it would be necessary that an officer should visit Naipal itself. It is only an officer possessing special qualifications as a medical man and botanist who should be deputed for a task of this kind ; but it is advisable that he should have the assistance of a linguist to ensure careful rendering of vernacular terms. If all the qualities can be combined in one officer so much the better.

Anil, or Anilbent, also, called **Chitah** and **Chitra** *(Plumbago zeylanica* and *Europœa)* is an herb used as a blister by rubbing to a paste with flour. It is a powerful irritant, used to cure skin diseases and aid digestion ; applied also with oil to relieve rheumatism and paralysis.

Atis *(aconitum heterophyllum)* is devoid of all poisonous principle, and is used as a tonic and febrifuge, and to check diarrhœa. Native practitioners employ it in diabetes, gonorrhœa, gleet, and uterine hemorrhage.

Balchir, called also **Budhabudhi, Sambul tib, Jatamasi** *(Nardostachys jatamasi)* is spikenard. It is used as a perfume and stimulant, and to scent tobacco and disguise the taste of medicines. It is valuable in hysteria, dyspepsia, epilepsy, cholic, and delirium tremens.

Bikhma, the root of the *Aconitum ferox*, is the most deadly variety of aconite, and Naipal is famed as a field rich in its growth.

Burhna (*genus usnea)* denotes lichens in general, stringy masses of which are gathered from trees and woven in wreaths for the hair by hill women, who at the same time dye their hair yellow with the leaves of the *Symplocos racemosa.* An extract is also made from these lichens to perfume hair oil, and give an aroma to tobacco.

Chab is the small 'drupe' or fruit of the *jharberi (zizyphus nummularia),* and is used in bilious complaints.

Chiraita *(gentiana chiraita)* is too well known to need more than mention.

Chiriya Kand, an esculent root, (probably *arum companulatum,)* noted by Hooker as a farinaceous tuber, in which is an acrid poisonous juice which may be dissipated by washing or by heat. ·Butler describes **Chiriya Kand** as an aphrodisiac, but notes it as indigenous to the plains.

Darchini, bark of the *Laurus cinnamomum*, is an aromatic, stomachic and carminative astringent; used in cholic and diarrhœa, and in low fever and vomiting. An oil prepared from it is a remedy for toothache.

Dalhard, the yellow wood of the *Berberis Asiatica ;* used in affections of the skin, eye and ear, and injected in gonorrhœa.

Dhup is a broad term meaning incense, and is applied to many fragrant things, used for burning, *e. g.*, to the root of *Dolomœa macrocephala*, to juniper, and to benzoin. The twigs of the pencil cedar (*juniperus excelsa)* are burnt as a fumigatory for delirium in fever.

Ghorbach also called **Bach-khushbu** (*Acorus Calamus)* is the plant which yields the medicine called *calamus aromaticus.* It is a reedy flag growing in marshy places. The dried stem is used as a carminative. It is also administered to horses in splenitis, and is made up as a plaster and applied to sores and galls in cattle to prevent suppuration. The name by its derivation indicates its uses as a 'horse-preserver.'

Hadhjora or **Harjori** is a medicinal preparation from the *Nyctanthes arbortristis,* used in ringworm and to unite broken bones (hence its name), and in disorders of·the wind, mucus, and bile. The flowers of the *nyctanthes* yield a good yellow dye, and combine with red to modify its shade.

Hathjori is given in Powell's 'Panjáb Products' as the *Martynia diandra,* but he makes no note on the drug. This is probably because of doubt. The word is used in India as the equivalent of the Arabic *bisfátij* or *bisfáij,* which is the *polypodium imbricatum.* allied to ferns, found throughout the hills in Northern Asia. Its uses are as a purgative and alterative.

Jamalgota (*croton tiglium*) is croton. Both the seeds and the oil extracted from them are used as drastic purgatives.

Kaiphal is the box-tree (*myrica sapida).* Its bark is highly aromatic, and is tied to the head as a cure for headache and cold.

Kahruba is oriental anise (*vateria indica).* A resin exudes from the tree, which is highly aromatic, and is used for rheumatism and chronic ulcers : also in varnishes and to make candles. It has been erroneously supposed to be the same thing as *sundaros,* which is obtained from another tree.

Kakar Singhi is a hollow, horn-like, curved gall, with a rough, brown exterior, and is dry, hot, and astringent, used as a remedy in coughs, asthma, &c. It is the nut of the *khus acuminata*; but has been sometimes confounded with the Sumach nut, which is also gathered in the hills from the *Summáq (khus coriaria)*, and is known to possess valuable properties in tanning, but is used in India only as an astringent and tonic.

Kamraj (*Sonchus*) is a weed with yellow flower heads. Its twigs are reputed to be aphrodisiac.

Katha is catechu, the inspissated juice of the *khair (areca catechu)* obtained by boiling the chipped wood. It is used as an astringent, and is a most efficacious wash in gonorrhœa.

Kuchilá is *nux vomica, strychnos nux vomica*, used externally in rheumatism and paralysis; believed to assist in breaking the habit of opium eating.

Kumkum is a corruption of the Arabic wood **Karkam** or **Kurkum**, which has been converted into 'Curcuma,' and applied to turmeric. The Arabic word signifies the plant *crocus sativus*, which yields the saffron used as a spice. Leaves of a plant brought from the Naipal hills, and said to be used as an aromatic ingredient in the *hom* sacrifice, appear to be named Kumkum, but apparently their only affinity with the *crocus sativus* is the fragrance they yield when burnt. The *Carthamus tinctoria*, which yields the saffron dye, is called in Arabic *qurtum*.

Katkaleji is a nut, or rather a hard round seed, possessed of tonic properties, used as a febrifuge ; also in piles and splenitis. It is applied externally to reduce hydrocele. The tree from which it is obtained is the *cisalpina bonducella* (var. *guilandina bonduc.*)

Kali-kutki *(Picrorhiza kurrooa)* is a gentian root used as a febrifuge. The term is also used to denote the *Helleborus niger*.

Luban (*Styrax benzoin*) is a resin mixed with benzoic acid, used as a stimulant, expectorant and diuretic. It is also burnt as a fumigator.

Lodh is the bark of the *Symplocos racemosa*, used as a remedy for ophthalmia and also as a dye-stuff.

Majith, or madder, is the root of the *Rubia majistha*, which produces a famous red dye, and is also used as a cosmetic.

Nirbisi (*curcuma zedoaria*), or **Jadwar**, is not (as stated in the N-W. P. and Oudh Trade Report for 1878-79) a poison. It is the most celebrated antidote to poison found in the hills north of Hindustan, and the variety found in Naipal is the best, and is exported to Le, Yarkand, Kashmir, and the Punjab, as well as to the nearer province of Oudh. Natives say that it grows wherever *bikhma* (aconite) is found, and that it is a remarkable provision of nature that the bane (*bish* or *bikhma*) and the antidote (*nirbisi*, Sansc. *nirvisha*) should be found together. The drug styled **Nirbisi** in the Report referred to is probably **Kachur** (*Curcuma zerumbet.*)

Nirmali or **Daran,** (*strychnos potatorum*) is a nut used to clarify water, gathered in the plains, but also brought from the hills of Naipal and Tibet.

Pakanbed (properly **Pathanbed**) is a gentian root, used in fevers, rheumatism and dyspepsia. It is a pure and bitter tonic.

Ral, or **Karayal,** called **kala** or **safed,** according to the prevailing tinge of colour, is the resin of the *shorea robusta* (sál tree), used as an ointment for sores and ulcers, also much esteemed as an astringent in dysentery.

Rasaut is the extract of **Dalhard** (*q. v.*), and is used to stop hemorrhage.

Rewand Chini (*genus Rheum*) is the Himalayan rhubarb, used as a laxative and tonic. It is said to be also called **Padamchal.**

Salajit-siyah is a black gum or resin, or perhaps it may more correctly be described as a balsam (borax), and is said to be obtained from the *Styrax officinale.* It is administered as a remedy for impotence. It is regarded as a specific in this disease.

Salajit safed seems, from the description given of it in the Trade Report already referred to, to be talc steatite. There is another steatite called **Sang-i-jarahat,** and also a substance called **Sang-i-salajit,** in use in native medicine. The latter is lignite.

Sana (*cassia senna*) is a widely known purgative.

Sandal-surkh (*Pterocarpus Santolinus*), red Sandal-wood, is used as a dye, and its medical properties are tonic and sedative. It is used to allay palpitation of the heart.

Sandal-safed (*Sirium myrtifolium*) is Sandal-wood proper, and is used as a refrigerant, and it also yields an aromatic oil.

Singiya is the root of the *Aconitum palmatum* and of other poisonous varieties, except *ferox.*

Sugandh-kokila, called also, it is said, **Haubar,** is an aromatic berry used for a perfume with tobacco. It is also called **Maliagir-ka-phal,** from the place where it grows most abundantly, the sacred mountain of Maliagir, in the Himalayan range. At this place sandal grows in abundance, and hence sandal-wood is also called *maliagir.*

Sugandhbala (*Andropogon muricatum*) is a plant which is found both in the plains and hills. It is used as a perfume and as a plaster.

Tagar is wild spikenard (*Asarum*), a substitute for Asarum Europœum. The Arabic name is Asárún, which is derived from the Greek (ASARON), and thus indicates the source whence a knowledge of it was derived. It is used in splenitis and hepatitis.

Taj is the bark of *cinnamomum albiflorum,* used in dysentry and other diseases.

Tejpat, or **Patraj,** is the leaf of the last named tree, and is used as a tonic and nervine. It is administered in cases of poisoning and serpent bite.

Timmal (var. **Timur**) is an aromatic berry, the fruit of a small tree (*Xanthoxylum hostile*), which is cut to make walking sticks. The berry is used as a condiment and as a remedy for toothache.

PART II.

PART II.

THE TRADE OF LUCKNOW.

It is impossible that any one should visit the native City of Lucknow, and examine its streets, buildings, and markets, and converse freely with its traders and other residents without being forcibly struck by a strange admixture of prosperity and decay, poverty and wealth. There are in one place heard loud praises of the benefits of British rule and in another there are sighings for the return of native rule. This contrast of feeling is explicable.

The Subah of Oudh though nominally a subject province of the Delhi Empire was from the time of Nawab Saádat Ali virtually an independent province though the title of king was not conferred on its rulers until a much later time. The province is naturally by far the most fertile in Hindustan and the revenue, after the payment of a large subsidy to the English, left a vast surplus in the hands of the king. The prodigality with which this wealth was lavished on court favorites stands almost without parallel. There flocked to the Oudh Court from Delhi in its decline all the reduced dependants of the imperial court, and although there thus arose in Lucknow a school of learning and poetry which has rivalled the Augustan age of Delhi, that does not balance the evil which now hangs about Lucknow in the poverty and licentiousness of the improvident and beggared descendants of the servants and favorites of the Oudh Court.

The whole revenues of the province of Oudh were, after payment of the subsidy to the East India Company, spent within the province: and all that was to be thus spent found its way to the capital. The buildings of this City are a monument of the waste of wealth under native rule and the wasiqas, pensions, and endowments on which the progeny of court favorites and retainers are still maintained in idleness but daily growing deeper in distress show how vast must have been the body of unproductive consumers who fed on the revenue. As soon as Oudh was annexed and brought under the imperial administration of the British its revenues went to the imperial exchequer and calamity overtook that great section of the population which were supported by the native court. This is the class which openly laments the effect of British rule.

There was a large field for the employment of the cadets of superior Hindu and Muhamadan families in the native army of Oudh and other independent provinces. Younger sons left their homes and sought fortune in war. But this opening has now been almost entirely closed to them and the effect is felt disastrously in the pressure of an increased number of claimants to share in landed property. Subdivision of estates results to a degree prejudicial to the honour and comfort of Brahmin, Thakur, Saiyad, Pathan and other high-caste families of landed proprietors. This is a second class which is unfortunately discontented with British rule.

Lucknow being the capital of the kingdom of Oudh was the centre of security for property. Here too was the mint. The precious metal poured into the capital. The business of bankers was in an extremely flourishing state. There were no state banks and there was no money-order system and no currency notes. This gave a great impetus to the business of a native banker and hundis were issued by Lucknow bankers on their correspondents in other cities and cashed in return. The coin of other states when it came to Lucknow was discounted by sarrafs. With British rule came the abolition of the Lucknow mint: the extension of security for property to other places than the capital, and the so-to-speak decentralization of money business: the introduction of money-orders and currency notes; the decline in hundi-business; the investment of money in Government promissory notes; uniformity of currency and reduction of the functions of the sarraf. The banking business of native firms is rapidly declining, not in Lucknow only, but in all Indian cities. The mahajan is no longer a banker, an issuer of bills or receiver of deposits to the extent which he was, but he is only a money lender and pawnbroker. Security for property has been extended. The present form of the mahajan's business does not tie him to the capital, and mahajans have spread to every bazar. The gain to the public by the system of money-order and currency notes has been infinitely great compared to the losses which native bankers have sustained in the decline of hundis. While, therefore, Lucknow bankers lament the consequences to themselves of British rule, theirs is a trivial loss compared to the gain which the public reap by modern changes, in the decentralization of money and capital, the increased convenience in the transfer of money and the more secure investment of savings.

Another class of traders who have suffered by the annexation of Oudh are the dealers in precious stones. Jauharis are the extreme case of suppliers of what are purely the luxuries of life. They depend on a demand made chiefly by unproductive consumers. The local demand is now reduced to a low ebb as one great class which made the demand, the native court and the minions who squandered the revenues of the province, are no longer in the local market. There are no mines in this province and few in India. The cheapest markets are at Calcutta and Bombay. There being no longer the special local demand which favoured the Jauharis of Lucknow they have rapidly declined. A further and, within the last five years, very appreciable influence has been felt by the fall in the value of the accumulated stock, caused by the influx of Cape diamonds and the discovery of new emerald and ruby mines in other parts of the world.

The manufacture of gold and silver embroidery and lace has not declined although these commodities are luxuries rather than necessaries of life and directed to supply the wants of unproductive rather than of productive consumers. The cause of this is not far to seek. The exceptionally great skill of Lucknow workmen in these departments which found them support in the local markets under native rule, has since the establishment of our rule found a new outlet in external markets in Bengal and the south of India. This outlet is the result of improved communication, and there being no special advantages in the cost of production of materials enjoyed by any other places in India, Lucknow and Delhi, which are the oldest centres of these manufactures and hold the most skilled laborers, must command the custom of external markets until workmen migrate or there arise in another place some improvement in the art or means of production.

Another trade which has not suffered but has perhaps increased by the annexation of Oudh is the trade in horns, hides, and catgut. The number of cattle slaughtered in this vast Muhammadan city is great. Take 1878, the number of large cattle imported for slaughter was 12,146, and the number of sheep and goats 1,54,127. This is exclusive of the number bred and fed within the city itself for slaughter. The total cannot have been less, and was probably greater, when the city was the capital of a Mussulman kingdom. The hides of these animals cannot be all absorbed locally, and Lucknow has consequently been always a hide emporium from which exports are made. Through it pass all hides from the north and west of Oudh. It is almost certain that since a railway has been opened the export of this class of goods has increased. There is no waste now, though the want of facilities for export in all probability caused waste in former days. Owing to the great local consumption of animal food, the manufacture and export of catgut has always been a thriving trade in Lucknow. The local demand for strings for musical instruments is also very great.

There was under former rule and still is, a considerable business done in manufacture and export of zangár (acetate of copper). This is a concomitant of the trade in copper vessels which has always been a prominent branch of commerce in Lucknow. Copper goods are exported in large quantities. The manufacture of brass vessels is perhaps as extensive but they are chiefly absorbed locally and export is insignificant. The import of specialities in brass vessels is considerable.

The effect produced on certain trades by the increased security to goods in transit under an improved system of police, and by the opening up of better lines of communication by road and rail, has been very marked. Communication with Bombay was absolutely unheard of under native rule, and it is only since the opening of a railway between Allahabad and Bombay that the name of the latter city has become at all familiar to traders in Lucknow. The whole of the trade in export of country manufactures and import of foreign goods, such as it was in the king's time, was done with Calcutta through Mirzapur and Allahabad. All large consignments of goods were passed on from place to place by professional carriers who charged what was termed *bíma*, an insurance at a percent rate on the value of the goods and the rate was determined by the risk The chief risk on certain roads was from dacoits and convoys of goods were escorted by armed men. The business of *bíma* has disappeared *in toto* since railways have overspread the country. Boats were much resorted to by carriers as a means of conveyance and river traffic was enormous. It has now fallen off and boats are in demand only for the conveyance of fuel, and other articles of commerce in the case of which the place of production renders their use a necessity.

The improvements in communication between Lucknow and the ports of Bombay and Calcutta have brought English piece goods into the local market and caused a decline in local manufacture. The weavers of Lucknow have been ruined by the import of English goods. In the king's time prohibitive dues on foreign goods and the expenses attaching to the carriage of imported fabrics combined to keep up the weaving industry of this City. Silk-weaving, especially of the fabric called daryáí, was well established but it has been now quite crushed out by the import of European silks, (sarcenet supplanting daryáí for instance) and Indian silks from other seats of manufacture. Cotton fabrics were woven and even much exported. A material called *sallam*, used to make floor-cloths, was extensively manufactured in Lucknow, and was in great demand, in fact a speciality, under native rule, and went to Calcutta, Delhi, and other cities. This has quite ceased to be an article of commerce : and although there is still a small industry in the weaving of dosútí, malmal, tanzeb and other country fabrics, it is at its last gasp. The spinning of cotton has dwindled to almost nothing for it has been found cheaper to import European twist and yarn for weaving purposes than to spin the cotton produced locally. The Joláhás of Lucknow are fast leaving the city of Lucknow and seeking a livelihood in service.

There is one industry which has grown to great proportions within the last 20 years. It was almost unknown in the nawábí. It is chikan-dozí. The class of embroidery denominated chikan is in great demand and the export of it to Calcutta, Patna, Bombay, Haidarábád and other cities is an important trade. It is not easy to see why this industry has taken so fast a hold in Lucknow. But I may venture an explanation. When one wanders through the mohullas of the City where reduced Muhammadan families reside and where there are poor Hindu families who need to add to the scant subsistence afforded by a small shop or by service, one sees women and even small children busy with needle and muslin. Thus the labor at the manufacturer's command is cheap and abundant. He is able to undersell those who go into the market from other places. This is one reason why the chikan business has taken a deep root in Lucknow. It is the natural vent found for the labour of persons thrown out of employ by failure of other trades and of those who seek a not irksome means of supplementing small incomes. As a domestic pursuit chikan was always a favorite employment of the women of some castes. It is also of the same class with zardozi and kámdání, forms of embroidery which afford scope for both men and women and which throve even in nawábí rule. Hence there was a natural soil in which the similar industry should take root.

It is believed that for a few years after the Mutiny the population of Lucknow suffered a sudden decrease. All persons who were connected with other parts of the province and of India generally, whom accidents of service and fortune had brought to Lucknow, left it. That section of the population who were attached to the City by the special conditions of trade under native rule also left. The proportion these bore to the total population was, however, small: and the population has as a whole increased. Not only has the population increased but, by the withdrawal of the funds squandered in unproductive consumption, the number of persons who press on capital for wages of labour has greatly increased. There has been neither a corresponding increase of capital nor improvement in local production. This has been the cause of a fall in wages. The rate of wages expressed in money may or may not have fallen, but the purchasing power of money is less now than it was twenty years ago. The price of food has risen partly owing to the exit of grain to other markets and the withdrawal of prohibitive restrictions on exports. This has been accompanied, it is true, by a cheapening of other necessaries of life, clothing for instance, but the rise in one is not balanced by the fall of the other. The condition, therefore, of the labouring class has deteriorated.

There has been a rise of rents in the province of Oudh owing to the increased pressure of population and a not corresponding improvement in the processes of agriculture. By this the landlords should have benefited, but it is notorious that the landlords of Oudh are not in a progressive state. There should have been an improvement in the condition of the agriculturist apace with the rise in the value of agricultural produce, but it is doubtful if there has been. The causes and remedies of these evils are matter for thought but foreign to this report.

Lucknow suffers from a want of capital, or, perhaps I should rather say, from a want of a field for the employment of already existing capital in local manufactures and productive industries. In this respect it is a poor city. The fact that Rs. 105,65,500, savings of private individuals in Lucknow, are at the present time lying locked up, invested in Government promissory notes, is enough to show that capital does exist locally which might be employed more profitably to the owners were there manufactures in Lucknow affording a quick and steady return of profit combined with security of investment. I use the words 'local' and 'locally' because the native of India (in the province of Oudh, at any rate) will not invest capital in what, I may call, foreign fields. He cannot trust his money in an investment out of sight and personal reach and supervision unless the ' Sirkár' is somehow connected with it. Hence the tendency of the owner of capital to seek a local field for employment of capital in trading and, if he cannot find it, to purchase Government notes.

There are also two other causes which operate to hinder Lucknow in commercial progress. The first of these is the proximity of Cawnpore. Lucknow will hardly ever compete with that city in some manufactures. The Elgin Mills and Muir Mills give Cawnpore a start in the manufacture of cotton goods.

It is exceedingly difficult to say whether there is or is not a market for goods to such an extent beyond that produced by those factories as would open a prospect to capitalists of realizing a profit at Lucknow if they built cotton mills there.

The damage done to Lucknow by Cawnpore is chiefly by the diverting of wholesale business from Lucknow to Cawnpore. The present cheapest and most direct route between Lucknow and Calcutta is viâ Cawnpore. Hence Lucknow retailers of imported goods, cloth and iron for instance, and retailers from all places beyond Lucknow buy in the Cawnpore market. The more direct route between Calcutta and Lucknow is viâ Banáras but the break in railway communication at the Ganges in the last named place operates to prevent the adoption of this line.

The position of Lucknow traders would undoubtedly be vastly improved by the construction of a bridge over the Ganges at Banáras to unite the O. & R. Railway and the E. I. Railway. The distance between Lucknow and Calcutta viâ Cawnpore is 730 miles viâ Banáras it is 677. The saving this difference would make in cost of placing goods in the market at Lucknow would be further greatly enhanced by the fact that goods would be carried on the O. & R. Railway Company's line for a longer distance than before and the goods rates are cheaper on this line than on the East Indian. Take as an instance the case of sheet iron. The carriage for 100 mds. from Calcutta to Lucknow viâ Cawnpore is Rs. 124-12, and from Calcutta to Lucknow viâ Banáras is Rs. 108-7-5. The latter route is not used because of the break of the line at Banáras. This sheet iron sells at Cawnpore for Rs. 6 per nawábí maund and if carriage be struck off, the cost price plus profit would be Rs. 475-4-4 per 100 mds. If the Lucknow trader imported viâ Banáras and sold at the same rates his cost price plus profit would be Rs. 475-4-4 per 100 mds. He could then afford to sell cheaper than the Cawnpore dealer by Rs. 11-12-4 per 100 mds. and make the same rate of profit per maund as the Cawnpore trader now makes. The octroi charges at Lucknow are Rs. 1-8 per cent. on value and this item. I have omitted but were it added in, the Lucknow trader would still be able to sell at a lower rate than the Cawnpore dealer. A slight calculation will show still more. It would pay the Cawnpore trader to import viâ Banáras and Lucknow.

What would the effect be to the Lucknow manufacturer of iron goods who would then buy his materials at Lucknow? The wholesale iron vendor who buys at Cawnpore sheet iron for Rs. 6 per nawábi maund sells it at Lucknow for Rs. 6-8 per md. He has incurred a charge of about 2 as. 8 p. per maund carriage. Thus, comparing present wholesale prices with the prices which would prevail if iron were imported to Lucknow via Banáras, the saving to the manufacturer would be Rs. 45-1-8 per 100 mds. nawábí in cost of material.

By two events the position of Lucknow as to chances of commercial prosperity would be vastly improved : (1) by the construction of a railway bridge over the Ganges at Banáras. (2) the abolition of octroi. The former would make

Lucknow the depôt for wholesale dealing in imported goods and would by lowering cost of production attract capital to Lucknow. The former combined with the latter would draw to Lucknow export traffic now diverted to Cawnpore.

That octroi does operate as a transit duty is, I fear, too true. The refunds claimed on goods exported are but a trifle and if this be due to the fact that certain goods on which octroi duty is paid in Lucknow can be exported at a profit without claiming a refund, this is not an economical argument in favour of octroi but only an indication of the exceptionally favourable conditions under which those goods are produced and put into the market. All goods exported to Calcutta now go through Cawnpore, and as viâ Banáras over a bridge at the Ganges would be a cheaper route, so long as any given place of production of goods for export is equidistant from Cawnpore and Lucknow they would (if there was no octroi duty,) on the establishment of the improved route cease to go to Cawnpore and come to Lucknow. This then brings us to the limit of the interference of octroi with transit of goods in export. When octroi exists in Lucknow and not in Cawnpore equidistance ceases to be the sole determinant of the choice as to route in export. Goods will come to Lucknow only from distances where the addition of octroi duty does not operate as a charge in export to outweigh the difference of railway charge in favour of the Lucknow and Banáras route.

The octroi duty may be a necessity for the maintenance of conservancy and police in Lucknow but that its abolition would be a benefit to trade there can be little doubt. It is a delicate point and I pass it without further comment.

Communication between Lucknow and other places is by river, road and railway. Traffic by river is chiefly in fuel. During the year 1878 the number of boats which imported commodities liable to octroi duty and their cargoes were as follows :—

Firewood, ...	1,184 boats.
Charcoal, ...	51 ,,
Kanda, ...	49 ,,
Reeds and grasses for thatching, sirki, matting, sentha, } ...	25 ,,
Bambus, ...	17 ,,

Total, ... 1,326 boat cargoes.

This does not, however, represent fairly the total traffic by boat. It excludes the traffic in lime between ghats in the city and immediate neighbourhood and is solely import traffic from distant points. It has been quite impossible to collect any statistics of export trade by boat. In addition to cargoes carried on boat, there is also river traffic by *bera bandi* or by raft, chiefly bambus and timber. The preponderance of firewood in the cargoes ascertained points to a more extensive traffic between Lucknow and the districts up stream, especially the north of Sitapur and Kheri district than with places down stream.

5

Pulapatáwar, sentha, and other materials for thatching &c., and khusa come by boat as well as by cart from Sultanpur and bambus from Jounpur. Both these places are down stream.

The road traffic is very extensive and the lines of communication between Lucknow and other places by road are well laid and open. There are two roads leave the city north of the river. That which turns to the east goes to Bara-banki-Nawabganj and there divides into two branches. The one keeps towards the east and passes on to Faizabad. The other goes to Bahramghat and through a ferry at that place joins communication with Bahraich, Nanpara, and Naipal. It is the grand channel of trade with trans-Gogra districts. The second road leaving Lucknow by the north goes almost due north to Sitapur and on to Kheri. A branch deflects at Sitapur to the west and leads to Shabjehanpur. These roads which communicate with the north and west of Oudh are of immense importance to Lucknow because chiefly of the grain trade. In the year 1878 as much as 9,60,388 maunds of grain came into the ganjes north of the river from the north of Oudh, and a further quantity not separately noted from the general total came to ganjes south of the river by the same route. The other imports from this direction are chiefly hides and horns, drugs, ganja, bhang, charas, tobacco, wax, lac, resins and other forest produce. The return traffic is in cotton, and woollen goods, salt, spices, metals and hardware goods, but this export trade is not, properly speaking, from Lucknow but from Cawnpore. It is purely an accident that it passes through Lucknow. These goods while moving from Cawnpore to the north do not to any important extent, change hands at Lucknow.

There are many roads through which communication may be had between Lucknow and various parts of the Unao district. The main line is the road to Cawnpore. The next in importance is that running through Mohan and Rasulabad to Safipur and to Unao. This was the oldest route from Lucknow to Cawnpore, Bithur, and other places on the Ganges banks. It is now little used as a line of commerce. The only important traffic is in grain and the imports to Lucknow of brass vessels from Mahrajganj and Nawalganj.

There is a road from Lucknow to Hurdoi cutting through some important qasbas of Lucknow District.

By far the most important roads south of the Gumti are those leading into Lucknow from Sultanpur and Rai Bareli. They have many branches and are the channels along which at least half the gráin is carried which comes into Lucknow and also gur, firewood, kanda, and charcoal. The return traffic is so miscellaneous it would be difficult to specify any commodities for which a special demand is shown.

It would be very interesting if a complete table could be prepared of all the imports and exports of Lucknow City for any given term, but full data are not obtainable. I have, however, procured from the Audit Office of the O. & R. Ry. Company returns of all goods imported and exported by the three branches of their line during 1878. The statistics were furnished to me under heads which had been given to the Company by the department of Agriculture and Commerce. I have not been able to adhere to the classification of that department : for my other source of information was the octroi department and the classification adopted by the latter differs.   I have assimilated the classification as far as possible.   The octroi department can furnish no reliable returns of exports and hence the exports from the city are not shown in full but only so far as they were by rail.   The octroi returns of imports as furnished to me included goods imported by rail and I therefore examined the books of the barriers which record imports by rail, and, deducting those imports, have shown the balance as imports otherwise than by rail.

The following is the table I have thus prepared :—

Import and Export Trade of Lucknow City during 1878.

		IMPORTS.												EXPORTS.							
		By Rail.								Otherwise.		Grand Total.		By Rail.							
		Banáras branch.		Cawnpore branch.		Aligarh branch.		Total.						Banáras branch.		Cawnpore branch.		Aligarh branch.		Total.	
		M.	S.	M.	S.	M.	S.	M.	S.	M.	S.	M.	S.	M.	S.	M.	S.	M.	S.	M.	S.
Animals, living.	Horses, Ponies & Mules,			*3				*3				*3									
	Cattle, ...									*12146		*12146									
	Sheep and Goats, ...			*26				*26		*154101		*154127									
	Other kinds,...			*91				*91				*91									
Bambus and Canes, ...								*90191		*232836		*323027									
Bricks, ...										*493610		*493610									
Canes and Rattans, ...		170	0	15	30	...	...	185	30	...	...	185	30	...	...	13	0	...	...	13	0
Cotton Raw, ...		94	20	1110	0	133	30	1338	10	...	..	1338	10	626	0	2	0	..	20	628	20
Cotton Twist and Yarn, ...		315	10	1375	20	...	...	1690	30	...	...	1690	30	273	30	17	10	8	0	299	0
Drugs and Medicines.	Asafœtida, ...	..	...	162	0	...	...	162	0	1	12	163	12	4	0	40	0	2	10	46	10
	Other sorts not intoxicating, ...	286	10	825	20	8	30	1120	20	1572	31	2693	11	49	20	169	0	64	10	282	30
	Pán, ...	...	...	...	...	...	...	...	...	5452	18	5452	18	...	...	...	...	1	10	1	10
	Opium, ...	...	...	39	20	...	...	39	20	...	...	39	20	...	..	...	...	..	...	...	...
	Gánja, ...	..	...	76	0	...	...	76	0	...	...	76	0	...	...	...	...	...	...	...	..
	Bhang, ...	140	0	...	...	...	...	140	0	...	...	140	0	14	20	...	...	...	...	14	20
	Charas, ...	...	...	5	20	...	...	5	20	...	...	5	20	...	...	...	...	1	20	1	20
Dyeing Materials.	Indigo, ...	...	...	1	20	12	30	14	10	...	...	14	10	2	30	12	30	...	...	15	20
	Maddar or Majith, ..	...	..	82	30	3	10	86	0	...	...	86	0	2	0	...	...	...	...	2	0
	Safflower, ...	...	...	6	30	...	...	6	30	...	...	6	30	...	...	70	10	...	...	70	10
	Turmeric, ...	503	0	220	0	233	20	956	20	838	12	1794	32	15	20	123	0	2	20	139	0
	Al, ...	...	...	...	...	...	...	...	...	...	...	...	...	...	...	...	...	...	...	...	...
	Other kinds,...	...	...	62	0	...	..	62	0	...	...	62	0	...	...	8	30	...	...	8	30
Fibres and fibrous products, Sirki, San, etc.	Raw, ...	3708	30	77	0	8	10	3794	0					...	...	299	0	13	0		
	Munj,									4657	7	12689	27							1536	0
	Manufactured,..	912	10	2907	10	419	0	4238	20					2193	20	1486	30	1523	0		
Fruits, Vegetables, and Nuts.	Cocoanuts (khushk), ...	...	...	...	..	...	...	...	...	3864	38	3864	38	...	...	...	...	...	...	...	...
	" (tar), ...	12	0	206	30	...	...	218	30	64	7	282	37	7	30	12	10	2	30	22	30
	Betel nuts, ...	69	10	2365	20	...	...	2434	30	1430	30	3865	20	1	20	...	...	20	10	21	30
	Potatoes, ...	443	0	459	30	8018	10	8921	0	7714	0	16635	0	646	30	5331	10	2875	20	8853	20
	Mahuas, ...	...	..	...	...	...	..	...	...	89421	29	89421	29	...	...	...	...	...	...	...	...
	Foreign Fruits, ...	...	...	...	...	...	...	...	...	639	6	639	6	...	..	...	..	...	...	...	...
	Country Fruits and Vegetables, etc., ...	359	0	2122	10	629	30	3111	0	465567	8	469678	8	169	10	275	0	83	10	527	20

207212 Mds.

Fuel. { Coal and Coke,	...	...	...	...	...	...	...	...	...	...	...	...	...	...	...	...
Charcoal,	...	...	...	...	...	...	...	...	...	...	...	...	...	...	...	...
Wood,	23980 0	17496 10	15225 0	5665 10	1571 0	17496 10	1367 0	31 10	1398 10
Kanda,									
Castor Cakes,									
Grains. { Wheat,	5399 20	55070 20	56038 30	116508 30	1571 0	167840 27	1089 30	7016 10
Grain and Pulse,	33486 30	149836 30	39680 20	223003 30	167840 27	47828 30	17204 10	24 11 20	29064 20	161480 10
Other Spring crops,	2223 10	7415 10	22855 20	32494 0	534936 0	160710 0	323 30	604 20	6664 0
Rice husked,	60899 0	43761 20	870 0	105470 20	160710 0	123058 13	2835 30	607 20	1462 20
Rice unhusked,	10730 20	4325 0	43 0	15098 20	123058 13	88 0	767 0	92 20	175 0
Other Rain crops,	15530 10	11078 10	1647 0	28255 20	5 0	77 20	37269 30
Horns,	22 0	121 20	384 0	527 20	2349402 0	1898571 0	942 30	28436 0	1097 20
Hides and { Hides of Cattle,	885 10	798 10	256 20	1940 20	399 10	667 20	30 30
Skins. { Skins of Sheep, Goats, etc.,					527 20	4519 10	10619 20	103 10
					1940 20			15224 0
Katha,	394 30	169 0	225 30	789 20	789 20	1514 20	887 30	4239 30	100 20	5227 30
Tallow and Wax,					1514 20	605 31		605 31
Borax,	28 0	6 0	5 0	11 0	11 0		1 0		8 0
Kirana { Gums and Resins,		148 20		176 20	176 20	116 25	1 0	6 0	1 0
(Grocery). { Saltpetre,		35 0		35 0	35 0	1876 31		
Mushk, Záfrán, etc.,					116 25	40637 24		
Kathái,					1876 31	516390 35		
Miscellaneous Grocery,	8 21	2 20	821 0	821 0	40637 24	2 20		
					517211 35			
Kunkar,		7 10		7 10	2 20	2 20		
Lac. { Dye,	35 30	127 30	163 20		222 9	114 39	246 20	2 30	13 0	15 30
Shell,		2024 20	26 20	2053 0	699 7	535 27	261 20	297 10	12 20	556 10
Stick and other kinds,	2 0				2053 0			208 0	69 0	538 20
Leather. { Unmanufactured,	5 20	656 30		662 10	662 10				239 10	239 10
Manufactured,		1087 0		1087 0	8235 10	8248 10	702 10	458 0	963 30	2124 0
Lime,	4257 0	6874 20	3303 0	14434 20	14434 20	74544 yds			
Liquors,					13285 nos	407 9			
Matting and Carpets,	427 30	560 30	30 20	1019 0	1426 9	554 5	453 10	114 30	87 30	655 30
Metals. { Brass and Copper,	3690 30	14986 30	857 30	19735 10	20289 15	3439 36	269 0	1763 20	128 30	3314 10
Iron,	365 20	397 0	1 30	764 10	4204 6	7707 9	44 30	45 30	9 30	10 10
Other Metals,					7707 9	4652 17			
Hardware Goods,	1439 0	5689 0	73 30	7201 30	11854 7	12849 2	1001 20	209 0	99 10	1309 30
Oils,	992 10	976 0	6 10	1974 20	1974 20		65 0	258 30	83 10	407 0
Oilman's Stores,			8 20	8 20	12857 22		750 20	8 20		758 20
Oilcake other than Castor,	190 20	1023 0	80 0	1293 20	1424 20	16770 35	169 20	31 0	114 30	345 10
Piece { Cotton,	3 30	104 30	22 30	131 10	21218 35		6 20	4 30	19 10	1910 0
Goods. { Wool,	3776 10	582 30	89 0	4448 0	1024 10		68 0	591 20	169 0	828 20
Provision. { Ghi,	423 20	578 20	22 10	1024 10	2460 10	*128218	458 0	175 10	98 0	731 10
Other kinds,					*128218				
Railway Materials,	17706 10	5698 30	1203 10	24608 10			7123 20	2740 0	12667 20	22531 0
Salita and Tat Bags,									

Figures marked with asterisks* represent number, not weight.

Import and Export Trade of Lucknow City during 1878.—(Concluded.)

IMPORTS · **EXPORTS**

Articles	Banáras br. (Imp. By Rail)		Cawnpore br. (Imp.)		Aligarh br. (Imp.)		Total (Imp.)		Otherwise (Imp.)		Grand Total (Imp.)		Banáras br. (Exp. By Rail)		Cawnpore br. (Exp.)		Aligarh br. (Exp.)		Total (Exp.)	
	M.	S.	M.	S.	M.	S.	M.	S.	M.	S.	M.	S.	M.	S.	M.	S.	M.	S.	M.	S.
Salt	1774	30	53506	10	1785	10	57066	10			57066	10	309	0	321	0	434	0	1064	0
Seeds — Oil Seeds: Linseed					89	0	89	0					633	30	8049	0	14	10		
Mustard and Rye	129	20	69	30	734	20	933	30	69681	0	72299	10	1887	20	19010	30	542	10	42845	30
Til	407	20	91	0	22	20	521	0					4	10	1615	20	1	10		
Other kinds	630	10	108	0	336	10	1074	20					311	10	10736	30	39	10	35	20
Other Seeds: Indigo									1470	35	1470	35	2	10	32	0	1	10		
Cotton																				
Other kinds	356	30	348	0	189	30	894	20			894	20	129	30	1235	0	15	10	1380	0
Silk — Raw	7	20	10	0			17	20			17	20								
Manufactured	4	30	28	30	1	0	34	20			34	20					12	30	12	30
Stationery	6373	30	3720	0	118	0	10211	30			10211	30	1346	30	1480	30	1068	20	3896	0
Stone	886	20	63234	10	263	20	64384	10			64384	10	437	10	985	30	1180	30	2603	30
Straw and Grasses for fodder, thatching, etc.									42543	17	42543	17								
Sugar — Refined	1479	20	1031	0	4509	20	7020	10	15303	23	22323	33	6	0	131	10	52	20	182	30
Unrefined	2973	0	2465	10	1108	0	6546	10	67960	11	74506	21	28	30	1986	20	420	20	2435	30
Tea	26	30	113	30	177	10	317	30	200	26	518	16	17	20	15	0	38	10	70	30
Timber	46630	10	11994	10	64	20	58689	0			58689	0	789	20	5857	0	731	30	7378	10
Tobacco	1189	30	331	0			1520	30	6003	14	7524	4	152	0	213	0	178	20	543	20
Wool Raw	58	20	227	30	7	20	293	30			293	30	1	0	11	0	5	0	17	0
Other articles of Merchandize	68592	30	38438	0	7637	20	114668	10			114668	10	5522	20	7340	0	908	10	21944	30
Military Stores	3221	30	39170	0	4297	10	46689	0			46689	0	8237	0	1870	0	1632	20	11739	20

The first head in the foregoing table represents in the fourth column animals imported for slaughter exclusive of animals supplied to the Commissariat. The average weight of flesh is in the case of a goat or sheep 12 seers and about 35 seers per head in the case of large animals. The total weight of flesh thus put in the market is 22,74,634 seer per years. The Muhammadan and Christian population of the City is 1,66,273.* This gives less than 14 seers per annum, or ·6 of a chittak per diem to each non-Hindu member of the population. The average consumption per diem of animal food is estimated by butchers in Lucknow at 4 chittaks per household of 5 persons or 8 of a chittak per head. This will show that the octroi returns of animals imported for slaughter do not adequately represent the number consumed and points to a very large business in the breeding of animals for slaughter within municipal limits or to the evasion of octroi duty, possibly to both.

BAMBUS AND CANES.—The octroi duty on these is levied at 4 per cent. on value and the price by which value is calculated is always given on the hundred. Hence the return which the octroi department has furnished is in numbers. I have separated the octroi number for railway imports from those by road and boat. The railway returns are by weight and the items Canes and Rattans include bambus, but as I could not be sure that the 90,191 bambus and canes entered in the octroi returns as imported by rail were actually the 185 mds. 30 seers of Canes and Rattans shown by the Railway Company (in fact the numbers are utterly inconsistent with the weight) I have shown both. Some interesting facts regarding trade in bambus will be found in Part III. under the head *Báns-farosh*.

The statistics regarding raw cotton and cotton twist and yarn being altogether railway returns require no comment. Their headings suggest all that can be said.

DRUGS AND MEDICINES.—I have had much difficulty in separating drugs and medicines from kirána (groceries) in octroi returns and it was often doubtful under which head I should place some items.

Asafœtida (hing) comes from Cabul. Other drugs not intoxicating have been restricted as far as possible to the ordinary bazar medicines sold by attars and pansaris. The bulk of these are wild products brought from jungles and village waste lands.

Pán is imported by rail as well as by cart and yet the Railway columns in the return furnished me are blank. It is imported by rail from Bardwán, Mahoba, and Bengal generally and from Unao, Barabanki and Rai Bareli districts by cart and headload. For further notes *vide* Tamboli in Part III.

Opium shows only the Government drug.

† Ganja is the leaf, branch and seed of the hemp-plant gathered and pressed together when damp with dew. It is imported from Gwaliyár, Sheopur, Kularas, Khandwa, and Sanaud. There is a variety called Baluchar imported from Cabul and another called Kalidar from Naipal.

† Bhang comes in the form of crushed leaves from Hardoi and Bahraich and Gondah. Through the second named place the Nepalese product comes from Nepalganj.

---

* I have omitted Hindus altogether, although Kashmírís, Káyaths, Bangálís, Panjábís, Khatrís and some other Hindus in Lucknow eat animal food as a regular article of diet.

† Natives call gánja a male plant and bháng female (not grammatically) but whether the difference is botanically correct I cannot say.

Charas is of three kinds (1) sáljaháni which comes from Naipal in long sticks. This is in much demand by saqins. (2) Yárkandi which comes through Amritsar (3) Kashmiri which is the cheapest and is imported to Lucknow by Mughal pedlars. The first-named quality is the best.

The statistics given of gánja, bháng and charas though reliable as far as they go do not represent the total import. There is no return of the drugs imported by cart although the imports from the north are chiefly by that means. I should have inquired as to his imports from the lessee of Muskirát at Lucknow but that I deemed it would hardly be fair to demand information on the point.

DYEING MATERIALS.—The returns in the table for 1878 are only of the materials imported by rail. Octroi duty is not levied on dye-stuffs and therefore the fifth column is blank. The last year in which octroi was levied in Lucknow on these goods was 1876. I have procured the returns of the octroi department for that year.

Name.	Weight.			Value.		
A'l (morinda citrifolia), ...	29	9	8	387	5	6
Bakkal babúl (bark of babúl), ...	7318	24	8	4,821	3	2
Pewri, ...	5	0	6	402	9	3
Phitkari (alum), ...	60	22	0	422	14	0
Tunn (flower of cedrela toona), ...	29	7	2	354	15	9
Lájawardi (lapis lazuli), ...	1	16	0	138	10	0
Dháni (light green), ...	17	5	4	263	1	3
Yellow, ...	37	29	8	620	2	6
Green, ...	1	6	0	22	10	0
Black, ...	16	12	0	248	2	3
Sendur (red lead), ...	74	9	8	1,509	10	0
Tútiya (sulphate of copper), ...	19	33	0	453	8	0
Kasis (sulphate of iron), ...	82	31	0	526	9	9
Kathá, ...	1121	27	12	13,103	9	9
Kusum (safflower), ...	790	32	12	10,071	6	9
Multáni matti (Armenian bole), ...	121	8	0	336	10	0
Gulál (red powder), ...	45	26	4	373	9	3
Tesu (flower of palas, Butea frondosa),	29	18	8	46	3	3
Patang (sappan wood), ...	296	9	4	1,482	0	0
Majenta, ...	447	13	4	845	12	0
Majíth (rubía munjít), ...	188	24	0	2546	6	0
Máju phal (gall-nut), ...	5	35	8	180	15	6
Níl (indigo), ...	18	28	9	2,459	14	0
Náspál (pomegranade rind), ...	4	37	0	29	11	0
Harsingár (nyctanthes arbor tristis), ...	13	39	12	386	10	6
Haldi (turmeric), ...	2,430	33	6	18,703	2	6
Hirmizi (red earth), ...	79	33	8	321	8	6
Har (terminalia citrina), ...	114	31	8	345	13	3
Total, ...	3528	25	7	61,605	5	8

Fibres and fibrous products call for no remark. I am not sure that the railway returns and octroi returns cover the same materials in all respects.

FRUITS, VEGETABLES, NUTS, &c.—The distinction preserved in the detail of cocoa-nut is between those used to make huqqahs (naryal khushk) and those imported as fruit (naryal tar). The former are imported with and without the external fibrous coating. No business in cocoanut fibre has yet been developed in Lucknow. I refer the reader for further notes on cocoa-nuts to the article *huqqawala* in Part III.

Betel nuts (supári, nut of the Areca Catechu) come chiefly from Bengal. They are now imported via Cawnpore and not by Benares because of the break in railway communication at the latter place.

Mahuas are brought into Lucknow from Unao, Barabanki and Bahraich districts, and to some extent from Raï Bareli. They are absorbed in the Sadr Distillery.

The import of foreign fruit is very inadequately shown by the octroi return of 632 maunds. I regret I have not received details of imports by rail.

FUEL.—The import of coal and coke for consumption in the city is almost nil. Charcoal is largely imported. Dhák and tamarind charcoal are chiefly in demand for huqqahs and angethis. Lohars prefer sákhu and dhobis and qalai-gars use mango charcoal. Sakho charcoal comes chiefly from Bahraich by the Naipalgunj road and mango, mahua, babul and tamarind charcoal from Haidar-gahr. The Muhamdi jaugals are the chief source of supply. The same place is also the chief source from which firewood is drawn but mango and mahua are imported from the east by cart. The calculation of fuel dealers is that it does not pay to import by cart from distances beyond 25 kos from the city. The cost of carriage beyond that becomes so heavy that the fuel so imported cannot be sold side by side with that in ported by boat. Kanda (cow-dung cake) is brought in on carts, by boat, and by headload. Castor cakes are imported from all places round the city.

GRAIN.—The total of grain imported is shown at 23,49,402 maunds but the amount on which octroi duty was levied during the year 1878 was 21,24,844 maunds. The reason of the difference is this. The octroi moharrirs at the barriers have no scales or weighing platforms and cannot correctly estimate the weights conveyed in carts and pack-loads. The Chaudhris and brokers of ganjes gave me an average weight for each mode of conveyance and I had the octroi cheque-books of all the nákas examined and the conveyances carrying grain tabulated, and applied the weights (as may be seen in the assessment of a ganj *vide* arhat-ghalla in Part III). This gave a total of 23,49,402 maunds from which I deducted the railway total (which must be correct) and I showed the ba-lance as imported otherwise than by rail. It is optional to take the total of grain imported at 23,49,402 maunds or 21,24,844 maunds, but the former is, I believe, nearer the correct amount. The reason is that octroi duty is not levied on weight of grain but at so much per bullock or other animal drawing or car-rying grain. Hence beopáris bring up a cart of grain with, say, five bullocks

6

to very near a barrier and then drop one and go through with four. The octroi moharrir notes in his cheque-book only the weight as stated by the beopári. I should think it worth while, if octroi be maintained in Lucknow, to introduce weighing platforms and make a fixed allowance for the weight of carts : deduct the cart weight so fixed from the weight registered at the platform and charge octroi on the balance weight according to the value of the grain carried.

The grain exported by rail is but a trifle compared to the total imported whichever total of the two given above, be accepted. The balance cannot be all consumed locally, and it is matter for regret that there is no means of ascertaining correctly the total exported.

HORNS, HIDES AND SKINS.—There is no octroi duty levied on this class of goods and hence there is no return procurable of the import other than by rail. The export by rail is 21,567 maunds 10 seers against 3,257 maunds and 20 seers imports. The reason is that the greatest amount of imports are by road from the north of the Gumti and there being no octroi duty there is no registration of the traffic. As to exports the railway returns, though correct, do not represent total exports for there is considerable export by road to Cawnpore.

KIRANA.—Though I have explained this word by grocery it is an inadequate explanation. Kirána includes all that a pansári sells and he sells sugar, ghi, oil, dye stuffs, raw silk, drugs, medicines, salts and all kinds of dry goods. I have under this head, however, shown only what it would hardly be proper to put under another.

Tallow and wax come from the north, wax chiefly from Nepal hills ; and gums and resins from the Tarai forests. Mishk and záfrán come from Kabul but chiefly from the port of Bombay to Lucknow through Cawnpore.

Kathái is the name given to dried mango stones used as spice in cooking and katha is a preparation of the bark of a tree eaten with pán.*

LAC,—(properly lákh), is a resinous substance which flows from the bargat (Ficus Indica), pákar (ficus venosa), pípal (ficus religiosa), beri (zizyphus jujuba) and perhaps other trees, on account of the puncture made by an insect (the coccus ficus) in the branches for the deposit of its eggs. It is extensively produced, and even the insect artificially propagated, in jungles in the north of Oudh, especially in Gonda and Bahraich Districts.

Dye-lac is used in scarlet dyeing. Stick-lac is dissolved in soda and solution of alum added. This gives a most brilliant colour.

Stick-lac is the substance in its natural state. Shell-lac is the refined stuff used in varnishes, japanning, and sealing wax.

MATTING AND CARPETS.—These are the manufactures of the Central Jail.

METALS.—Closer details than those given in the general table may be given. A few of the more important items imported are :—

Made-up goods, { Iron ware, ... 4,435 maunds 14 seers.
{ Brass vessels, ... 2,530 „ 6 „

These come chiefly from Mahrájganj and Newalganj but also include specialities (vide zaruf birinji farosh).

---

* It is catechu and, although popularly supposed by baniyas to be prepared from the bark only, it is extracted from the chopped wood of the khair (Acacia Catecha), vide p. 23.

Jasta, zinc, ... 2,109 maunds 20 seers.
Sísá, lead, ... 36 ,, 24 ,,
Rángá, pewter, ...
Kánsá, bellmetal, ... 1,017 ,, 38 ,,

PIECE GOODS.—The figures given under this head are incomplete. The Railway Company charges by weight and shows these goods by weight. The octroi department charges on value and by bundle as the case may be. I have been utterly unable to reduce the octroi return to weight and I therefore omit it in the table and note it here :

Piece goods including haberdashery, ... 4,51,348 pieces.
Hosiery and gloves, ... 775 ,,

The latter item is an absurdity : and a total of pieces in the former case without details is useless as a key to the local trade.

GHI, SALTS.—(vide *ghi-farosh,* and *nimak-farosh,* Part III).

SEEDS.—The statistics in this case are reliable.

SILK.—The figures under this head are worth nothing. The consumption of raw silk in Lucknow is enormous in zardozi, kamdani, embroidery, and gold and silver lace weaving.

SUGAR.—Under the head ' refined' sugar I have shown sugar, sugar-candy and khand : under ' unrefined' are classed gur, shira, ráb, and treacle. The import of gur alone was 38,625 maunds.

TIMBER.—Here again I have been unable to assimilate the octroi returns : and I am therefore compelled to show them here separately. I regret that I cannot state the amount which the octroi department would make out to have come by rail. It is perhaps as well I should not attempt to make a calculation for much timber comes by rail which is exempted from the payment of octroi and the Company's returns and the octroi total for import by rail would not tally.

Timber on which octroi was charged in 1878.

Logs, (shisham, tunn, sál, etc.) ... ... 34,263 cubic feet.
Sawn timber (do.) carried on carts, ... 4,654 pieces.
  Do.   (other kinds)   do.   ... 10,038 ,,
  Do.   (of all kinds) carried otherwise,... { 14,062 ,, measuring 12,008 cubic feet
Ballis, ... 12,845.

TOBACCO.—The export must be deducted before local consumption of tobacco can be approximated. It leaves about 7000 maunds of leaf imported in the year. Tobacconists make up the leaf with shira and sajji for the market adding 3 seers of the latter to 2 of the former. This amount of imported leaf would therefore represent 21,000 maunds of made-up tobacco. The annual consumption at 4 maunds per head of population would in Lucknow where the population is 2,73,126 be 27,312 maunds.*

* As a fact the consumption is much greater for I have omitted tobacco which is eaten. Besides the Government estimate of 4 maunds per annum per head of population is small for a city like Lucknow where opium is largely consumed. Opium smoking induces a larger consumption of tobacco.

This leaves 6,312 maunds of made up tobacco consumed in Lucknow in a year unaccounted for. This item represents 2,525 maunds of leaf. The average produce of tobacco is 12 maunds per bigah. At this rate there must be 210 bigahs of land within municipal limits under tobacco cultivation. As much as 176 bigahs have been ascertained by measurement.

Besides the trades to which the statistics given in the table of imports and exports refer there are some interesting figures which I have collected regarding other trades and which may be most conveniently given in this place.

For some years a tax was levied on the precious stones, gold and silver (both ornaments and bullion), and materials for use in manufacture of embroidery (zardozi) and lace (gota) imported into Lucknow and also on the kandilas (*vide* gotawála in Part III.) melted in the gotawálas kachahri in the Chauk. The collection was farmed to one Jagarnath the Daroga of the last named guild. He has placed his registers for three years before me and I have tabulated the imports. The tax was abolished in 1869. He has given me the accounts of the kandila factory for 1876-79 and I have put in the figures for three years.

Year.	Precious Stones.		Made up Jewellery.				Foreign market gold and silver lace etc				Bullion.						Kandilas.		
			Gold.		Silver.		Gold wire.		Lace.		Gold.		Silver.		Total.		Gold.	Silver.	TOTAL.
	Rs.	A.	Rs.	A.	Rs.	A.	Rs.	A.	Rs.	A.	Rs.	A.	Rs.	A.	Rs.	A.	Number.	Number.	Number.
64-65	48907	4	9564	3	621	9	583	8	423	11	...	..	...	...	...	....	1438	1021	2459
65-66	...		...		...		...		...		...		...		...		...	...	
66-67	154618	0	4212	2	1203	1	...	...	145	8	2831	10	3814	13	6646	7	1705	901	2606
67-68	96949	9	12311	1	8839	14	...	...	2415	15	14088	6	14951	5	29039	11	1947	1203	3150
76-77	...	...	...		...	...	...	...	...	...	...		...		...		..	...	4543
77-78	...	...	...	..	...	...	..	...	...		.		...	..	...	...	...	...	4040
78-79	...	...	...	..	...	...	...		...		...		...		..	...	.	..	4502

There is nothing in the table which is so remarkable as the number of Kandilas pointing to an increase in the manufacture of gold and silver lace and of gold embroidery to which I have already referred as one of the staple manufactures of Lucknow. The import of foreign wire has altogether ceased, and all the processes of manufacture are now carried on locally. For further information the reader is referred to the heads bearing on these trades in Part III.

MONEY LENDERS.—It is impossible to give any idea of the money lent in Lucknow. The loans on bahi are innumerable and the Rastogis who lend by augahi and rozahi and practice pawnbroking must have many lakhs of rupees lent in these ways. One of the family of the 'Panchbahiyas,' as a certain firm in Rastogi Tola is called, has over 3 lakhs of rupees lent in pawnbroking alone.

The only statistics available are from the Registrar's office and from this source I have procured statistics for four years past of all deeds registered which are of a class which usually bear interest or are deeds to cover closed loans on interest. I have given the city of Lucknow and the Pargana separately, but the loans are all made by Lucknow money-lenders.

Year.	Deeds of sale Rs. 100 and upwards.		Deeds of sale (less than Rs. 100).		Deeds of mortgage (Rs. 100 and upwards.		Deeds of mortgage (less than Rs. 100).		Deeds of sale.		Obligation for payment of money.		GRAND TOTAL OF BOTH CLASSES.	
	No.	Value.	No.	Value.	No.	Value.	No.	Value.	No.	Value.	No.	Value.	No.	Value.
76-77	318	206436	887	32635	333	286239	550	28344	38	5930	195	165635	2321	725319
77-78	270	255755	964	32862	403	370515	878	37831	101	49283	224	184023	2840	930274
78-79	314	226152	964	36757	396	267816	807	35586	80	22242	143	127347	2704	716600
79-80	363	168905	826	33203	449	232377	680	42333	54	10448	191	192419	2563	679685
Total.	1265	857248	3641	135457	1581	1156947	2915	144094	273	87903	753	669429	10428	3051878
Aver.	316	214312	910	33864	395	289236	728	36023	68	21975	188	167357	2607	762969
76 77	38	35548	26	1023	40	22949	48	2392	69	13016	975	289593	1196	364529
77-78	45	119833	59	2611	61	30637	172	7709	57	7068	904	256640	1298	424498
78-79	38	25162	45	2109	82	52518	152	7047	50	8201	798	268320	1165	363357
79-80	31	19287	32	1826	68	56272	93	4837	42	6800	27	2567	293	91589
Total,	152	199830	162	7569	251	162376	465	21985	218	35085	2704	817120	3952	1243965
Aver.	38	49957	40	1892	62	40594	116	5496	54	8771	676	204280	988	310991

It will be seen how suddenly the total of money lent at interest on mortgaged deeds rose in 1877-78, (the year of drought and distress) and how it is again falling. If the average of the city figures for the four years is taken to represent deeds executed by residents of the city for debt the incidence per head of population is over 2 Rs. 12 annas. If the average of both pargana and city be added together and taken to be money lent and secured or wiped off by deed within the city the total is Rs. 10,73,960 This gives almost Rs. 4 per head of city population. The true incidence of debt secured or wiped off by deed lies somewhere between the two.

The following is a detailed list of the amount of money invested in Government promissory notes in Lucknow, giving the year of the loan and the amount of each loan held. It excludes all money invested as endowments and all notes held by banks. It shows only savings of private individuals invested in Government notes of which the interest is drawn at Lucknow treasury :—

				Rs.
1832-33,	...	...	...	1,37,000
1833-36,	...	...	...	4,56,400
1842-43,	...	...	...	33,59,400
1853-54,	...	...	...	15,500
1854-55,	...	...	...	18,80,700
1854-55,	...	...	...	30,00,000
1865,	...	...	...	11,82,900
1870,	...	...	...	74,500
1872,	...	...	...	3,26,000

				Rs.
1878,	...	...	...	16,500
1879,	...	...	...	97,000
1879,	...	...	...	19,600

Total Rs. ... 105,65,500

The incidence is 38 Rs. 11 as. per head of population. This is a strong contrast to the average of indebtedness and would seem to indicate that there is more a want of field for the employment of capital in productive industry in Lucknow than a want of capital.

ADDENDUM TO PART II.

It is a question of some importance to answer, what is the amount of the necessaries of life consumed within the municipal limits of the native city of Lucknow. I have taken the figures for the four first-class municipalities of the Panjab as a standard, and have calculated what the figures should be for Lucknow. The population of Delhi is taken to be 155,000; of Amritsar 130,000; of Lahaur 100,000; of Multan 55,000; and of Lucknow 275,000. I have been compelled to leave a few items blank here and there in the case of some municipalities, e. g., when exports exceed imports. I have, therefore, calculated only on the average of those municipalities which show a balance of imports.

	Delhi.	Amritsar.	Lahaur.	Multan.	Lucknow.
	Mds.	Mds.	Mds.	Mds.	Mds.
Raw cotton, ..	577	1,880	2,971	..	3,877
European twist and yarn,	13,250	7,069	527	1,087	10,967
Indian do. do.	380	94	1,922	1,266	1.831
European piece goods, ..	121,596	5,411	6,414	9,938	71,680
Indian do. do. ..	..	5,467	1,699	1,856	8,705
Wheat, ..	..	637,277	599,619	1,49,319	11,62,137)
Other food grains, ..	..	522,780	442,884	65,893	9,95,362) *
Ghi, ...	21,295	17,462	18,012	8,130	32,450
Salt, ...	14,789	21,207	15,370	5,664	40,735†
Spices, ..	5,916	..	2,258	..	8,815
Sugar, refined, ..	40,714	31,468	25,075	26,657	61,957
Sugar, unrefined, ..	..	90,506	49,582	32,731	1,66,753
Tea, Indian, ..	499	3,154	1,964	..	4,012
Tea, foreign, ..	1	131	8	15	78

* There should be some regard paid to the fact that Lucknow is the central depôt to which the grain of the north-west of Oudh all comes for export to Cawnpore and other places. The grain comes on bullock-carts and pack animals, and the average stay of a conveyance or pack animal in a gunj is from one morning to another. Thus each animal is three times fed within municipal limits. Bullocks and buffalos used in grain carriage are fed with bhusa, khali and grain. The average of grain given as fodder is 1½ seers per diem to each head of cattle : which would be 2¼ seers for the three times it is fed within municipal limits. The number of bullocks and buffalos which come into Lucknow carrying grain is 1,62,700 per annum (on an average calculation). This means a consumption of 9,177 maunds of grain which has passed municipal barriers. Add this to the other items of food grains, and the total of food grains consumed within Lucknow city rises to 21,66,676 maunds per annum. The average number of persons coming in charge of conveyances and pack animals carrying grain, exclusive of those coming with grain carried by rail, is 6,93,300. Calculating at the rate given in the statement above, they consume 1,490 maunds of grain in the day and-a-half that they are in the City with conveyances. This gives a grand total of 21,68,166 maunds, or, as near as may be, 8⅞ maunds per annum per head of the population of Lucknow.

† Of which 24,584 maunds would be Lahauri.

PART III.

PART III.

NOTES ON TRADERS AND PROFITS OF TRADES.

A.

Abkar.—Distiller of country spirits.

All country spirits are made within a Government distillery, called ábkárí godown by licensed distillers. The distiller (kashíd dár) pays Government Rs. 1 fee per annum for license to distil and Rs. 2 per mensem for license to issue spirits. Government also levies one rupee still head duty on each gallon of liquor which is issued from the godown.

Country spirit is made from *mahua* or from *shíra,* which is first steeped in large earthen jars buried up to the neck in the ground. In a jar are placed 30 seers of *mahuas* and on them is poured half a *ghara* of water. The quantity of *shira* infused is a maund per jar and on this are poured five *gharas* of water and three *gharas* of *ghúra* (the refuse emptied out of the copper caldrons or *degs* used in distilling). It is optional to the distiller to manufacture from *shíra* or *mahuas,* but the bulk of country spirit is made from the latter. Shíra ferments in fifteen days in cold weather and in eight in hot weather. Mahua requires only nine in the coldest weather and but five in the hottest.

Whether the stuff steeped in the jar (*mathor*) be shíra or mahua the contents of one jar suffice to supply one caldron (*deg*). The *deg* is covered with an inverted earthen pan (*nánd*) closed air tight and from their cover come two worms (*naicha*) made of bambu through which the vapour passes down into two vessels called *bhapkas* which rest buried in water up to their necks in a *hauz* or cistern placed at ground level.

The *deg* is emptied of the ghúra or refuse as each batch (*táo*) of stuff is distilled and when two batches have been distilled once (*ekbára*), the deposit of both is thrown together into one *deg* and redistilled. This is called *doátasha* and all country spirit now issued is *doátasha.* In this way one *deg* is used nine times in 27 hours—six times for *ekbára* and three times for *doátashá* liquor.

The expense of the distiller are 1½ maunds of wood for each time a *deg* is used. He pays also 2½ as. to the water contractor each time a *deg* is used for *ekbára* distilling, and Rs. 3-14 per mensem for chokídárí and conservancy. He requires two servants at Rs. 5 each per mensem and he expends Rs. 2 a month in lighting his shed at night.

To determine the present cost of production and profit of distilling at the Sadr distillery of Lucknow—take a long term of days to avoid fractions and suppose the prices of all things to remain as now. Shíra is now Rs. 2-14 the maund and mahua 30 seers the rupee. Wood (which distillers buy wholesale) is Rs. 30 the 100 maunds. The yield of mahua is six gallons per *deg* and of shíra 7 gallons.

A period of 360 days gives 320 terms of 27 hours each. Take the yield for that time of mahua from one *deg* which will be 11,520 gallons and as it is almost a year take the expenses of production and fees for a whole year. The account is :—

	Rs.	As.	P.	Rs.	As.	P.
1,690 maunds of mahuas, ...				1,920	0	0
4,320 ,, firewood, ...1,296	0	0				
1,920 degs (water for, @ 2½ as. per deg), ... 300	0	0				
12 months lighting (at Rs. 2 p. m. per deg), 24	0	0				
12 ,, chokídárí and conservancy, at Rs. 3-14 per mensem per deg , ... 46	8	0				
12 months, two servants at Rs. 5 each p. m.,... 120	0	0	1,786	8	0	
Duty on 11,520 gallons at Re. 1 per gallon, ...				11,520	0	0
License fees annual and monthly, ...				25	0	0
Total Rs.				15,251	8	0

This liquor now sells wholesale at the godown for Rs. 1-12 per gallon ; that is, the whole yield will be worth Rs. 20,160. The profit is Rs. 4,908-8 or slightly over 5 annas 3 pie per gallon.

Take now the yield of shíra-sharáb for the same term and calculate in the same way.

The yield will in this case be 13,440 gallons.

	Rs.	As.	P.
1,920 maunds of shíra, ...	5,120	0	0
Firewood and other items as before, ...	1,786	8	0
Duty on 13,440 gallons, ...	13,440	0	0
License fee annual and monthly, ...	25	0	0
Total Rs....	20,371	8	0

This liquor now sells wholesale at the godown for Rs. 2-2 per gallon : that is, the whole yield will be worth Rs. 28,560. The profit is Rs. 8,188-8 or almost 9 annas 9 pie per gallon.

It is not to be supposed that the prices of all materials required in the manufactures of country spirit are stationary, or that the prices at which spirits are issued or the profits per gallon always the same : but the object of the preceding calculation is to show the cost of production, price, and profit of manufacture of country liquor at the present time : and, I may add, that having made similar calculations for other periods I have not found the rate of profit differ materially. The season of the year does not very much affect the price of country spirit, that is, country spirit, of mahuas forinstance, is not necessarily cheaper when the fruit is in season, for the purchase and storing of the fruit are practically a monopoly in the hands of the licensed distillers who enjoy a monopoly of manufacture. There is no such competition between licensed distillers as will operate to greatly reduce the price at which spirit is issued from the Government distillery.

The abkári year runs from 1st October to the 30th September and the following table shows the amount of country spirit issued from the Sadr distillery Lucknow in 1878-79 and in the first four months of 1879-80 : also the number of distillers and the number of shops for the whole district of Lucknow :—

	No. of distillers.	No. of gallons issued.	No. of retail shops.	Fees on retail shops.	No. of thoks.	Fees on thoks.
1878-79	9	51,589	142	23,895	6	144
1st Oct. 1878 to 31st Jan. 1879,	...	14,594	...	...	...	...
1879-80,	7	...	132	31,795	6	1,542
1st Oct. 1879 to 31st Jan. 1880,	...	19,384	...	...	...	...

The term thok means a wholesale shop lying without city limits sanctioned for the convenience of shop-keepers buying wholesale but residing far from the Sadr distillery. There are six of these. They were let at fixed rates in 1878-79 but were auctioned in 1879-80. The vast enhancement of revenue which resulted on the adoption of the system of auctioning leases of thoks indicates the lucrativeness of the trade in country spirits.

The liquor issued to thoks is included in the total issue for the District. Hence to estimate profits of the retail shops by the district figures would be misleading. I therefore take the number of shops in the city and the number of gallons issued to city shops as a basis of calculation (there being no thok in the city) and calculate minimum profits of retail shop-keepers (gaddidár).

Within the abkári year 1878-79 there were issued to city shops 34,910 gallons. Suppose this liquor to have been all mahua spirit. It is less profitable than shíra-sharáb and will therefore not vitiate calculation by causing an overestimate of retailer's profits. The number of shops was 40 and these were let at auction sale of leases for Rs. 20,074. The average selling price of mahua spirit at retail shops was 8 annas the bottle. Six bottles go to the gallon, that is, the retail shops in Lucknow realized at least Rs. 1,04,730 by the liquor issued to them in the year. They paid to Government Rs. 20,074 on their leases and hence have had Rs. 83,656 to cover original wholesale cost of spirit. The cost of spirit at the godown was in 1878-79 on the average certainly not more than it now is, and was probably less, but take it to have been as at present : price of issue Re. 1-12 per gallon. The cost price was Rs. 55,842. Thus the balance of profits in favour of the retailers in city limits was Rs. 27,814. As I have before remarked the average wholesale price of mahua spirit was in 1878-79 probably lower than it now is (February 1880) and mahua spirit is less profitable than shíra-sharáb. Further, I have taken all liquor as mahua spirit and have supposed all spirit to be sold unadulterated. Therefore, when, having put all the conditions down in the form least favorable to the trader I have made out Rs. 27,814 profits to retailers where they pay Rs. 20,074 to Government for their licenses or fees on leases, I think I may fairly conclude that as a rule a retailer of country spirit will realize within a year profits at least equal to the fee, rent, or whatever it may be called, that he pays to Government for his shop-lease.

Acharwala.—This trader makes pickles (áchár), chatnis, and preserves (murabba) from mangos, date (chúhárah), raisins (kishmish), lemon, (nebu), jackfruit (kathal and barhal), ginger (adrakh), turnips (shaljam), cucumber (khírá), papaw (papaiya, rund kharbúza), oranges, gourd (petha), myrobalan (ánwala and har), pears (náspáti), quince (bihi) bámbú, apple (seb), pineapple (anánás), guava (amrúd), tamarind (imli) and other fruits. The ingredients used to make syrup (qíwám) are sugar (kand) and lemon juice : but the latter is seldom added to the syrup except in the case of apple-preserves.

Preserves are sold at 8 as., 12 as., or 1 Re. per seer. Take one of each class. Preserved ginger is sold at 12 as. the seer. The achárwála takes $\frac{3}{4}$ seer of kand which costs 5 as : half a seer of ginger which costs 2 as. The kand is placed in a vessel containing $2\frac{1}{4}$ seers of water and boiled until it is reduced to such a consistency that it adheres to a slip of bambu when thrust in and pulled out of the vessel. The ginger is then boiled in water and when it becomes soft and clear it is thrown into the syrup. A paisa worth of essence of keora (Pandanus odoratissimus) is added for perfume. This gives about a nawábí seer (96 Rs. weight) of preserved ginger which has cost $7\frac{1}{4}$ as., excluding firewood which would be an anna at most. Total cost $8\frac{1}{4}$ as. This preserve is sold at 12 as. the English seer, or 14 as. 4 p. the nawábí seer.

Apple preserve is sold at Re. 1 per seer. The cost is : 6 apples 6 annas ; $\frac{1}{2}$ seer kand (good quality) 3 as.; lemon 6 pies ; *keora* 3 pies ; firewood 1 anna. Total cost 10 as. 9 pies for making a nawábí seer which is sold at Re. 1 per English seer for Re. 1-3-2.

Preserved *ánwalas* are sold at the cheápest rate, 8 as. a seer. In this case $\frac{1}{2}$ seer of *shakkar* (unrefined sugar) is issued. This costs 2 as. 6 pies. Fresh *anwalas* $\frac{1}{2}$ seer, 6 pies. Keora in larger quantity than in the former cases as *ánwalas* are bitter, viz. 2 paisa worth. One anna's worth of wood is needed as before. This will give a nawábi seer, costing 4 as. 6 pies—to sell at 8 as. the nawábi seer, or for 9 as. 7 pies when sold at 8 as. the English seer.

Pickles are sold at 6 as. or 8 as. per seer.

Mango pickles are made thus :—¾ seer vinegar, 9 pies: mangos (dried) ⅛ seer, 3 pies; cheap shakkar, ⅛ seer 6 pies : red pepper one chhatánk, 3 pies : *kalaunji* (Nigella Indica) 3 pies : ginger 3 pies : mint (podína) 3 pies ; salt 1½ pies ; miscellaneous small fruit (raisins &c.) one anna. Total 3 as. 7½ p. This gives one seer pickles and profits of sale at 6 as. per seer are 2 as 4½ pies.

The manufacturer and vendor of pickles are usually one and the same person. There is no wholesale and retail dealing as separate businesses; and all dealing in pickles is by the *sirkári* seer. On the other hand dealing in preserves is in two hands—the manufacturer's and the retailer's.

The former buys his ingredients and manufactures and sells at nawábi seer rates The retailer purchases at nawábi seer rate and sells by the lumbari seer. Their relative cost prices and profits in the sample cases stand thus :—

	Cost of materials etc. at nawábi rate			Sold by manufacturer and retailer at nawábi rate for			Sold by retailer at lumbari seer rate for		
	Rs.	As.	P.	Rs.	As.	P.	Rs.	As.	P.
Kuwalas,	... 0	4	6	0	8	0	9	7	0
Ginger,	... 0	8	3	0	12	0	0	14	4
Apples,	... 0	10	9	1	0	0	1	3	2

The demand for preserves and pickles is not large. They are articles of luxury and the profits of manufacture must be high. Further, the demand is so far precarious that there is risk of loss and deterioration of the value of stock and this necessitates a high rate of profit in goods sold to compensate for potential loss on goods unsold.

Addadar.—This word properly signifies the owner of a stand or station where persons of the same profession, porters, bearers, carriers, carters, and the like congregate, and who receive from them a portion of their earnings in return for the advantage given them by connection with the stand as a means of securing employment. The word is now seldom used in cities except for the proprietor of a station of doli-bearers : and the term *adda kaháran* is met with in lists of licensed traders.

The system of business is this. A kahár having some capital and a connection makes up a number of dolis and settles at a central part of a city. He enters into an agreement with a number of kahárs, professional doli-bearers, and retains two for each doli. The kahárs hold themselves in readiness to carry a doli for the *addadár* when he calls on them to attend and whatever their earnings be, they pay two annas in the rupee to the *addadár*. There is a fixed charge for every well-known distance in the city and there is a separate charge made for the time the kahárs and doli are detained beyond the time spent in carrying. Thus the fare from the Chauk to the Kachahri and back is 4 as. for a doli with two bearers and 1 anna extra for every half hour that the doli is detained, or 4 as. extra for the whole hours of business. It must be added that where the person hiring the doli lives at a distance from the adda, he must pay for the distance from the aḍḍa to his residence and thence to place of destination; but as a rule aḍḍas are sufficiently numerous and so well placed that any person needing a doli has no great distance to send to procure one. Dolis are most in demand for short distances within native quarters of large cities where pardah-nishins and others go through narrow streets to visit neighbours. There is also a great call on aḍḍas at night for the conveyance of ladies of the demi-monde and especially of the many not openly unchaste females who are to be found in large cities. The poverty to which many families, chiefly Muhammadan, formerly maintained by the bounty and extravagance of the native court have been reduced in Lucknow since English rule began, unfortunately drives many well connected females to ply a trade under cover of the night. The chief aḍḍas of Lucknow are close to the residences of pimps: and indeed one sometimes hears the term aḍḍa randiyán used to denote a bawd's business connection. The aḍḍa kahárán and the aḍḍa randiyán will generally be found not far apart.

Adda-gari *vide* Argarah.

Afiun-farosh.—The opium vendor has a license from Government and is supposed to sell only opium issued from the Government Treasury. He is required to keep a register of sales. The Government price is Rs. 15 per seer and the vendor can sell at his own price. He sells in various ways, *e. g.* in pills (golis) of from 4 to 5 máshas each, and in lumps of so many anna's worth as demanded by purchasers. If he sells *golis* he makes them and prices them so that he vends at the rate of Rs. 24 per seer, and the chief demand is for these pills. If the vend is by anna's worth he arranges his price at from Rs. 18 to 19 per seer, and in this case the vendor has increased his weight by damping and adulterating the Government standard opium so that he really sells at the lowest computation at about Rs. 20 per seer.

Opium vendors undoubtedly drive a large trade in contraband opium. This they purchase for Rs. 8 per seer at most and keep concealed somewhere on their premises, generally in a small mud vessel hid in a hole in the wall or ground. There is something facetious about the method of illicit sale as described to me. The licensed opium-vendor places before him at his shop a small pile of Government opium which he calls ' sirkárí maḥádeo.' A purchaser comes up and takes his seat. The vendor seeing he has before him a hardened opium consumer asks ' Do you not prefer the *dúdhi afiún*.' This term is that given to the smuggled opium which inveterate opium eaters much prefer to the standard article. The purchaser remarks it is hard to get *dúdhi afiún* and the vendor says he has a very little which he has with much difficulty stored, and after much feigned reluctance he slips inside and produces a little which he sells. This sale will of course not appear in the shop register and indeed the opium disposed of in golis is not all entered, for the opium sold by the anna's worth system has generally been sufficiently weighted by moisture and adulteration to account when shown in the register for all that the vendor purchased from the Government.

The expenses of the opium shop are Government fees for license and rent of shop. To which must be added the pay of the shopkeeper where the licensee is not himself the vendor. Allowing for all these expenses—there is still, by the system of sale practised by licensees, a sure profit of 25 per cent. at least to the licensee on the Government price of all opium issued to licensee; but the illicit profits by dealing in contraband opium are practically limited only by risk of detection.

The chief opium shops in Lucknow are seven:—

1.	That at	Chauk Khass,	Thánah	Chauk.
2.	do.	Amínábád,	do.	Ganeshgunj.
3.	do.	Huzratgunj,	do.	do.
4.	do.	Saádatgunj Kalán,	do.	Saádatgunj.
5.	do.	Dáliganj.	do.	Husanganj.
6.	do.	Husenábád,	do.	Daulatganj.
7.	do.	Deori Agha Mir,	do.	Wazirganj.

Ahir *vide* **Dudh-farosh.**

Ainak-saz.—This is the oculist and optician but his name does not imply the same scope and skill of manufacture as the English words. Indeed the ordinary ainak-saz is merely one who sets in frames and guards glasses which he has procured from bisátís; but there will in most large cities be found manufactures of lenses who also set those lenses to order and these are sometimes exceedingly skilful men. There is in Lucknow behind the Tahsín Masjid near the Chauk an ainak-saz called Muhamad Abrahim who commands a very large custom. He has a moderate scientific knowledge and extensive practical experience. He purchases the materials for manufacture—Crystal and pebbles—and makes concave (kulhiya) and convex (nigáhdár) lenses and also a very strong magnifying lens used by persons afflicted with the disease called *motiyabind*. He has stones with prepared curved surfaces both convex and concave adapted by determined curvature to the manufacture of lenses of required power, and all lenses are made up to order. An applicant for a pair of spectacles consults this optician and his eyesight is tested on the same principles as a European oculist adopts, and the power of lens required being determined, it is made up. There are sixteen degrees of power of lenses whether kulhiya, nigáhdár, or motiyabind, and these are termed chhitánks. It sounds strange to hear one's eyes spoken of as requiring glasses of so many chhitanks power but it is the oriental idiom.

The materials used for manufacture are glass and crystal, but chiefly crystal, of various colours, the best being *dhunaila, sufaid,* and *nilkanthi*. The *dhunaila* is said to relieve the eyes, *sufaid* is clearest, and *nilkanthi* is a light grayish-blue tint, a neutal colour. Crystal is imported in blocks or rough lumps from Kabul, Naipál, Haidarábád, and Birhma: and is delivered in Lucknow at from Rs. 3-2 to Rs. 4 per seer. It is held in the hand and cut in thin layers or slices by means of a steel wire strung from horn to horn of a bow and these slices are cut into elliptical or round pieces and ground on the convex or concave stones already alluded to. The triturating medium used in grinding the lenses is a substance called *mal*, a paste made of the powder which falls from precious stones when they are in the hands of the almas-tarash or begri. When the lens has been prepared of required strength it is given a smoothness and polish by rubbing on a leather strop and the polishing medium is *bari*.

Aina-saz.—This is a looking-glass manufacturer. The quality of glass necessary for this trader's business is not made in Lucknow. Light but clear glass is brought from Calcutta and sold by bisátís, but a thick and clear glass imported from Aleppo through Bombay is most highly esteemed. The aina-sáz merely cuts the glass and covers it on one side with tinfoil (panní) and quicksilver (párá). There are no famous aina-sázes in Lucknow and the best looking-glasses are imported from Cawnpore and Delhi, and no trader of this class in Lucknow can be called on to pay License Tax.

Almas Tarash.—This term is indifferently used in describing the diamond-cutter proper and the begri, nagíná sáz and others, all of whom perform different operations of trade and are really quite separate traders. It will be convenient, however, to deal with all of them under this head as they are all concerned with precious stones : and this article read with that on Jauharí will give a complete view of the whole trade in precious stones and their counterfeits.

The almás tarásh (also called hakkák) cuts diamonds at a lathe with a revolving steel disc called *patsán*. This is set in motion with the ordinary *kamání* and *tasmá* such as carpenters use to move the *barmá*. Close to the patsán but not quite touching it is a second disc which is stationary ; on the circumference of this disc are fixed clasps called *ghoriyá*. In one of these the diamond is fastened. The *patsán* is set in motion and the *ghoriyá* holding the diamond is pressed against the *patsán* by a lever called *ánkurá*. The diamond is cut by the surface of the disc not by the circumference, else the facet cut would not be a plane but a curve. The *patsán* is kept moist by the application of a paste or starch (*máwá*) made of the powder of diamonds gathered as the dust falls from the lathe.

Diamonds are cut either *parab, polkí,* or *kanwál* (*vide* Jauharí) and the diamond cutter is paid accordingly.

Parab	Rs. 3	per rati.
Polki	,, 4	,,
Kanwal	,, 5 to 6	,,

The *begri* is the cutter of other precious stones. There are many begris in Lucknow but the last almás-tarásh remaining in Lucknow in 1879 has gone to Banáras.

There are three discs used for cutting precious stones other than diamonds· The first is called *ragrái sán*, the second is called *mahín sán*, and the third *jilą sán*. The first and second are made of *kuranḍ*, corundum stone (adamantinus corundum). The first is of rougher manufacture than the second. It is used to bring the stone roughly into shape while the second is much finer and cuts the facets. The third disc is made of *phul* (bell-metal) for topáz (pukhráj), garnet (yáqút), emerald (panná), and sapphire (nílam): and of *rángá* (pewter), for the *lálrí* and other soft stones. The last sán gives the smooth polish (*opní*). In all cases the máwá used to moisten the sán must be made of the powder of the stone to be cut, emerald powder for emeralds, ruby for rubies, and so on.

Precious stones other than diamonds are cut *taurá*, *mathailá*, and *tilákridár* terms which are explained (Part II. Jauharí) and the *begrí* is paid accordingly.

	Taura.	Mathailá	Tilakri-dár.
Panna, yáqút, Nílam, pukhráj, & Lálri,	Re. 1 per rati.	8 as. per rati.	8 as. per rati.
Gomedak,	ditto.	ditto.	not cut in this form.

Coral (munga) is cut either in dánas (beads) or in nagínas for setting : but in either case the begri receives Rs. 4 per toláh for cutting up the *shákh* (branch) as coral is termed in the rough form.

Next after the almástarash and begri comes the *bidhiya*. This is the workman who perforates precious stones, pearls, coral, &c. The instrument used for piercing is a steel *barma* worked with a *tasma* and *kamani*. The object to be pierced is placed in a tipahi on the ground before which the bidhiya squats and a cup is placed at a little distance above and so contrived that water comes falling drop by drop on the hole which is being pierced. The wages of the *bidhiya* are :—

Hira,	...	...	...	5 Rs. per rati
Panna,	...	•••	...,	1 an do.
Yáqút,	...	...	...,	1 ,,· do.
Nílam,	...	...	...,	2 ,, do.
Pukhráj,	...	...	...,	1 ,, do.
Gomedak,	...	...	...	½ an. do.
Lálri,	...	...	...	1 ,, do.
Firoza,	...	...	...	1 ,, do.
Munga,	...	..	...	1 Re per tolah.
Moti,	...	...	...	8 as. per tánk.*

There is still another workman to be noticed, the *kataiya*. His business is to cut into smaller pieces the large mass of crystal, topáz or whatever it be, which a jauharí buys or imports. He does this with a steel wire strung from horn to horn of a semi-circular bow. He either works at daily wages of 8 as. or at task rates from 4 as. to 8 as. per score of smaller pieces, to which he reduces the larger mass. The smaller the pieces to which it is reduced the higher the rate paid to the *kataiya*.

---

* Tank is equal to 24 rati.

8

There was under native rule a large business done in precious stones in Lucknow and skilful diamond cutters were not uncommon, but since the British occupation of Oudh there has been a decline in this trade and in its place has sprung up a very extensive business in the manufacture and sale of imitation gems, counterfeit stones, etc. The manufacture of these imitations and counterfeits is carried on to great perfection by Kallan Khán. He manufactures glass brilliants into which he infuses colour so skilfully as to deceive dealers in precious stones, not to say the ordinary unwary public. His work is called *do palka* (do pallah ká kám) as it combines two operations, the manufacturing and colouring, as opposed to the work of the *naginasáz* who merely cuts up pieces of coloured glass.

The naginasáz uses the same sáns as the *begri :* but in the case of counterfeits made of glass the third *sán* is made of wood and the second is called *mal sán.* The latter and the first are both made of *kurand.* The *máwá* is made from a substance resembling powdered slate. Instead of the *ghoriya* a slip of bambu called *kánid* is used, held in the hand for applying the *nag* (piece of glass or other substance being cut) to the sán glass and pebbles are not the only materials sought after by the nagína-sáz. He will not despise fragments of glazed porcelain and he will eagerly clutch pieces of the coloured borders of English crockery. A nagína-sáz may be either a manufacturer and vendor or merely a labourer working for wages. In the latter case he receives 8 as. per score of *nags* which he turns out and in the former case 12 as. per score is the average selling price. The retailer who vends in broken lots (*phut kar*) or singly will sell such *nags* for the most he can get and it may be taken that he sells at double his cost price.

The class of business carried on by a manufacturer like Kallan Khán is of course more profitable than that of the ordinary nagína-sáz, for he can deceive the skilful jauhari as well as the undiscerning public and a jauharí will often close with a skilful counterfeiter for the sake of the great profit which such a partnership will obviously afford.

Arad-farosh *vide* Chakkiwala.

Araishwala.—This is the class of trader that makes up takhts, táziyas, toys, flowers, fruits, and nosegays, pitáras, belis, doors, and other festive decorations such as paper and talc lanterns, and horses and other figures of paper-pulp. The materials required in this business are paper of all kinds and colours, talc of all colours, bambus, brass tinsel, paste, catgut and thread.

The demand for the goods produced is confined to occasions of festivity such as marriage processions, and of mourning as in the Muharram : but there is of course a larger demand in a wealthy city than in villages and especially in a Muhammadan city like Lucknow. At best an áráishwálá can hardly ever earn Rs. 500. profits of trade in a year.

Araq-kash.—This is the distiller of extracts and essences of flowers, etc., which are widely consumed as beverages and as medicinal draughts. They are retailed by aṭṭárs.

The preparations most in demand are made from guláb (rose), keoṛá (pandanus odoratisimus), mandí (sphœranthus Indicus), makoí (Sarsaparilla), laung (clove), iláchí (cardamom), nímbú (lemon), dhaniyá (coriander), podína mint), and saunf (aniseed).

The mode of distilling is that adopted in making country spirit with *deg, naicha* and *bhapka,* and the case of *guláb ká araq* will serve as a sample for all.

The average *deg* holds three gharas of water and into it are poured two gharas of water and about 10,000 roses. The fire is applied about 10 A.M., and the whole is distilled by sunset. This *ek bára araq* is re-distilled next day and yields finally doátasha araq about 12 seers. The consumption of wood is 4 mds. per diem which is at most a rupee, certainly seldom more and generally less. There are two servants to attend the *deg* at 1½ as. per diem each. The present price of roses is 1250 the rupee : but they have been as dear as 800 and are generally as cheap as 2,000 the rupee.

Cost of production of 12 seers guláb ká araq :—

10,000 roses,	... Rs.	8	0	0
Two maunds firewood,	... ,,	2	0	0
Two servants two days at 1½ as. each per diem,	... ,,	0	6	0
Total Rs.		10	6	0

The araq-kash sells the araq at Re. 1 per seer thus realizing profit Re. 1-10 or within a trifle of 16 per cent. on his outlay.

Roses are procurable everywhere but the variety usually used is what natives call the 'faslí guláb' which comes into market in Chait after the Holí.

Keoṛá araq is not made in Lucknow but imported in qarábás or glass flagons from Jaunpur. The carriage is by boat.

Mundí is procurable at all places. Lucknow grass-cutters bring it to market in bundles which sell at 4 as. each. One bundle will suffice for two degs and the araq-kash sells at Re. 1-8 per maund to retailers who sell at 1 anna per seer.

Makoí is imported dry and sold by *Márwáris* to araq-kashes at Rs. 8 per maund. The araq is sold by them at Rs. 2 per maund to aṭṭárs who retail at 2 as. the seer.

Laung ká araq is not made in Lucknow.

Iláchi ká araq is made up to order, from either *baṛí* or *chhoṭí iláichí.* The former is purchased from *pansáris* by the person giving the order for 14 as. the seer, and the latter for from Rs. 10 to Rs. 15 the seer and delivered by him to the araq-kash.

Podína is bought by the araq-kash at 2½ as. the panseri. He sells the araq at Rs. 2 per maund to aṭṭárs who retail at 2 as. the seer.

Saunf ranges in price according to the state of the market from Rs. 6 to Rs. 20 per maund. It is at present Rs. 12 per maund. The araq is sold at Rs. 4 per maund to attárs who retail at 2 as. per seer.

Argarah is the name given to the employment of livery stable keepers who send out vehicles for hire. The word is said to be a corruption of addá-gár and to have denoted originally hackery carriage stands at Railway stations. This may be so.

Some livery keepers have as many as ten gárís and others only one or two, but in Lucknow all are required to take out a Municipal License for each such conveyance and conveyances are classed in two grades and the fares regulated accordingly. If, therefore, the probable profits of a first and second-class conveyance be determined it is a very simple matter to tax the owner according to the number of gárís he has running.

The second class vehicles convey native passengers to and from trains. The average chance, as far as I have been able to ascertain, is six fares of 4 as. each per diem. This is Re. 1-8 and excludes odd jobs from place to place in the city : and gives Rs. 557-8 per annum.

The cost of keeping this class of gárí, supposing it to run with a pair of ponies is :—

Grass 2 as. per diem,	... Rs.	45	10	0
Grain (cheap kinds 20 seers the rupee or thereabouts,)	... „	54	12	0
Driver, at Rs. 4 per mensem,	... „	48	0	0
One bálgír, ...	... „	36	0	0
Nalbandí, ...	... „	9	0	0
Ghí and guṛ, (occasionally),	... „	12	0	0
Oiling wheels, ...	... „	2	8	0
Lighting with oil, ...	... „	5	11	3
Repairs to gárí and loss by selling worn out and buying fresher tattús,...	„	60	0	0
Allow ten days not running owing to repairs, ...	... „	15	0	0
	Total Rs.	288	9	3

This will leave profits Rs. 258-14-9.

Now, take a first class pálkí-gárí. If it run to and from trains and if the average is the same as in the last case—six fares per diem and the pay 8 as. per fare—the daily income will be Rs. 3 : but the chance of fares is really less than six for European passengers who create demand for first class vehicles are fewer than native passengers who engage 2nd class gárís. Say the average is 5 fares per diem. That gives Rs. 2-8 per diem or Rs. 9-12-8 per annum, and it is hardly an overestimate for the hire of a first class vehicle is in Lucknow as much as Rs. 3 per diem.

The cost of keeping the conveyance is about as follows :—

Grass for a pair of ponies at 3 as. per diem, Rs.	68	7	0
Gram eight seers per diem @ 16 seer the rupee, average price, ... „	182	8	0
Driver, at Rs. 5 per mensem, ... „	60	0	0
Bálgír, at Rs. 3 do., ... „	36	0	0
Nálbandí, ... „	12	0	0
Ghí, gur & occasionally, ... „	24	0	0
Candles, ... „	9	0	0
Oil for wheels,... ... ... „	2	8	0
Repairs and loss by selling old and buying other tattús, ... „	100	0	0
Ten days hire lost by vehicle being under repair, ... „	25	0	0
Total ... „	519	7	0

This will leave Rs. 383-1-0 profits in the year and it is a very low estimate, for I have set the average daily hire at only Rs. 2-8. I should say that a first-class pálkí-gárí kept by a stable-man who has a good connection is worth about Rs. 500 per annum and a second class vehicle about Rs. 250.

Arhat-ghalla.—This is the business of grain-broking but it will be as well under this head to dispose of grain-dealers in general.

The grain trade of Lucknow is conducted on a system which needs explanation but which when understood much facilitates the taxation of grain-brokers. In the first place it must be understood that all grain brought within the limits of the Lucknow Municipality is brought to some ganj and the *beopári* importing the grain, or his servant in charge who passes the grain, at the octroi barriers (conveyed by cart, beast of burden or headload), declares the ganj to which he is taking the grain and the octroi muharrir registers the mode of conveyance, the weight and kind of grain which the carrier alleges he is conveying, and the amount of duty paid at the barrier. The importer—generally called beopári in all large transactions—brings this grain on to a ganj and there through a middle-man, *arhatiya* or broker, vends to a purchaser or purchasers. The grain is generally purchased in a lump sum by some storer or factor, or exporter : and sometimes in lots by *pharyas*. A *pharya* generally squats in a ganj under the wing of a broker and buys each day various lots of grain which he retails in the ganj : and the word may be taken to mean 'retailer of grain within limits of a ganj.' The grain storer or cornfactor is called *bharsárwálá*. The word is a corruption from *bhandsál* a grain-store and the proper name for a grain-storer is *bhandsáli*. The exporter is termed *dasáwar* and the derivation is obvious.

There are two classes of *ganjes*. The first is the ganj built as an enclosure somewhat like a sarai and the proprietor lets it out to a lessee and this lessee is termed the *chaudhri*. The shops in this class of ganj are let to grain-brokers and they rent according to the space occupied. Each arhatiya receives all the profits of his own business and pays the chaudhri the customary dues. The other class of ganj is that in which the brokers are a coparcenary body termed a *panth*. Of this class is Thakurganj where there are four brokers who recognise one of their number as chaudhri and they treat their income as a common fund which they throw together and divide in four 4-anna shares. He who is the chaudhri also takes chaudhri's dues. He is so to speak lambardar and the others are co-sharers in a corporate ganj.

Of whatever class the ganj may be, the chaudhri and proprietor keep muharrirs who each day register the number and details of conveyances that come to each broker. From these books the details of each broker's business as such can be discovered for any given period. The octroi books do not give this detail. The latter show only the gáris or other conveyances declared at the barriers to be about to proceed to certain destinations. The chaudhri's and proprietor's or lessee's books show the number of gáris, beasts of burden or headloads that come to each broker each day because the chaudhri's and proprietor's dues are levied accordingly from the brokers.

What are the customs of ganjes, the chaudhri's and proprietor's dues, and the commission charged by brokers? This is a question which is easy in one part and extremely difficult in the other part to answer.

As to chaudhris and proprietors, there cannot be the slightest doubt that the general rule in all ganjes in Lucknow is that these parties receive through the brokers :—

				Proprietor	Chaudhri.
Per 4-bullock cart,	...	4 as.	*i. e.*	3 annas	1 anna.
„ 3 ditto,	...	3 „	„	2¼ „	9 pies.
„ 2 ditto,	...	2 „	„	1½ „	½ anna.
„ 1 ditto,	...	1 „	„	9 pies	3 pies.
„ buffalo, ...	...	6½ pies „		4½ „	2 „
„ bullock, } „ tattu, }	...	4 „	„	3 „	1 pie.
„ buqcha (headload), ...					nil.

The only exceptions I know of are (1) to Dakshinaganj where the rates are a trifle lower, but the difference is made up in grain: and (2) other ganjes in which there is something levied on buqchas.

The difficult part of the question to answer is as regards the commission charged by brokers. The first point ascertained beyond doubt is that the broker is paid both by the beopári who brings him the grain and by the purchaser who buys through him. I have taken statements of many beopáris, brokers, purchasers both for export and storage, and of some mahájans who have large transactions as bankers to grain-brokers. It is a universal rule in Lucknow that the broker takes ' taka fi rupiya.' He takes two paisa in the rupee on the ganj price.

Next, what does the broker take from the beopári? The brokers in ganjes north of the Gumti levy from beopáris one rupee per 4-bullock cart, and rateably four annas per bullock on each mode of conveyance. This amount is not always taken wholly in cash but sometimes partly in grain and partly in cash : it being understood that the grain given will with the cash make up a rupee per 4-bullock cart, and so on. I am not clearly satisfied that this rule exists in exactly the same form in all ganjes south of the Gumti but in those ganjes there is also some fixed understanding which is probably much the same as that prevailing north of the Gumti.

Custom has also prescribed certain other pickings which the broker takes from the beopári, grain for bihishti who fills water for the bullocks, for the faqír of the ganj, for the brahmins, for the broker's son, for the chokidár, for the lad who hands round tobacco, and so on, an endless loot.

The arhatiya takes all he can get from the beopári and so manages that he gets what covers his expenses : e. g. take Dakshinagunj. The broker takes from the beopári one rupee cash and 5 seers of grain on a 4-bullock cart. Out of this pays :—

To chaudhri cash 1 anna 4½ pies.

„ proprietor „ 2 annas 4½ „

„ proprietor grain 3¼ seers
$\begin{cases} \text{chokidár,} & \frac{1}{2} \text{ seer.} \\ \text{brahmin,} & 1\frac{1}{4} \text{ ,,} \\ \text{dandiya,} & \frac{3}{4} \text{ ,,} \\ \text{chaprassy,} & \frac{3}{4} \text{ ,,} \end{cases}$

He has left 12 annas 3 pies and 1¾ seers grain on the 4-bullock cart.

It is true that he also treats the beopári to tobacco and provides him with vegetables and kanda out of this but still he has ample margin left to pay weighmen and other servants.

It is thus clear that it is quite fair towards a broker and, indeed, very mild treatment, to take his profits as ½ anna in the rupee on total price of grain sold through him during the year and tax him thereon.

As the chaudhri's books will show all conveyances which have come to each broker in a year, it is obvious that to tabulate his books and calculate weight and price of grain is a fair mode of taxation. No broker can object to the details of the chaudhri's books, for he has bound himself by paying chaudhri's dues according to those books.

The average weights I have ascertained to be :—

4-bullock cart.	...	...	36½	mds.
3 do.,	...	...	27½	„
2 do.,	...	...	22½	„
1 do.,	...	...	10	„
Buffalo,	...	...	7	„
Bullock,	...	...	5	„
Tattu,	...	...	3	„
Buqcha,	...	...	1	„

These rates are somewhat lower than prevail (for carts at least) in some parts of the city as admitted by chaudhris, but they are rates which if applied as an average can cause no hardship. The books on which I was compelled to proceed were those of 1878 as I commenced work in January 1879, and hence I applied the average price of grain for that year. That was Rs. 2-14 per maund.

The following is a sample of a ganj assessed on these principles :—

NAZIRGANJ.

Broker's name.	4-bullock-carts.	2-bullock cart.	Buffalos.	Bullocks.	Tattus.	Buqchas.	Total weight mds.	Total value Rs.	Broker's pro-fits, Commn. taka fi rupiya.	Tax.
Rám Dass, ...	...	...	25	258	5236	4762	21957	63122	1972	20
Raghobar, ...	9	43	29	158	1727	2366	7540	216n8	677	10
Nanku, ...	925	626	1	...	242	27	48611	139767	4367	75
Raghu Mal, ...	46	97	...	...	...	...	3802	10931	342	5
Narain, ...	24	63	...	...	...	...	2294	6596	206	2
Manik, ...	765	458	...	1	1	...	38458	111567	3486	75
Chandi, ...	310	244	...	...	...	...	16805	48315	1509	25
Kálka, ...	22	23	...	...	...	...	1310	3767	117	...
Jola Mal, ...	331	340	...	...	...	...	18731	53852	1683	25
Baldeo, ...	73	111	...	...	24	18	5253	15103	472	10
Srikishn, ...	14	18	...	...	...	...	916	2634	82	...
Badlu, ...	25	33	...	...	...	...	1650	4744	148	...
Dási, ...	...	10	...	...	...	...	225	637	19	...
Durga, ...	1	7	...	...	...	...	194	558	17	...
Anant Rám & Shabráti.	44	25	...	...	...	..	2169	6236	195	2

The foregoing will show that grain-brokers may have profits which far eqxceed Rs. 3,750 per annum, and yet the Act as it stands by the schedule annexed does not admit of a grain-broker going higher than class II grade I. There are many brokers in Lucknow, who should go into the first class, but the Schedule forbids it. This is an error which should be corrected by amendment of the Schedule, It causes loss to Government and the class benefitting is that which above all others derives a benefit by the high prices consequent on the dearths, scarcity, and famine, for the meeting of which the License Tax Act provides a fund.

It must not be supposed that this ' taka rupiya' commission is the broker's sole source of income. The arhatiya is a money-lender lending either his own or borrowed money to beopáris to enable them to buy up grain. On those advances the arhatiya receives interest not less than one paisa the rupee per mensem and in busy seasons the interest will be as high as an anna the rupee. These are prevailing rates, but there is no absolute rule. The beopáris come by borrowing into the clutches of the arhatiya and are, so to speak, his *jajmáns* and sons will deal with the brokers to whom their fathers have brought grain.

A broker who seeks to have his license tax decided by his books should produce not only his roz-námcha showing daily ‘batta’ or gains but also his account of loans to beopáris and (where, as is generally the case, he is a storer as well as broker) his account of *bhandsál*. It is not proper to tax a grain-broker *solely* on the profits shown in the Schedule of the ganj made out as before shown until it is clear beyond doubt that he is not a storer or money-lender as well as broker.

The business of the grain-broker is secure : not so that of the grain-storer or cornfactor. The latter trade is very precarious and the profits of one year may be more than swallowed up by losses in the next. Storing of grain and transport from one market to another in India to take advantage of prices is but in the infancy of its development. The extension of railways has much aided trade and tended to diminish the chances of high prices continuing long in any one part of India. There are traders so alive to the benefits of knowing intimately the state of the market in other places that they receive telegrams on the subject from correspondents.

Ata-farosh *vide* Chakkiwala.

Atashbaz.—It would be idle to enumerate all the names of the many fireworks which a native átashbáz manufactures. The chief favorites are the *anars* or grenades, *mahtábi* or rocket and *chachhundar* or squib.

The anár will serve to give some idea of the profit of a firework-maker.

Anárs are of several sizes : panserah, adhserah, tipaiya, serah and others to order, even to a maund. The átashbáz purchases the mud-shells for these from kumhars at Rs. 1 per 800. The kumhar reckons 105 to the 100. The átashbáz makes his own gun-powder—with *koela*, *gandhak*, and *shora-qalmi*. He mixes these in proportion of 10 chittaks koela, 4 chittaks gandhak, and 2 chittaks shora-qalmi to make a seer of gunpowder. The átashbáz takes one seer of this gun-powder to make 25 panserah anárs and he adds 2 chittaks gandhak, 4 chittaks koela, and one chittak lohchan (iron filings.) He has expended:—

25 Mud-shells for anars, ...	0	6	0
1 seer gun-powder (home-made),	0	4	0
Gandhak, ...	0	1	0
Koela, ...	0	0	3
Lohchan, ...	0	0	3
Total, ...	0	6	0

and has made up 25 anárs which he sells at 2 paisa per anár for 12¼ as. and his profit is 6½ as. on the lot.

The occupation of an átashbáz is not constant for the demand for fire-works fluctuates with the season—being most brisk in Baisakh, Jeth, and Asárh when Hindu marriages take place; and slowest between Muharram and Chahlam when Muhamadans do not marry.

Attar.—A native druggist has large profits. Two-thirds of the drugs he keeps are wild flowers, herbs, leaves, fruits, nuts, and roots, which women gather in jungles and sell for a trifling price. The rest of his medicines are purchased for something like four to six annas per seer. Yet when he places these varied drugs in stock he prices all alike at a high price regardless of cost-price. If an attar could sell off his whole stock at his shop-prices he would realize perhaps 400 per cent. on cost-price but he cannot hope to sell the whole of a stock, for native drugs being chiefly vegetable, deteriorate in virtue by time. Still his profits are very high.

Another source of profit, really excessive profit, is the collusive connection which exists between hakíms and attárs in large cities. They play into one another's hands thus. A hakím gives a patient a prescription which he takes to an attár who does not happen to be on good terms with the hakím who wrote it. It is made up. The hakím asks the patient to show the medicine. He condemns it and tells his patient to try another attár, naming a friend. The patient goes to this second attár and has to buy the same articles over again, paying Rs. 5 for what the first after gave for Rs. 3. The hakím receives from the friendly attár a share of the loot.

In a large city like Lucknow an attár with a connection among hakíms can well pay Rs. 10 License Tax and perhaps more.

B.

Balliwala.—This is a trader in beams of undressed wood used for scaffolding by masons and others, and also as rafters in thatched and tiled roofing. Ballis are of three kinds :—*tarak* (used in roofing), *gola* (shorter and thicker than tarak but used for same purposes), and *balli* proper which is used to erect scaffolding. All these are made of the long, straight, tapering trunks of trees from which the branches are lopped and the bark removed. The wood is generally *tákhú*.

The importer of ballis buys a plot of forest, at Muhamdi or Dilawarpur, hews the trees and roughly dresses the trunks as taraks, golas, or ballis as the case may be. They are then carried to the Gumti and floated down in *berabandi, i. e.,* chained rafts of 400 ballis each, to the *kalan kothi ghat* near Husenabad, at Lucknow. Here they are sold by the hundred to retailers. The retailer estimates the general quality of the lot and pays accordingly,

Rs. 25 to Rs. 60 per cent. *ballis.*
,, 20 to ,, 28 do. *taraks.*
,, 20 to ,, 30 do. *golas.*

The retailer sells these singly—

As. 8 to Re. 1 per balli.
,, 4 to as. 8 per tarak.
,, 5 to ,, 8 per gola.

Retailers of these beams being in the dark as to the quality of a great many of the beams in a lot of a hundred buy at a risk, but profit is secured by high retail prices. The rate of profit on retail sales is high because the stock is combustible and insurance against loss enters into the determination of profit.

Both importers and retailers lend out ballis (but not golas or taraks) on hire to building contractors for the erection of scaffolding and receive from Rs. 5 to Rs. 8 (according to length and strength of the bullis lent) per hundred ballis per month. If the ballis are detained in use beyond a month a higher rate is charged for each successive month. The increase of rate charged for hire arises because the value of the ballis as goods threafter saleable deteriorates by lengthened use.

The importer is at no expense for carriage by water beyond pay of servants in charge of the bera. His chief charges after purchase of a plot in the jungle are hewage and carriage to the river bank.

The retailer who purchases at the ghat in Lucknow pays Rs. 3 per hundred beams to carriers who convey them to his shop, which like the bambu vendor's is called a *theki.*

Ban-farosh, ban-saz, rassi-but.—Rope-makers are chiefly Kahárs and Malláhs. They make twine and rope from múnj, san, káns, and hathi chingár.

Two men combine, purchase múnj (saccharum múnja) pound it, tease it, steep it in water, and spin it on *charkhis* of special construction. Thus strands are produced which are attached to horizontal bambu poles or to branches of trees and twisted together and made into *bán.* These lines stretched out to be wound together are called *algani.* In all the operations of rope-making females of the family assist.

Rope-makers usually buy múnj at 1½ maund per rupee, and they sell coarse bán (*rasri*) at 16 seers the rupee to *bánfaroshes,* but the quality (*bárík bán*) used for weaving charpoys they sell at 10 to 12 seers the rupee. Two Malláhs or Kahárs cannot make up more than 7½ maunds of múnj into bán in one month, and the loss of múnj in preparation for the *charkhi* is 2 seers per maund. Thus a maund of múnj will yield 38 seers of bán. Each Kahár or Malláh will earn about Rs. 3-4 per mensem if he manufactures only the coarse quality, but if he make fine quality bán, although it sell for a higher price, he will not make greater profits, for labour is heavier and production slower.

San is cultivated as a crop, and thus it differs from múnj, káns, and hathí chingár which are all wild products.

Thirty seers of seed which cost Rs. 1-8 are required for a bigah of land and it is sown in poor soil which rents at about Rs. 2 per bigah. A bigah is ploughed well enough for san in one day and is sown on the same day. Irrigation is not needed. Sowing is in Asárh and reaping in Kátik. Six labourers will cut a bigah of san in one day, but the cultivator's family usually cut the crop. When the san is cut the *sathéra* is separated from the san. The sathera or stalks are used to make matches and spills for the native market. The expense of reaping the crop and of cleaning and separating the sathera and san is about Rs. 2-5-6 per bigah, and the out-turn of clean san is about 3 mds. per bigah. This is sold at 10 seers the rupee. The sathera is about 20 bundles to the bigah and sells by the head-load for about Rs. 2-8 the lot. The seed which is taken from the produce is about 3 maunds per bigah and sells for 20 seers the rupee.

The expense of raising a bigah of san is Rs. 7-1, and the produce is worth Rs. 20-8.

As in múnj rope-making, so in san rope manufacture, there is combination of two operators. They purchase san, steep it for a night, tease it out next morning and twist it in an aintha. This consists of two pieces of wood, a short thick piece called *langar* with a hole at one end thurst over another larger and thinner piece of wood. The latter piece is held in the hand as an axis and san is attached to that end of the *langar* which is farthest from the axis, and as the axsis is swung round and round the san receives a twist from the revolution of the langar. When in this way these strands have been made they are further twisted on a charkha and their ends attached to a hook some distance off; and one of the operators passes the three strands over a wooden instrument called *kálbhút* while the other operator unwinds them from the charkha. The strands as they pass over the kálbhút unite and become a rope.

The rass ibats who make san rope do not buy san themselves but are supplied by shop-keepers with san and they make up rope. They receive one rupee per maund wages and their work is wholly piece-work by contract at that rate. The rate never varies. From one maund of san 20 ropes are made, kúá bhar lambá. These ropes are examined by shop-keepers on delivery and classified in two classes and sold at 4½ as. or 5 as. each. They fall in these classes in about equal proportion.

The cost of manufacture is Rs. 5 and the lot will sell for Rs. 5-15. The shopkeeper thus makes 3 as. per rupee.

The foregoing is merely a sample case. It is when the maund of san is made into 20 ropes. But when 30 ropes are made their prices will differ. The cost of manufacture and the total selling prices are, however, the same. The profit dies not vary.

The shop-keepers who give out san and sell the ropes made therefrom are the persons who buy the bán made by Malláhs and others and are generally described as *bán-faroshes*. Their profits on san rope are defined but are not so much a matter of rule in the case of bán. They vend both wholesale and retail. They frequently vend for 11 or 12 seers the rupee bán which they have purchased at 16 seers. In a dry year their profits are much higher than in an ordinary year. The reason is obvious. Where crops fail through drought múnj though a wild product also fails as well as san. There being thus a want of raw material for the *bán-sáz* or *rassí-bat*, to manufacture, the shop-keeper who holds a stock of the made up article sells to great advantage.

Banswala.—There are four kinds of bambus imported into Lucknow and sold either wholesale at the gháts on the river or retail at an enclosure much like a timber yard, called *theki báns.*

(1) *Danwás.*—This bambu is long and of great diameter but is hollow (pola) and the shell is not thick (dal thora). If it be cut green it is weak and insects attack it and perforate it with holes (ghun jata). If it be cut yellow it is not thus eaten (na ghunega). Danwás bambus come from Jaunpur to Lucknow by boat and are sold at the ghát for Rs. 50 per cent. bambus. They are brought laden on boats and each boat brings large bundles tied together floating on each side. These bundles are *tátiyas*, but are made up of no fixed number as is the case with kathiya bambus. The purchaser for retail buys at the ghát wholesale unassorted lots (pachmel) and carries them home, assorts and vends them. He will also sell *pachmel* lots by retail if demanded.

This kind of bambu is used for making thelas or thél-gáris (hand-carts); for beams of houses (barer); scaffolding; flagstaffs (jhanda kí chhar), pigeon-stands (kabútar kí chhatrí) and similar uses.

(2) *Chao.*—These are very long and thin, they are hollow but the shell is thick (*pola kam dal bahut*) and they are very springy (lochdár). They are much used in making chhappars for dolis and doli poles, for bahngis, oars and sculls of boats, shafts of tumtums and other vehicles. They are imported from Sultanpur by boat and from Azimgahr, Partabgahr, etc. and sold wholesale unassorted (pachmel) at 15 per cent and retailers assort them and sell in classes ranging from 10 per cent. to 25 per cent. bambus.

Danwás and cháo bambus may be said to be of one class because they are all produced in the one line of country and the uninitiated call both alike cháo but bambu-dealers make a distinction as above.

(3) *Katiya.*—These come from the west chiefly by berabandi on the river Gumti. They are produced in zillahs Muhamdi and Hardoi and come chiefly from those places but not unfrequently are brought from Hurdwar (through Cawnpore). They are cut in the jungle into three pieces—the upper part (*palai*), the middle (*manjhá*), and lower (*peri*). They are almost solid (bhartu) and the knots are close together. They are very strong and are used in roofing. They do not bend (loch nabín hota).

The *bera* (raft) in which they come consists of from six to eight *tatiyas* chained together and a *tátiya* is either *kachcha* (250 bambus) or *pakka* (1000 bambus). The custom is to sell by the *tátiya* at the ghát and the prevailing price is Rs. 12 per *kachcha* and Rs. 50 per *pakka* *tátiya*. The purchaser sees the *tátiya* unopened and buys at a guess. If the importer sells by tale an opened *tátiya* he will still sell pachmel and charge Rs. 6 per cent. bambus. Retailers assort their purchases and sell in five classes at from Rs. 2-8 to Rs. 12 per cent. bambus.

(4) *Purbi.*—This variety of bambu comes from Dhámpur-Nagína beyond Bijnor and is floated down the Ganges to Cawnpore. The bera in this case is not divided into *tátiyás* but is sold *en masse*. The customary tale is 13,200 bambus to a bera and the average price Rs. 320 for the bera. The cost of carriage from Cawnpore to Lucknow is 10 as. per 100 bambus, *bahar* and *sirancha* (*vide* (*postea* and 5 as. per 100 bambus *sirbojhi* and *kandelawa* (*vide postea*). They are conveyed by *gári* and in addition to this the *gáriwán* receives 1½ as. per 100 bambus for feeding chokidars at halting places *en route*. These bambus have the cavity large and the shell thin. They are of four classes :—

Bahar, about 12 feet long used for making chiks.

Sirancha,	ditto	ditto	mondhas, chairs, couches, &c.
Sirbojhi, }			
Kandelawa, }	very slight	ditto	tátis and chhappars.

The retail prices in Lucknow are Rs. 4 per 100 for the first two and Rs. 2 per 100 for the last two kinds.

Barhai.—(Arabic and Persian Najjár). Carpenter.

The *barhai* was originally a village servant and still exists as such and receives 30 seers khám in each fasl (kharif and rabí) for each plough which he attends to in the village. This right of the barhai is called *tihái*. He also receives one seer of each kind of grain from each cultivator's *khaliyán* when the grain is leaving it, this is called *anjali*. For seven months his services are required, from Jeth to Agahan. He has the remaining five months to practise his trade on charpoys, gháris, domestic utensils of wood, and building wood. For this he receives wages other than his *tihái* and *anjali*.

The city *barhai* is of two class, the journey-man and the master-carpenter (kárkhánadár). A high class workman employed on building materials will earn 6 as. or 8 as. per diem, while the inferior workman who corresponds to the village barhai will get but 3 as. or 4 as. per diem. The kárkhánadár barhai employs journey-men and makes up furniture, yikkahs, boxes and building timber. He generally calculates his charges so that on paying wages of labour and cost of materials he shall have at least one rupee per diem for himself as wages of superintendence. This is his profit. Such a trader often adds to this business a small trade in new timber and buys up the timber of demolished houses, and sometimes takes small building contracts.

Bariya.—This is the knife-grinder, razor-setter, &c., of India. He is a trader of no worth and his whole stock in trade is a sán, or circular whetstone moved by a leather strap on an axle between two posts fixed in the ground. He gets a paisa for a four-bladed knife or a pair of scissors or two razors. It sometimes falls to his lot to sharpen a sword and his pay for the job is according to the quality of the metal from 4 as. to Rs. 2. The edge of a sword is tested by turning it up and sweeping down on it a handkerchief. If the handkerchief be cut the edge is good. No báriya can have profits to justify demand of License Tax.

Batashewala.—Batashas are those small round sweetmeats, light and porous in appearance, which one sees offered up to deities at shrines and temples. They are a very favorite sweetmeat in the East and there is a class of confectioner who devotes himself solely to their manufacture.

The batáshewálá buys kachcha shakkar and receives 46 seers (nawábi taul) to the maund. He mixes this with water and boils it in a large pan called *karáhi ;* when it reaches the consistency of a syrup he takes a little from the *karáhi* in a smaller iron pan called *dohara*, which has a long upright wooden handle and much resembles a soup-ladle with a perpendicular handle. The ryrup is reboiled in the dohara and when it begins to thicken the confectioner lifts the dohara and dashing the syrup against the handle with an iron instrument called *katarni*, somewhat like a knife, allows it to fall in large drops on a clean white sheet spread on the ground. The syrup hardens as it falls and thus *batáshás* are formed. The syrup remaining in the *karáhi* when the best part has been taken for batáshás, is allowed to thicken and is then pulled out in long threads about as thick as a cane and these are chopped into small pieces called *kuntiyan* (chopped sugarstick). The loss of *kachcha shakkar* in manufacture is 4½ seers in the maund. A batáshewálá with four journeymen can dispose of 1½ maund shakkar per diem.

The cost of production and produce are :—

	Rs.	As.	P.		Rs.	As.	P.
1½ maunds of shakkar at Rs. 14 per maund, ...	21	0	0	60¾ seers batasha sold at 2½ seers the rupee, ...	24	4	9
Kanda for fuel 4 as. to a md. of shakkar, ...	0	4	0	3¾ seers kuntiyán at 5 seers the rupee, (4½ seers waste),	0	12	0
Four servants at 2 as. each,	0	8	0				
Total Rs. ...	21	12	0	Total Rs. ...	25	0	9

Batti-saz.—Chandler. The process of candle-making as practised in Lucknow is very simple and only the rudest kinds are made, resembling what are called in England ' dips.'

The native chandler splits a long bambu and makes a large hoop with it and this he suspends from the ceiling or else he has a rough round table. At intervals in the circumference he cuts notches or grooves and from these he sus-pends country cotton thread. He boils up fat (charbi)in a cauldron and when it is at boiling point he takes a huge spoon or ladle (karchhá) with a hole in the bottom and filling it so places it that the cooling liquid trickles down the suspended thread. These candles are made without reference to weight but solely with reference to length—which ranges from a span (bálisht) to an ell (háth bhar).

Six seers of raw charbi cost about one rupee and when boiled are reduced to 5½ seers. The fuel consumed is 5 seers of wood, costing one anna. Two men will make up a *pachmel* (miscellaneous) lot of candles in a day with these materials and one and a half chhitáks of country thread to make wicks. The cost of thread will be about one anna. The workmen receive only 6 paisa each per diem, and one anna for miscellaneous expenses : total Re. 1-6 per diem. Thus for an expenditure of Re. 1-6 the battisáz produces 5½ seers of candles. These he sells wholesale at 2¾ seers for the rupee. This gives him 10 as. profit. The retailer also sells by weight at 2½ seers the rupee.

Coloured candles are manufactured in the same way. The colour is added to the fat when it is boiling and is estimated to add about one anna to the cost price per seer. Wholesale dealers sell coloured candles by weight but retailers sell them by number.

Bazzaz.—There are three classes of cloth-merchants. The first of these is the wholesale dealer who is called thokfarosh and kothiwál to distinguish him from the retail dealer or dukándar. The whole of the European fabrics brought to Lucknow are imported from Cawnpore by wholesale dealers chiefly residents of Cawnpore. Country fabrics both woollen and cotton are brought to Lucknow by importers who sell in the local markets wholesale and these im-porters are usually either manufacturers as in the case of weavers, etc., or travelling merchants like the Kabulis and Kashmiris who import pashmina, etc.

The second class of bazzaz is the shop-keeper who sells by retai (phutkar), He generally buys from wholesale dealers in the city but sometimes he imports supplies from Cawnpore.

The average of a large number of cases in which account books have been produced shows the prevailing rate of profit on sales in these cases to be:—

Purely wholesale dealers, ... 3½ per cent.
Do. retail dealers, ... 7½ ,,
Retail dealers who import their stock or part of it from Cawnpore, ... 9½ ... ,,
These rates are not, however, a hard and fast rule. They are an average of a number of cases. It is easy to ascertain the exact profits of a bazzaz, for

a cloth-merchant always keeps account-books, and if his books are regularly kept, they should in a moment show the following particulars :—

1	2	3	4	5	6
Year.	Balance of stock of last year at cost prices.	Cost price of amount of stock sold in the year.	Retail price realized on account of stock sold in the year.	Balance of stock at end of the year at cost price.	

By deducting the total of columns 2 and 3 from the total of columns 4 and 5 the profit on sales is ascertained. In case a retail dealer should try to defeat inquiry made in this way he should be asked to produce his *jai khata*. This is a bahi in which he keeps a jotting of the profit on his sales each day. The total which it gives for the year should correspond pretty closely with the profits determined by the method already explained. The *jai khata* as a rule actually shows more. Two other items are generally to be found in a bazzáz's account-books. (1) *Batta*, forecharge of interest on credit sales and discount received on purchases of stock for cash payment; (2) *kasarát*, miscellaneous profits by interest, for instance, on credit accounts. These should always be totalled and placed under the heads of jama (receipts) and nám (payments) and the profits or loss should be added to or deducted from the profits shown by the Schedule I have given or by *jai-khata*.

There is a third bazzáz, the pheríwálá or pedlar. There is no rule as to the profits of this class. It is known that the pedlar who visits a sahib's bungalow makes a good profit but the same trader if he visit houses of native customers and sell on credit will make much more. The extreme profit is made by the bazzáz who visits villages and sells to cultivators (muráos, káchhís,

10

&c.), lahngás and pharyás for their wives and daughters on credit and comes back in the harvest and obtains from the cultivator cash and grain from the khaliyán. The price actually realized is limited only by the measure of the cultivators satisfaction with his harvest.

Behna *vide* **Rui-farosh.**

Bhandsar *vide* **Arhat-ghalla.**

Bed-baf.—This term properly means a weaver of cane-work. But it will be as well to treat of all similar work under this head.

Canes are either *purbí*, imported from Calcutta, or *desí* grown up country and chiefly imported from Naipal, Bahraich, Gonda and Tarai tracts. The former are more substantial than the latter, and sell for as much as 3 seers a rupee, whereas *desí* canes are sold for 5 seers the rupee best quality. The weaver splits a cane into 8 strips called társ and clears off the inner portion of each strip with an instrument called tiraunthí (some thing resembling a lemon slicer). These inside cuttings he sells to bakers to make *sánchás*, used for applying cakes to the walls of ovens. The average length of a cane is 12 haths, and the very smallest pieces of each tár are used up. For instance, the pieces which remain from weaving a chair are used for small baskets and the like.

A béd-báf weaves the seats and backs of chairs and makes baskets, pitárás, etc. Chairs are woven either jálídár (open-work), or chatáidár (close-work). Holes are made round the frame work which is to hold the cane and three or four társ go to a hole in the former case and 5 or 6 in the latter. A seer of cane will suffice to weave the seat and back of a chair *jálídár;* this costs 3 as. 3 pies. One labourer will split this cane in one day and weave the chair in another day. He receives 2 as. per diem. The charge is 12 as. for the chair. Thus the master béd-báf makes 4 as. 9 pies. If the chair be woven chatáidár the charge is Rs. 1-8, and the expense is 12 as. 3 pies for 1½ seer cane and 4 days labor. In this case the profit is 11 as. 9 pies. If an arm-chair be woven 12 girahs wide and 1½ yards long the charge is, jálídár Rs. 1-8, and chatáidár Rs. 2-3. The profit is 8 as. in the former case and 12 as. in the latter; and the time required is 2 days and 4 days respectively. In all these cases the béd-báf works to order on chairs entrusted to him.

Pitárás, cane-chairs, and baskets of all kinds are made up by the béd-báf at his own risk speculatively. A pitárá in which there are 3 seers of cane sells for Rs. 1-8. The cane costs 9 as. 9 pies. Bambu costing about 6 pies is used as a frame-work on which to weave. One labourer in 3 days or 3 labourers in one day will split the cane and bambu and weave the pitárá. In either case the wages of labor are 6 as. The profit is 7 as. 9 pies.

Bánsphors also make baskets of various kinds and pitárás, but work only with bambu. They split bambus into slips called *pattas* and steep them in water. When these slips are soft they are woven into pitárás, and other baskets; but the chief demand is for pitárás which range from 9 inches to 2 feet on the average. The latter kind may be seen hung up in bisátí's shops covered with cloth, leather, or a substance resembling papier maché. The bánsphor when he has woven the pitárá of bambu takes sirkí, splits it, beats it on a stone so as to flatten it and with this lines the pitára. In this condition he sells these baskets to bisátís at Rs. 3 per score. He can turn out a score in 6 days. His profits is Rs. 1-9. His expense has been 8 as. for bambu; sirkí 3 as.; wages of labor, 12 as. The bisátí covers these pitáras as beforementioned, and affixes iron hinges and clasps. He calls in a rang-sáz and supplies materials. The outer surface of the pitáras is covered with putty made of saw-dust, khalí and másh flour; then old cloth purchased in the gúdarí bazár is sown over this and coated over with a mixture of glue and khariya mattí. When the pitáras are dry they are painted and picked out with lines and flowers. The painting is done with a mixture of resin, indigo, linseed oil, and yellow arsenic. The lines and flowers are painted with various colors but chiefly with white lead, indigo, lac, cinnabar and red ochre. Finally hinges and hasps are applied.

The whole expense of the bisátí is :—

		Rs.	As.	P.
Original cost of pitáras, per score, ...		3	0	0
Materials for making up, per score :—				

	Rs.	As.	P.			
Paste, etc., ...	0	12	0			
Gudar, ...	0	10	0			
Glue, etc., ...	0	6	0			
Colours, ...	3	11	9			
Hinges, etc., ...	0	5	0	5	12	9
Wages of labour (pánoh nafrí), ...				1	4	0
Total Rs. ...				10	0	9

He will sell these pitáras on an average for 10 as. each and will therefore make a profit of Rs. 2-7-3.

Similar to these are the makers of chairs, chiks, couches, etc. from séntha and bambus. These are korí chhappar-bands who make chiks, tattís, and chhappars, and parchhattís and gudariyas who make móndhas, and dharkars who make up furniture, fine door-chiks, baskets, fans, etc. from bambu. In fact a dharkár makes up all goods which the former make up, but he works in bambu and they work in séntha.

The chhappar-band buys séntha at the rate of 12 lungis (headloads) per rupee. He cleans off the patáwar and múnj and nips off the upper joint (sirkí) which he sells to bánsphors. He uses the patáwar and múnj in his own business. If the múnj be more than he requires he sells it to the rope-maker. Chiks are made at an adda or stand. This is of very simple construction. Two pieces of wood are driven into the ground so that their ends cross each other like the letter X standing on the ground; another similar pair of sticks is driven into the ground at the distance of some feet. A thick bambu is laid across from one support to the other. To this cross bambu are tied the long pieces of twine which are used to weave the chik. This twine is made of hemp and rolled in balls called *langars*. Large chiks are often woven as much as 9 feet wide and 10½ feet long. For this size of chik 21 langars are tied to the *adda* and the chhappar-band, when he has woven a couple of feet by putting reeds in between the twine and lapping them, turns the adda round and rolls up what he has woven. It is said that one man can make 12 chiks of this kind in 3 days, but of this there is some doubt; at any rate allowing one lungi to a chik the account of manufacture of 12 chiks is as follows:—

	Rs.	As.	P.
Cost of séntha, ...	1	0	0
Sutlí 3 seers, ...	0	15	0
Wages of workman who cleans the séntha } of patáwar and sirkí,	0	3	0
Wages of workman at the adda, ...	0	4	6
Total Rs. ...	2	6	6

He realizes :—

	Rs.	As.	P.
Twelve chiks at 3 as. each, ...	2	4	0
Patáwar, ...	0	4	0
Múnj, ...	0	6	0
Sirkí, ...	0	3	0
Kucharas, (thin tips of sirkí used to make } brooms),	0	1	6
Total Rs.	3	2	6

This gives a profit of 12 as. or one anna per chik.

The gadariya who makes chairs and móndhas purchases séntha in the same way as the chhappar-band and cleans it in the same way, but keeps the patáwar, as well as the reeds. He sells the other part of the séntha. He makes either plain round stools without backs called sáda-móndha, or chairs with backs (takiya-dár). Three of the latter or six of the former are made by one man in a day. One lungi gives three takiya-dár or six sáda móndas. Suppose a gadariya buys 12 lungis and makes takiya-dár móndhas his outlay is as follows :—

		Rs.	As.	P.
Cost of sentha	Re.	1	0	0
Ban 18 seers, ...	,,	1	2	0
Wages of workman who cleans the séntha } of patawar and sirki.	,,	0	3	0
Pay of chair maker at 6 pies per chair,	,,	1	2	0
Total Rs. ...		3	7	0

He realizes :—

36 chairs at 3 as. each, ...	Rs.	6 12 0
Munj, ...	,,	0 6 0
Sirki, ...	,,	0 3 0
Kucharas, ...	,,	0 1 0
Total, Rs. ...		7 6 0

His profit is therefore Rs. 3-15 on 36 chairs or exactly 1 anna. 6 pies per chair.

The dharkar works in bambu and makes chairs, couches, baskets and chiks. Take the last mentioned as a specimen of his work. Bambu chiks are either gol or chapti. The former are the fine chiks placed at doors and windows and are so called because the bambu is split into round strands like wire. One bambu is split into as many as 160 strands, and usually 200 strands are reckoned in 1 yard of a gol chik. Chapti chiks is so called because it is made of flat strands of bambu 80 to the bambu and 100 to the yard of chik. These chiks are made at an adda such as the chhapper-band uses : but the ball of twine attached to the adda in this case is called *dhima*. Gol chiks are dyed and some times painted ; but chapti chiks are made up plain. It is not necessary to go in to the details of the cost of making chiks. Suffice it to say that a gol chik 10 yards wide and 3 yards long is made for 7 as. 9 pies while it sells for 12 as. A chapti chik 3 yards long by 3 yards wide costs 5 as. 7 pies to make up and is sold for 8 as. In the former case the selling price is a much greater advance from the cost price than in the latter case. Because a gol chik takes two days to make while the chapti chik is easily made in one day.

Begri *vide* Almas-tarash.

Bhang-farosh.—Bháng (cannabis sativus) is imported from Hardoi and Bahraich districts by the zillah lessee of drugs (Tikadár mushkirát). This preparation is made of the crushed leaves of the plant and thus differs from gánjá which consists of the plant when in flower, gathered leaves, stem and flowers all together and pressed while damp with dew. It is also said that bháng is prepared from the male plant and gánjá from the female plant of the hemp *cannabis*.

Bháng grows luxuriantly in jungles and is purchased by the zillah contractor for from 12 as. to Re. 1 per maund, but by the time it reaches Lucknow the price rises by cost of carriage to Rs. 3-8 per maund. The contractor sells wholesale to retail dealers (bháng-farosh) at Rs. 2 per seer.

The retailer is but an humble trader and is generally a Brahmin. He mixes black pepper with the bháng and crushes them on a *sil* (stone slab prepared for crushing spices) with a *bata* (oblong stone) and when a customer comes he infuses this in water, strains it, and adds some shakkar. A paisa is all that he receives for a draught.

There are two bháng-faroshes of some importance in Lucknow, Sita Ram, of Ganeshganj, and Hulási of Aminabad. It is possible that these shop-keepers may have an income warranting a charge of License Tax but their cases are exceptional. They add *keora* and other aromatic spices to the draughts they prepare and they enjoy a reputation in the city which brings them many customers especially in hot weather. They are also the great vendors in this city of majúm, an aphrodisiac sweetmeat made of bháng.

Bhurji.—There are three classes of grain-parchers. The poorest are those who merely parch grain for persons who bring it. They receive one paisa per seer on expensive grain; and a pau per seer on cheap grain. A stage above these are grain-parchers who buy grain and store it and sell parched grain. These are termed charban-farosh. Above both of these is a much more comfortable class who buy rice in kharif and store it. They make láí, chiura and khíl, which are in daily demand and also in special demand in the Déwalí, and on the occasions of fairs, &c. There are some bhurjis especially well off who have their *bhára* in the immediate neighbourhood of large grain markets. Beopáris who import grain treat these very liberally and think nothing of flinging down a couple of seers of grain and taking in exchange a half seer of *chabéna*. There are a few grain-parchers in Lucknow who were taxed in the third grade in 1879. It was only after local inquiry that in any such cases the tax was imposed.

Bhusawala.—The bhúsáwálá is a dealer in chaff as an article of fodder for cattle. It may be observed that it is only the trader who buys up and stores bhúsá who can have profits sufficiently high to justify the imposition of a License Tax. He goes to villages and buys up the chaff at the threshing floors by the khárá or kút. Khárá is a net-like basket containing from a maund to a maund and five seers. Kút is valuation or guess. The purchaser stands on the threshing floor and buys the mass at a valuation. Whatever be the method of purchase the bhúsáwálá has the expense of carriage from the village to place of storage. Villagers, however, often bring bhúsá to the city market in khárás on their heads: and these khárás are eagerly bought by bhúsáwálás.

Wheat, barley, gojai, kiráo, gram, and arhar bhúsá are stored in the hot weather—when the rabi crops have been gathered in. Másh, múng, lobiya, and mothi bhusa are stored in October and November.

The demand for bhúsá is very great in Lucknow and bhúsáwálás import by the hundred or more maunds in boats. The only question with a bhadsár is: will the cost of carriage added to cost price leave a margin for profit if I sell at the price I expect to sell for when the bhúsá of this fasl has all been stored? If he answer this to himself in the affirmative he buys. The result is that when the bhúsáwálá has stored, say, bhusa from Rabi crops in the expectation of drought in the rains, his profit is in a great measure at the mercy of a rainfall of even two inches. His business is therefore in a measure speculative and whil the undoubtedly has at lest 25 per cent. profits in most years he is liable to ruin in one season.

Bhusiwala, vendor of the bran of gram and arhar. When gram and arhar are broken up to make ḍál the outer shell which peels off is called bhúsí. This is bought up by baniyás but chiefly by telis and sold as cattle fodder, with khalí, the refuse stuff of oil-mills. The profits of bhúsí-vending are small and to describe a trader as khalí-bhúsí-farosh implies no very profitable business.

Bidarsaz.—This is inlaid work in silver on a basis of inferior metal. This basis is a compound of three metals in the following proportion :—

Copper,	...	...	...	2	chittaks.
Steel powder,		...	...	2	ditto.
Zinc,	...	...	...	12	ditto.

These are melted together and cast in a mould for the manufacture of drinking vessels and of huqqahs, pándáns, and the like. The roughly cast vessel is cleaned on a lathe : then the pattern for the inlaid work is traced on it with a pencil and the necessary cuttings made. It is then weighed and silver is delivered to the workman who fills in the silver into the grooves and hollows cut on the vessel and when it is finally delivered the vessel is again weighed to ascertain the amount of silver used. The wages of the laborer are 6 as. per diem, and the employer charges his profit at a minimum rate of 4 as. per rupee on his outlay, making up the account much in the same way as a zardóz.

Bidhiya *vide* **Almash-tarash.**

Bisati.—The vendor of miscellaneous goods whose stock embraces stationery, hardware, china, glass, twines, thread, and in fact everything of English manufacture other than what the cloth-merchant sells and all small goods of native manufacture in general demand of the classes specified. These goods when imported from England come through Calcutta and the carriage from thence to Lucknow is high. They are great weight and little value in small bulk. Hence the charges incurred by bringing up-country are high in proportion to the value of the goods. This greatly reduces the profits of the vendor and a wholesale vendor does not enjoy more than about $4\frac{1}{2}$ per cent. profit. The bisátí who sells retail has a very much larger profit on the sales he makes but the daily amount of sales is small and hence few retailing bisátís can touch the Rs. 10 grade for License Tax.

Biskutwala.—Biscuit-manufacturer. There are always to be found in cantonments and cities bakers who drive a comfortable trade in biscuit baking. Sales are rapid and there is little loss by stale goods. The oven is generally

built to bake six seers of biscuits in a batch (táo). And the materials required
are :—

		Rs.	As.	P.
Fine flour 6 seers at 10¾ seers the rupee, ...		0	9	6
Salt, ...		0	0	3
Shakkar, Chíní, ...		0	1	0
Khamír (barm), ...		0	1	3
Firewood, ...		0	3	0
Pay of baker per batch, ...		0	2	0
Loss of weight in cooking, ...		0	1	0
Total Rs. ...		1	2	0

The rate of sale is 4 seers of biscuit to the rupee or Re. 1-8, the batch of
six seers. There is, however, a further gain to the baker of 1 anna per batch for
the charcoal which he takes from the oven. Thus the biscuit-baker cannot have
less than 7 as. per diem on each batch of biscuits if he employ a journeyman
baker nor less than 9 as. if he himself bake.

But-saz *vide* **Juta-farosh.**

<hr>

C.

Chakkiwala.—Flour-grinder or miller.

The Indian market is supplied with flour by persons who keep a large
number of *chakkis* or *jántás* and make flour-grinding their sole business or by
baniyás, parchunwálás, and others who add this business to other trades. There
are three cases of millers to consider.

The humblest of this class of traders is the Lodh or Kurmi who employs the
women of his house or neighbourhood to grind singly. Each písanári (as she is
called) grinds on an average 15 seers English in a day. She is paid two paisa
per panseri nawábi. The Nawábi seer is 2 chitáks over the English seer *i. e.*
17½ nawábi seers are equal to 20 seers English. In grinding wheat, in 10 seers
grain-one half seer bran is taken from the flour.

At present prices the following account will show the profit of a chakki
per diem worked by one písanári:

	Rs.	As.	P.		Rs.	As.	P.
15 seers of wheat at				14 seers 4 chs. átá			
18 seers the rupee,	0	13	4	at 14 seers the Rupee, ...	1	0	4
Wages of písanári,	0	1	3	12 chs. chokar at			
				25 seers the rupee,... ...	0	0	6
Rs.	0	14	7				
				Rs.	1	0	10

This gives 2 as. 3 ps. per chakki of this class per diem when pure wheat flour is ground and a hired pisanári is employed. Where the women of the house grind, the profit is 3 as. 6 ps. per diem. The wheat purchased is second quality and is brought by the men of the house in headloads (buqchas) from ganjes north of the Gumti where every grain is as a rule a seer cheaper than in ganjes south of the river.

Next there is the átá-farosh who employs a couple of písanáris to each chakki and pays them jointly 6 pies per panseri nawábi. The chakkis employed in this case are larger and are called *jántás*. The tale of work is on the average 5¼ panseris nawábi or 30 seers English per diem and the present cost of production and profit are shown in the following account:—

	Rs.	As.	P.		Rs.	As.	P.
30 seers of wheat at 28 seers the rupee, ...	1	10	8	28½ seers átá at 14 seers the rupee, ...	2	0	7
Pay of pisanáris, ...	0	2	7	1½ seers chokar at 25 seers the rupee, ...	0	1	0
Rs.	1	13	3	Rs.	2	1	7

The profit is thus to an átá farosh 4 as. 4 p. per diem on each *jántá*.

The átá farosh is sometimes called árad-farosh.

The third case is that of the maida-farosh. He also uses jántás. The amount ground and wages paid are as before : but the difference between this business and that of the átáwálá is that the latter grinds wheat dry while the maidawálá damps the wheat. Besides this the maidawálá turns out súji or ráwá, maida, and chokar. Súji is produced when the wheat has been so long damped that it is on the point of sprouting. Ráwá is produced when the wheat has been but slightly damped. In either case the wheat is ground and the flour thrown off is winnowed with a basket called súp. The súji or ráwá falls to the ground apart from the maida and chokar which are subsequently sifted with a chalni. The profit is in this case also about 4as. 4p. per jánta per diem.

Chanduwala.—Chándu is made from opium. The opium is steeped in water till it becomes soft and it is then placed on a fire and boiled. When it is at boiling point it is strained and the joga (foreign matters, dust &c,) left in the cloth thrown away. The opium is boiled till it is reduced to a syrup (qiwám) and then placed in a box. The opium which originally cost Rs. 16 per seer is sold in this state (chandu) for 8 as. per tolah. The chánduwálá sells, however, chiefly to persons who smoke on his premises small quantities of 6 or 8 máshas to the pipe. The pipe stem is called *nigáli* and also *bambu*. The bowl is called *dawát* and the idiom for smoking is *chándu bambu pína*.

It is worth one's while to visit the chándu-khána near the Akbari Darwáza between 6 and 8 P. M. A narrow lane leads to a square enclosure with sheds on three sides where there lie or loll a motley lot of men and women. In one corner a sickly-eyed man lies propped against the wall with his head hanging on his breast and in another is a female in man's clothes smoking a huqqah, while at another spot a half dozen human beings are lying mixed regardless of sex. Look into the shed where the chánduwálá sits and you see a couple of dissolute youths joking over the fumes of tobacco and waiting for the nigáli to pass. A young woman leaning ever a young man who is stretched in a corner near the chánduwálá calls for the bambu. The chanduwálá takes a girmit (a long wire) and cleans the stem. He places the pipe in her hand and she lies down on her side and pillows her head comfortably on the figure beside her. She places a lamp with a shade round it so that it just touches the dawát of the pipe and the chánduwálá hands her 6 máshas of chándu on a short iron spike (thak). She heats the chándu in the flame of the lamp till it becomes soft and then thrusts it into the dawát, turns it over on the flame and inhales a long breath. The smoke fills the mouth and throat and the chest seems to rise and then the girl emits one long puff and you wonder how that vast volume of smoke could have been contained in her. Then you ask 'what was the effect?' and the answer is ' jaisa dhakka sir húa?' (as if one had pushed my head) and she explains that the sensation was as of a pleasant shove in the crown of the head but she denies any symptoms of intoxication. The nigáli is then passed on and another customer has his turn. While one is smoking chándu another is puffing his huqqah and so they wait or come and go till 9 o'clock.

The chánduwálá supplies tobacco and water and lights to his customers, and he needs a water carrier and a chillamwálá for this purpose. He needs a servant to pass the nigális round and he furnishes his shop with farash, so that customers may have a comfortable recline. He has his rent to pay and lamps to buy. He pays the lessee of drugs as much as Re. 1-8 to Rs. 3 per diem. Allowing for all expenses a chándu shop where 12 chittaks are consumed in a day is worth Rs. 2-8 per diem.

Chanwalwala.—Dealer in rice.

Rice is brought into market in the ear, when it is cut and cleaned of the husk or is kept in villages for two, three, or more years before it is brought to market. The longer the rice is kept the higher the price it fetches. When brought into the city the rice dealer who purchases it from beoparis or from brokers adds one and a half seers of wheat flour to the maund of rice, crushes it with an iron bound pestle (musal), and sifts it with a sieve (chalna). This operation is repeated and the rice falls into four lots (1) istamáli, (2) pauna, (3) kanda, (4) reg aur kámún.

The first only of these is what passes for good rice and is stored and exported as well as sold in the local market. The others are looked upon as much inferior, and are consumed locally.

The only variety of rice used in Lucknow to prepare Istamáli birinj is hansráj, one of the (jarhan) winter rice crops. Darai is also sometimes use but only for the purpose of adulteration. The older the rice which is used the longer the time required to crush it and clean it. For instance, two workmen will prepare three maunds of new rice in one day, whereas in the same time they would turn out only one maund of very old rice. The following is an estimate based an present prices of cost of production and profit of dealing in istamáli rice:—

I.—Very old rice which has been kept in villages for three or more years before coming into market.

	Rs.	As.	P.			Rs.	As.	P.
One maund rice, ...	6	0	0	Istamálí, 22½ seers, ...		5	10	0
Wages of labour, two work-				Pauna 5 seers, ...		0	6	3
men 1 md. per diem,	0	5	0	Kanda, 10 seers, ...		0	10	0
Flour one seer, ...	0	1	6	Reg and kámún, 2½ seers,...		0	1	3
Total Rs.	6	6	6	Total Rs.		6	11	6

II.—Rice which comes to the market the year after it is cut.

	Rs.	As.	P.			Rs.	As.	P.
One maund rice, ...	5	0	0	Istamálí 30 seers, ...		4	14	0
Wages of labor, one work-				Pauna 3 seers, ...		0	3	9
man 1 md. per diem,	0	2	6	Kanda 5 seers, ...		0	5	0
Flour ⅓ seer, ...	0	0	6	Reg and kámún 2 seers, ...		0	0	9
Total Rs.	5	3	0	Total Rs.		5	7	6

III.—Rice brought into market in the year of harvest.

	Rs.	As.	P.			Rs.	As.	P.
One maund rice, ...	4	0	0	Istamálí 30 seers, ...		3	12	0
Wages of labor for one				Pauna, 3 seers, ...		0	3	9
md., two workmen be-				Kanda, 5 seers, ...		0	5	0
ing capable of turning out				Reg and kámún 2 seers, ...		0	0	9
3 mds. per diem, ...	0	1	9					
Flour ⅓ seer, ...	0	0	6					
Total Rs.	4	2	3	Total Rs.		4	5	6

These three classes yield to the rice dealer at present prices 5 as., 4 as. 6 pies, and 3 as. 3 pies respectively profit per maund. But this is the profit on trade prices (tájirána qímat) prevailing between one dealer and another. I have not calculated any thing on profits by retail sales at bazar rates. Dealers who sell retail as well as wholesale will of course have a higher profit per maund than one who sells purely wholesale. There is another source of profit in the first quality of rice. I have accounted for forty seers rice above, but there has been added a seer and a half of flour to the maund of rice. Most of the flour either adheres to the rice or passes off with the reg and kámún. There remains say about one seer of weight to be accounted for. This is about the weight per maund of picked rice which is taken from first quality of hansráj grains selected by sifting in a chalna and which have remained unbroken by the musal. This is called aglí or sire ká chánwal and is kept from year to year and sells for fancy prices.

Charas-farosh *vide* Saqin.

Charban-farosh *vide* Bhurji.

Chape-khana, Printing Press.—There are in Lucknow a great many proprietors of presses. The most famous is Newal Kishore whose press is at Hazrat Ganj in Civil Lines, but no reference will be made to cases like his under this head. This note refers to small publishers and jobbing printers within the native city. These persons print only by lithography and the following case is taken as typical:—

Sáligrám, whose printing-press is in Subhánnagar, is now printing a book called 'Khúliq Bárí' of 16 pages on white Serampore paper (20 × 26). 16 pages or 8 leaves make what is called a juz. One sheet of the paper in use suffices for 2 juz and one ream of this paper which costs Rs. 6 consists of 20 dastas (quires) of 25 sheets each. The press-man cuts each sheet into 4 pieces, and one sheet gives 2 juz. One quarter of a sheet can be printed from one stone at a time. Four copies, that is 4 stones, are required to print one juz. The copy writer who writes up the sheets which are transferred to stone receives 4 as. per copy or one rupee per juz. The copy is written on French paper and the materials with which the paper is prepared for copy-writing are applied by the printer, *usárá* (gamboge), arrowroot, and *nishásta* (starch). One sheet of French paper suffices for writing 2 pages and the cost is 1 an. 3 pies per dasta (quire). If bought by the ream it is only one rupee per ream. The materials used to prepare the paper come to Re. 1-9 per ream. A whole ream prepared costs Rs. 2-9. A copy when transferred to stone will give a thousand, nay, an almost unlimited number of impressions. Two sheets of French paper are necessary for one stone for printing this book. One side only of a paper is printed in a day, and one impression is called 'tao.' A thousand táus is the daily average for a press. Four labourers are employed in a press; one press-man, one péchkash, one isfanjia (sponge man), and one rulia (a lad who applies the ink roller to the stone). The press-man, receives 3 as.; pechkash 2 as.; isfanjia 2 as. and rulia 1 an. per diem. The press-man damps the paper for the press and cuts the sheets. When the sheets have been printed off the daftari who works by contract, folds and stitches the book. He receives 6 as. per thousand. The cost of printer's ink is about 6 as. per thousand impressions for one stone, and miscellaneous expenses for oil and cloths for each press are only one anna per diem. The proprieter of the press sells this book at 3 pies per copy wholesale price to retail book-sellers, who retail at two paisa.

A calculation from above data will show that an edition of 1000 copies costs Rs. 11-2 and sells for Rs. 15-10, that is an edition of 1000 copies of a vernacular work printed in this size, which happens to be that most current, brings the printer Rs. 4 per juz.

The more usual practise for printers who have a large business is to sell their publications to wholesale book-sellers who supply retailers at 40 juz the rupee and retailers vend at 32 juz the rupee. These are the prevailing prices for books printed on Serampore paper of the size 22 × 29, 20 × 26, and 18 × 22, and this system of sale is called *ajza qímat*. Registered books and school book printed by authority are sold at what is termed *pukhtá qímat* or a fixed price.

Chhipi.—This word has the exclusive meaning of cotton printer or stamper. There are three different classes of cotton-printers who pass under this name, but they all use similar dies. The dies are made of mango, shisham, or ebony by carpenters, but carpenters who adopt the profession of die-cutters relinquish other work. The remuneration of die-cutters is regulated by the class of die cut:—

1. *Bel hashiya*, for flowered borders, so cut that it can be used continuously, ...   4 as. per die.
2. *Bel buti*, (single flowers impressed by one stamp of the die), ...   4 ,, ,,
3. *Bel haazi*, flowered stripes used to print in long diagonal or transverse lines: also cut to be used continuously, ...   8 to 12 ,, ,,
4. *Tahrír*, (letters and quotations, also pictures and figures, requiring use of successive dies), ... Rs. 2 to Rs. 4 per set of dies.

A very skilful carpenter who works alone can earn about 8 as. per diem by cutting dies in wood, after defraying the cost of wood used. Qutb Ali of Chaupattiyán is an exceedingly skilful die-cutter and he can cut dies to print English or native patterns from a drawing or print or from the made-up materials.

The chhipí keeps at hand a large stock of dies (thappas) of various patterns and uses any pattern according to order.

The first class of cotton printer is the stamper of real or imitation gold or silver leaf on colored cotton fabrics for use in pálki coverings, pardahs, liháfs, razáis, toshaks, &c. Lucknow manufactures of this class are almost all genuine. The process is simple but ingenious. The chhipí makes a mixture of gum, chalk, and glue. He stamps the pattern on the fabrics with this mixture by means of a wooden die. He then lays strips of silver leaf over the pattern traced in this way and taps it gently with a pad. The leaf adheres to the gummy lines of the pattern stamped and comes away from the unstamped surface. The process of printing an imitation of silver differs. The chhipí in this case mixes ránga, gum, glue and chalk and stamps the pattern right off. After it dries he rubs the cloth over with a piece of wood called *muhra* and this gives a gloss to the surface of the inferior metal. This class of chhípí is purely a labourer earning about Rs. 4. per mensem.

The second chhípí is the stamper of patterns on tanzéb, muslin, &c., for chikan-workers. He uses the same wooden thappas as other chhípís and the colored fluid which he uses is a thick solution of gerú or of maháwar (red color extracted from lac). The rate of remuneration it will be seen, is very low when it is stated that a *thán* for a doputtah 10 yards long and 14 girahs wide is stamped for from 2 as. to 4 as., the chhípí supplying the color. A chhípí of this class cannot be fairly charged with License Tax.

The third chhípí is the printer of cotton fabrics in fast colors used as duláí, toshak, liháf, palang-pósh, jánamáz, dastarkhwán, &c. He also stamps chintzes. This is a staple business of Lucknow and the fabrics produced in this city are famed throughout the whole of India. Great difficulty has been experienced in getting any information regarding the process of manufacture but all that has been ascertained is as follows :—

Wholesale cloth-merchants supply chhípís with nainsukh which is stamped and returned by them : but the proprietors of large factories purchase webs themselves and stamp them and supply goods wholesale to bazzazes. The first process is oiling (tél chalána). This is performed by dhobis. The web is 20 yards long and is cut in four pieces (fard). These are steeped in oil (til or réndi) and sajjí (carbonate of soda). The latter is dissolved in water. The fards are placed in an open earthen vessel (nánd), and two men take, the one a vessel of oil and the other a vessel containing the solution of sajjí. They pour these on the fards from a height such that the spreading streams cross each other as they fall and produce a froth. They then press the fards in this mixture and wring them out. They then tie them up in a large cloth for a night and dry them next day. This process is repeated until the smell and gloss of the oil is not perceptible. Then the dhóbis wash out the pieces in the river.

The next process is to produce faint lines to guide the printers. The outmost edge of the four sides, what I may call the border of the pieces, is marked with black (siyáhkár). This is called *bel*. Within this is an inner frame marked on four sides called *háshiya*. This is marked brown (udá-kár). The whole of the inner surface is called *hauz*. The lines to guide the printer in this space are marked red. These lines are extremely faintly marked so that they are imperceptible except to a practised eye, and are of fleeting color.

The next process is to boil in water in a large pán (karáhí). When it is at boiling point blossoms of the palás tree (ṭesú) are thrown in. This is called *páni phárná*. Then manjith is thrown into the karáhí which is kept boiling and the pieces are placed in it and stirred round and round. After a time more manjith is thrown in and finally the *fards* are taken out, wrung out and dried. This makes the marks previously stamped fast, and the pieces come out clear and clean. Dhobis are then employed to wash them out at the river side and spread them on the sand and dry them very gradually sprinkling them occasionally with water.

The pieces are now ready for printing and are laid by folded up in the factory. The process of printing is tedious, for the patterns stamped, flowers, checks or whatever they be, cannot be produced at one printing. Each color is impressed with a different die. For instance, if a flower is to be stamped with brown stalks, green leaves, and blue blossom, the stalks are printed over the whole piece with a die cut for the purpose. Then the green leaves are stamped in the same way and then the blue flowers. Whatever be the number of colors so many are the number of times the sheet must pass under the hands of a printer. The number of colors sometimes reaches as much as twelve.

The printer sits on the round before a small bench called *aḍḍah* and holds the die in his left hand and strikes it with his right. To protect his right hand from hurt he wears a leather guard.

The colors used are all prepared by the chhípí and are :—

1. Siyáh (black). This color is kasís (sulphate of iron).

Old iron,	...	...	...	20 seers.
Gur, ...	...	...	...	5 ,,
Til, ...	...	...	...	10 chittaks.

The gur is dissolved in water, and the til ground and thrown in. In this is placed a lump of old iron of the weight given. In eight days this color is prepared and poured off and mixed with gum.

The cost of making this is Re. 1-6-9, and it will suffice a whole season round.

2. U'dá (brown).

Kasís (prepared as above),	...	4 chittaks.
Phitkarí (alum), ...	...	...	8 ,,
Gerú (red ochre), ...	...	...	4 ,,
Gum (of dhâk), ...	...	...	12 ,,

These are mixed up in water. The cost of preparation is 5 as. 3 pies and this supply will suffice for 3 score of fards.

3. Surkh (red).

Geru,	...	...	...	...	4 chittaks.
Phitkirí, ...	...	...	...	8 ,,
Lodh, (bark of *symplocus racemosa*),	4 ,,
Haldí, (turmeric),...	...	...	$\frac{1}{2}$,,
Gum (of Dhâk), ...	...	...	12 ,,

The lodh is ground and boiled in water. When it boils the ground haldí is added. It is then strained and the gerú phitkirí, and gum are added.

This supply costs 5 as. 9 pies and will suffice for 2 score.

4. Zard (yellow) khúb rang.

Tesú, (flower of pálás tree),	...	... 1 seer.
Harsingár, (weeping nyctanthes),		... 2 chittaks.
Phitkirí,	... ...	... 1 ,,

The palás flowers are boiled in water till they dissolve and then the harsingár and phitkirí are added and the infusion strained and gum added. Cost of the supply is 2 as. 6 pies and will suffice for 6 score.

5. Zard (yellow) kam rang.

Haldí,	... .	... $1\frac{1}{2}$ chattaks.
Náspál (husk of pomegranate),	...	4 ,,
Phitkirí,	... ...	... 4 ,,

These are all boiled up together, strained and gum added.

This will cost 3 as. $4\frac{1}{2}$ pies to make up and the supply is for 6 score

6. Guláb. This is prepared from *patang* (sappan wood).

One seer of this is split and steeped in a ghará of water, then boiled and when it reaches boiling point milk is poured on it, and it is boiled up again until half of a seer remains. This color is used while hot. The above supply will suffice for 3 score and costs 6 as. 9 pies.

7. Sausní (bluish).

This is guláb with kasís added in proportion of one-half.

8. Sabzí (green leaf color).

This is khúb rang zard with a chittak of indigo added.

9. Nílá (indigo blue).

This is not made from indigo alone but the secret of the manufacture is not disclosed.

This color comes to 8 as. per score of fards stamped.

10. Zangár (verdigris).

Verdigris,	... ...	... 2 chittaks.
Gum,	... ...	... 8 ,,

These are boiled in a ghara of water. This supply costs 8 as. and suffices for 20 score.

These are all the main colors. They are mixed together to make various shades as nafarmán, zafrání, etc.

The printing of cotton fabrics begins in March and continues to the end of October. Factories are closed for the five months of cold weather.

The wages of chhípís employed by master printers range from Rs. 2 to Rs. 4 per mensem : and an apprentice (shágird) is paid only one paisa per diem. He performs the preparatory processes of *siyáh kár*, etc. A fard will pass 6 times in a day under the hand of a chhípí for the processes of stamping. This is the average work of a first class printer. This means that 2 fards in each of which there are 9 colors will be stamped off in 3 days. For this class of work the master printer who stamps fards supplied by a bazzaz will receive Rs. 20 per score.

Suppose a master printer prepares a score of fards and uses all the ten colors noted in preparing them the account will stand :—

					Rs.	As.	P.
Oil (til) 1 seer 6 chittaks,	...	...	...		0	9	4
Oil (réndí) do.,	...	...	...		0	8	3
Sajjí 6 seers,	...	...	...		0	1	7
Manjith 2 seers 8 chittaks,	...	...	...		3	12	0
Tesú ,, ,,	...	...	...		0	2	6
Firewood for karáhís,	...	...	...		1	0	0
Wages of dhobis at Rs. 14 per hundred,			...		2	12	10
Do. printers 33 days at the rate of Rs. 3 per month,	...	...	...		3	5	0
Colors (at rates given above) about	...	...			1	4	0
Added a margin for miscellaneous expenses,					0	8	6
			Total Rs.	...	14	0	0

Thus the profit of a master printer who stamps fards supplied to him by a bazzáz is about Rs. 6 on a score of fards. If the master printer buy his own material and stamp it and sell printed fards, his profit will be much more. He buys the best quality of nainsukh used in this business for Rs. 6 per thán of 20 yards. He makes four fards and if he stamps them in the style I have calculated he will sell them at Rs. 3-2 per fard. In this case the account for a score will be :—

					Rs.	As.	P.
Cost of 5 tháns,	...	...	...	...	30	0	0
Printing,	...	...	...	...	14	0	0
			Total Rs.	...	44	0	0

The 20 fards will sell for Rs. 62-8. His profit is Rs. 18-8. This seems at first sight enormously high but it is not. The Rs. 30 laid out in March is sunk until the cold weather. Thus 8 months' interest is in the profit. That is Rs. 4-12-9 at the bazaar rate of interest, Rs. 2 per cent. per month. The other item of Rs. 14 is also money sunk and, as all such items are sunk for the greater or less part of the like term, interest for 4 months may be taken on it. That is Rs. 1-1-11. Knocking off Rs. 5-15-4, or say Rs. 6 even, from Rs. 18-8 the profit which the master printer who lays in his own stock of webs makes is clear Rs. 12-8 on a score of stamped sheets. If however he do not borrow money to carry on his business but has independent capital he makes the full Rs. 18-8 on a score.

Chikanwala.—Chikan is hand-worked flowered muslin and the chikan of Lucknow is in great demand in all parts of India. The most of this work is done on tanzeb, a kind of muslin of local manufacture, which is woven generally in webs of between 19 and 20 yards in length and 14 girahs in breadth. The chikanwala who gives out material to the chikan-doz or embroiderer cuts the web into two equal lengths, for the half web (about $9\frac{1}{2}$ yards long) is the length that is used for doputtahs, and is also convenient for cutting up to make angarkhas. Females generally cut the piece in two parts, one being double of the other, and the short piece is cut in two in the length and the three pieces then formed are sewed together so as to make a doputtah half as wide again as the web. Thus a web $9\frac{3}{4}$ yards long and 14 girahs wide makes a doputtah for females to wear $6\frac{1}{4}$ yards long 21 girahs wide. The same web might be cut into 4 angarkhas.

It is only when one wanders round the city enquiring into trade that one can get any idea of the extent to which the working of chikan is pushed. Little girls 5 or 6 years of age may be seen sitting at the doors of houses near Chob Mandi busily moving their tiny fingers, over a piece of tanzeb and working bútas (flowers) and helping home by their earnings which are little enough, only one paisa for 100 butas. It is by this early beginning that chikan workers attain the great skill they do in embroidery : but even when the greatest skill has been attained the wages paid to the chikandoz are but low. Take a piece of chikan $9\frac{3}{4}$ yds. long worked in good style which sells for Rs. 12. It is worked with diagonal bels about one inch wide at intervals of about 3 inches, and in each intermediate space there are twelve bútas worked. There are 560 yards of bel and 560 bútas in the piece. The chikandoz has been paid only Rs. 4 for all this work. The tanzeb has cost Rs. 3-8. The thread delivered to the embroiderer was 14 lachhas which @ 6 as. 6 pies per pola, cost 14 as. 6 pies. There is a little silk spent in picking out the hearts of the flowers, and the silk and labor come to only 4 as. 6 pies. The stamping of the pattern by a chhípí before giving out the web to the chikandoz cost only 4 as., and the charge of the dhobi for washing and stiffening when the web is returned by the chikandoz to the chikanwala is 4 as. Thus the whole cost of production is Rs. 9-3 and the selling price is Rs. 12. This gives a profit of 32 per cent. This rate is high because the chikanwálá has his capital sunk in the piece of web while it is in the hands of the embroiders, and he has a brisk market for his goods only during the hot weather and rains.

The foregoing will serve as a sample of the rate of profit enjoyed by chikanwálás, and, as far as I can ascertain, this rate prevails whatever be the form of goods made up,—whether rúmáls, doputtahs, bels (for insertion), or chádars.

Chikan is largely exported from Lucknow to Agra in the N.-W., to Mirzapur, Patna, and Calcutta in the east, and to Haidarábád, Dakhan. All this work is wrought by chikandozes who are given out work and paid by the piece and the wages paid are determined by the skill of the workman and the difficulty of the work.

Among the best workers in Lucknow are a small settlement of Mahomedans on the north side of the river at Hasanganj and after them are the workmen employed by Ilahi Bakhsh, and Damodhar in the Chauk.

Women of the Agarwála and Khattri castes are very clever needlewomen and embroider their own doputtahs. Some specimens of their workmanship, are quite equal to anything turned out by skilled Mahomedan men, professional chikan-workers.

Chikni-daliwala.—This is a dealer in supári or betel-nut, which is of 2 classes (1) chikni dali which comes from Amraoti and (2) ním chikni which comes from Bombay. Márwáris import both and sell wholesale : the former kind at from Rs. 34 to Rs. 42 per maund and the latter at from Rs. 24 to Rs. 28 per maund. The chikni daliwála buys from márwáris nuts wholesale, and cuts up the nuts and sells by retail. The nut is almost round, a slice is cut of the nut on two sides and there remains a round piece about ⅛ inch thick. This piece is then hollowed on both sides so as to be like a double concave lens. Its edges are then clipped. This is called *dó-rukhi*, the two pieces first clipped off are called *chúras*. The scrapings made in hollowing the dó-rukhi are called dó-rukhi chúra. Márwáris sell supári at 48 seers to the maund. Suppose a chikni daliwála buys 10 seers of nuts at Rs. 34 a maund, he gets 12 lambari seers for Rs. 8-4. He sells by the lambari seer and the outturn and classification of the pieces of nuts when cut up will be :—

							Rs.	A.	P.
	⎧ 1st quality	1¼	seer at Rs. 4	per seer,	...		5	0	0
Dó-rukhi 3¾ seers,	⎨ 2nd do.	1¼	,, ,, 3	,,	...		3	12	0
	⎪ 3rd do.	⅝	,, ,, 2	,,	...		1	4	0
	⎩ 4th do.	⅝	,, ,, 1	,,	...		0	10	0
Chúra,	...	... 6⅜	,, as. 12	,,	...		4	12	6
Chúra durukhi,	...	... ⅝	,, Re. 1	,,	...		1	10	0
Barra nákas,	...	... 1¼	,, as. 4	,,	...		0	5	0
					Total Rs.	...	16	5	6

One seer only can be prepared in a day by one labourer and his pay is 3 as. per seer nawábi. Rs. 1-14 must therefore be added to expenses. This leaves Rs. 6-3-6 profit to the chikni daliwála on 10 seers or almost 10 as. per seer nawábi weight of betel-nuts which he purchases from márwári dealers. I give the rate in this form because most chikni daliwálas do not keep accounts and the extent of their business can only be known from the wholesale dealers from whom they purchase their stock. There are, however, some very extensive traders of this class in the Chauk who keep their own accounts. Dó-rukhi dali is eaten as an astringent, generally alone but some times with ilaichi (cardamum). Chúra is used in preparing *gota* (a mixture of spices eaten by Mahomedans during the Muharram) and in gilauri or bíra (pán leaf rolled up for eating). Barra nákas is sold by chikni daliwálás to pansáris, who vend it as spice.

It is hardly necessary to go into the account of ním chikni or inferior quality of supári. Suffice it to say that the profit is about 5 as. 6 pies per seer nawábi purchased from márwári dealers. At the same time, being a cheaper commodity than chikni dali it is in greater demand. It is made up more quickly also, and is not always made up dorukhi but generally only ekrukhi. It is not less profitable to the dealer than the more expensive quality.

Chikwa.—The chikwa is a dealer in small slaughter animals, goats and sheep, as opposed to the qassáb who deals in large cattle. The distinction is sometimes made by calling the former buz-qassáb, and the latter gáo-qassábi

Chikwas sometimes combine in a partnership of three or more. One remains in charge of a cattle yard in the city and the other two go to villages round the city and into other districts to buy up goats and sheep and drive them into the city to the cattle yard. These chikwas do not fatten up the animals they sell, but drive stock to bakar-mandi near the Góldarwaza and sell there. They graze their stock on roadsides and on field pasture. The rule with them is to sell *ba hisáb deora*. These partnerships sometimes extends to five. In this case one of the partners keeps a meat-shop and another deals in hides. The other three carry on the business in stock.

Next there are chikwas who buy up goats and sheep at the bakar-mandi and take them to private slaughter-houses. Some kill as many as a score and even two score in a day. They sell goat's flesh at the rate of 10 seers the rupee and from these the khurda farosh (retailing) chikwas purchase at this rate and retail at 8 seers the rupee.

The chikwas who fatten small cattle for slaughter generally choose sheep for the reason that they are in demand to supply Europeans with mutton. They are at the expense of keeping a herdman and they fatten their stock on grain, gram or barley. Their rate at which they sell the fattened animals, if they sell to butchers, is *das ka chaudah* and, if they kill and sell the flesh, they make Rs. 7 in Rs. 16. This is somewhat less than Rs. 2 more. The reason of this difference is that a chikwa looks to the four quarters to give him *das ka chaudah* and the skin and smaller pieces are worth about a couple of rupees, more in the case of a sheep which it has cost the chikwa Rs. 10 to buy and feed up. This last item of Rs. 2 is the margin which the chikwa leaves for profit to the butcher to whom he sells a fattened sheep.

For a view of the business of leather dealing in which chikwas engage *vide Chirmfarosh.*

Chirmfarosh.—This term is used to cover all classes of leather dealers and conveys no clear idea of the varied business in leather which is carried on in Lucknow. It will therefore be convenient under this head to give a general sketch of all trades connected with leather dressing.

All sides are either *halláli* or *murdári*. The former means skins stripped from animals slaughtered for human food and the latter includes all other skins but properly means skins stripped off unclean animals or carrion. *Halláli* hides are chiefly of two kinds, (1) skins of large and small cattle, chiefly bullocks and goats killed by the Commissariat Department, and these usually are all bought by a contractor and are generally passed on to Calcutta and shipped to the English market either by the contractor or middlemen who purchase from him. The contractors are chiefly Europeans and their business is not within my scope. (2) skins of large and small cattle, bullocks, buffalos, sheep and goats, killed by butchers for private consumers. These are mostly tanned and dressed for the Indian market, but also go in large quantities to the European market. *Murdári* hides include skins stripped from bulls, buffalos, bullocks, cows, &c., which either die naturally or accidentally, or by violence and poisoning, and also skins of horses, mules, and donkeys. The former class of *murdári* hides are mostly brought into Lucknow by chamárs from villages and it is well known that chamárs having a jajmáni of dead animals resort to poisoning to procure death of animals that they may have the skins. A very large export trade in hides is done from Lucknow, and buyers who have godowns in Lucknow have branches in Sitapur, Khíri, Bahraich and Nawabgunj Districts. It would be interesting to trace the connection, if there be any, between the demand for leather in these places and cattle poisoning—does cattle poisoning increase with increase of demand in a particular year and does it within the year increase as the period of purchase comes round ? Buyers up of hides, begin to purchase in Kátik and draw off gradually from Chait to Asárh.

En passant it may be remarked that only buffalo horns are of any value. These are either absorbed locally in the manufacture of combs or go to Calcutta, Bombay, &c., with the hides, and are converted into umbrella-handles and combs in those cities or in Europe.

Native exporters of leather do not export bullock hides but only buffalo and goat skins. These they purchase chiefly from butchers in the city but occasionally from other sources. They usually have butchers attached to them like jajmáns and give them advances which are gradually repaid by delivery of skins. In this way a number of skins are delivered daily and these are spread inside upon the earth in a large enclosure, pegged down, sprinkled with *khári nimak* ($\frac{1}{2}$ pau to a goat skin, $1\frac{1}{2}$ pau to a bullock skin) and either permitted to dry or folded up wet. Skins exported to Bombay and Madras are exported wet and to Calcutta dried. In both cases the hair is not removed. Native exporters do not deal in bullock skins. Sheep skins (except of animals killed for the Commissariat) do not leave Lucknow. Dressers of skins and hides find it to their advantage to import khári nimak from Dánapur. This is done by sacks (borah) containing each 2½ maunds. This quantity costs Rs. 6 in that market and in Lucknow is worth Rs. 10.

Bullock, buffalo, and cow hides are dressed for the native market by chamárs. They purchase bullock and cow hides for prices ranging from Rs. 2 to Rs. 3-8 and buffalo hides from Rs. 3 to Rs. 5. Twelve skins are thrown into a pit and covered with water. Into this is thrown chúna (lime) and sajji (impure carbonate of soda) after ten days the skins are taken out and scraped with an iron called (khurpí) scraper. All hair is removed. There is a second pit containing babúl bark and water. In this the hides are steeped for eight days, taken out, and sewed up with múnj—the edges being made to meet where they were united on the animal—and suspended from trees and filled with the infusion of babúl bark. They are taken down after five days, opened, spread out and sprinkled with khári nimak and dried. A hide is a month in the hands of the leather dresser and the expense of dressing one lot of twelve skins (suppose buffalo hides) would be :—

		Rs.	As.	P.
Cost of raw hides @ Rs. 4 per hide, ...	...	58	0	0
Huqq Dallalí @ 1 an. per hide to middleman,	...	0	12	0
Chúna, 30 seers, ...	...	0	3	0
Sajjí, 2 seers, ...	...	0	1	6
Chhílan (pay of scraper @ 2 paisa per hide),	...	0	6	0
Babúl bark, 2½ mds., ...	...	1	4	0
Huqq Dallálí, to middleman purchasing do.,	...	0	2	6
Múnj one pau per hide @ 3 as. the seer,...	...	0	9	0
Khári nimak 3 pau per hide @ 10 seers the rupee,	...	0	14	0
One servant, ...	...	4	0	0
	Total Rs.	56	4	0

These 12 skins will sell on the average for Rs. 6 each i. e. for Rs. 72. The profit remaining to the tanner is Rs. 15-12 or Re. 1-5 per hide.

The rule is 12 hides to a táo or batch put into a pit, and while one batch is in lime and soda another batch may be in the infusion of babúl bark and for eight days at most a batch is in either pit. A tanner with two pits, one for first process and one for second process, can pass at least three batches completely dressed through his hands in a month and his profits will be Rs. 47-2 per month. It is necessary that a chamar who carries on a business of this extent should have capital. There are many such in Lucknow.

Sheep-skins; (mesha) are dressed by Muhammadans chiefly chikwas : and are turned out, either badámí or red (lal) or blue (nílak). They are bought up raw either with wool attached at Rs. 5 per score or without wool at Rs. 7 per hundred. The method of tanning is much as in the case of large hides. Twenty make a táo and are steeped first for four days in chúna (lime) and flour of makrá.

When taken out the wool is removed with a *khurpi* and the skins are steeped in babul bark. They are taken out, dried, spirinkle.l with khári nimak, and are then ready for the market. The cost, etc., of the batch of 20 skins is :—

	Rs.	As.	P.
Twenty skins with wool, ...	5	0	0
Chúna 5 seers, ...	0	1	0
Átá makrá ká 3 seers, ...	0	2	0
Babul bark 10 seers, ...	0	2	0
Khárí namak, 2½ seers, ...	0	4	0
Total Rs. ...	5	9	0

These skins when dressed sell for 4 as. each, *i. e.*, the batch will sell for Rs. 5. The trader has thus apparently lost 9 as. but he has also got 6 seers of wool from the 20 skins and this is worth Rs. 2. He has thus really gained Re. 1-7 on the score.

To dye sheepskins red the tanner does all as before, but after taking them out of the babul infusion he steeps them in an infusion of kachcha lákh, sajjí and lodh (bark of *symplocos racemosa*). These are mixed in proportions— one seer of lákh, half a chittak of lodh, and one chittak sajjí. The lákh costs Re. 1, the others one paisa at most. The prepared red-sheepskins sell at 6 as. per skin and thus the profit of the tanner is Rs. 2-14-9 per score.

Goatskins as well as sheepskins are dyed blue and called nilak. This is one of the exceptional purposes for which goatskins are kept back, otherwise they go almost entirely to the European market. The skins are steeped in lime and the hair or wool removed. They are then steeped in copper filings (tánba ká lohchan), naushádar (sal ammoniac) and lemon juice.

The account of production is as follows :—

	Rs.	As.	P.
Four sheepskins, ...	1	0	0
Chúna (one seer), ...	0	0	3
Copper filings 1¼ pau, ...	0	4	6
Naushádar do., ...	0	3	0
Lemon, ...	0	0	3
Total Rs. ...	1	8	0

These skins will sell at 7 as. 6 pies each. The tanner will also have a seer of wool—5 as. 3 pies. The total produce will be Rs. 2-3-3 as against Rs. 1-8. Four skins per diem can be turned out by one man but the demand for nilak is limited and small account need be taken of its manufacture as a staple trade.

The *luk-saz* is another leather dresser worthy of mention. *Luk* is varnish and the term is applied to varnished or patent leather. The hides used for this class of leather are cow, bullock and sheepskins, sometimes goatskins. The luk-sáz buys dressed cow and bullock hides of the lighter class suitable for uppers of boots from chamárs and he prepares sheepskins himself. The composition applied as varnish is made of printers' ink, linseed oil and resin (rál). The skin is spread on a wooden frame and covered with a paste of printers' ink and resin. It is then washed over with linseed oil and placed in the sun to dry. The process is repeated *ad libitum*.

The cost of preparing three large cowhides is :—

						Rs.	As.	P.
Three hides,	...	...	...	...	...	10	8	0
Printers' ink one bundle,		...	...	...		0	3	6
Linseed oil 2½ seers,	...	...	...	...		0	15	0
Rál ½ seer,	...	...	...	...	...	0	3	0
				Total Re.	...	11	13	6

These hides sell for Rs. 5 each, so that the tanner clears Rs. 3-2-6. If he employs labourers he pays them 2 as. per head per diem, and a labourer passes ten hides through his hands in a day : but each hide is five days in hand. This gives cost of labour 1 anna per hide. The tanner clears thus 3 pies less than, Rs. 3 on three hides or roughly Re. 1 per hide.

There is no need to go into the account for sheepskins (bhera ká luk). Only the largest of these are used. Eight of these require the same amount of stuff as three cowhides and cost about Rs. 4. They are bought by the luk-saz raw and he tans and dresses them. He makes something by selling the wool. Taking all into account I find the profit to be about 6 as. per skin.

It remains to notice the manufacture of kímukht and kirkin. These are fancy leather made from the skins of horses, mules, and donkeys. The process is the same whichever animal's skin be made up. The kímukht-sáz buys horse skins for Rs. 20 the score and others for 5 as. and 4 as. per skin. I shall take horse skins as a sample case. The skins are steeped in water for three days, then taken out, stretched and pegged down to a large flat board standing against a wall. The hair is scraped off with a scraper called *dhás*. The skin is then dried and *sáwán* (a grain) spread over the damp skin while drying. In two days the skin is dried and the effect of the sáwán is to cause the surface of the skin to assume a rough and granulated appearance. The skin is again pegged to the board and scraped with the *dhás*. Then the skin is placed in a large earthen pot containing water and *khárí namak* over a fire and boiled. When the skin has been thoroughly softened it is steeped in copper filings and sal ammoniac. It then becomes green. The extremely thin edges the legs of the skin have been cut off as refuse and sold to *kuppesázes* before the dyeing process. After dyeing the thickest parts of the dressed leather are cut out and placed apart from the lighter parts and sold separately as *kímukht* and *karkin* respectively.

The account of cost of preparing one score of skins is :—

			Rs.	A.	P.
One score of skin,	...	...	20	0	0
6 seers of sáwán,	...	...	0	6	0
5 ,, khári namak,	...	...	0	8	0
Fuel, ...	...	...	0	2	0
One labourer,	...	...	2	8	0
5 seers copper filings,	...	...	3	12	0
Nausbádar (brick kiln refuse),		...	0	0	6
Total Rs.		...	27	4	6

Each skin gives *kimukht* and *karhin* to value of about Rs. 1-12 and the cuttings, (katran) sold to kuppesaz are about 6 pies per skin. The total is Rs. 35-10. The profit is Rs. 8-5-6.

Chitəra *vide* Sunar.

Chuna kamp farosh.—This means vendor of lime made from the deposit of river beds, but the word is used in a wider sense, and all lime dealing may be treated under this head.

Lime is made in Lucknow from mud brought from Dulármau to Gao ghat, and Kurya ghat by Bhaisakund. The mud is mixed with charcoal-dust damped and made into cakes which are dried in the sun. These are burnt in a kiln and produce lime.

The lime-burner rents a piece of land which yields the kind of earth called chúr, and pays generally Rs. 2 per biswa, and digs on the average 200 maunds from a biswa. The expense of digging is about Re. 1 the hundred maunds. The earth is brought to the rivers's edge by cart by a carrier who receives Rs. 5 per 100 maunds, and thence by boat to Lucknow at Rs. 2 per 100 maunds. Say it is brought by Bhaisakund. It is there made up with charcoal dust in cakes (tikiyas) and burned in the kiln : 20 coolies at 2 as. each per diem make up 200 maunds of chúra in tikyas in one day and 24 maunds charcoal dust, which sells at 4 as. per maund, go to 200 maunds of chúr, and as 50 maunds of chúr go to a kiln and the kiln needs 8 maunds charcoal to fire it, there will be an expense of 32 maunds of charcoal, this costs Rs. 32.

When the kiln is burnt, the lime is thrown into a hauz or tank of water and stirred with a stick. One labourer is allowed to a kiln for this purpose and gets 2 as. per diem. The prepared lime is then brought to a place between Moti Mahal and Bruce's Bridge. Two kishtís at 6 as. each will convey the whole. The octroi charge is levied not on the made up lime, but on the chúr at Bhaisakund. The charge is Re. 1 per boat load.

13

From 200 maunds of chúr 450 maunds of lime are produced. When it is placed in the hauz and up to time of sale, the weight is increased to 775 maunds by the addition of sand which is mixed in the proportion of 20 seers to 40 seers of lime. The cost of production of the whole as detailed above is Rs. 61-4 and the average price of sale is Rs. 17-8 a hundred maunds or Rs. 118 for the whole. The lime-vendors deliver the lime to order of purchasers and the average cost of delivery is Rs. 2-3 per 100 maunds. This is a further charge on the lime vendor.

Kunkur lime comes from Nawabgunj ready for use and is merely broken and dissolved in water in Lucknow. It is chiefly used for eating with pán or tobacco. The selling price at Nawabgunj is Rs. 20 per 100 maunds and five maunds are equal to 2 maunds lumbari, and carriage to Lucknow is Rs. 8 per 100 maunds lumbari. One hundred maunds lambari will be broken up and moistened by 3 men in 5 days receiving $2\frac{1}{2}$ as. each per diem. The weight is doubled by the moistening process, and the lime sells at 2 maunds a rupee. The cost of the dry lime is Rs. 60-4 and the moistened lime (200 maunds at 2 maunds a rupee) will realise Rs. 100. In this case as in the former the cost of delivery lies with the lime-vendor. This is a charge of about $1\frac{1}{2}$ as. per rupee. The profit to the lime-vendor is thus Rs. 30-6 per 200 maunds.

Kali, quicklime is not prepared in Lucknow, but it is imported and sold by pansáris.

Churihar *vide* Manihar.

D.

Dal-farosh.—This term refers to those traders who purchase unbroken másh (úrd), múng, chana, arhar, matar, móth, masúr, break these grains on a grinding-stone called dharéti, and supply baniyas who sell retail. When the grain has been broken it is called dál.

All kinds of dál enumerated above are prepared in one way except arhar.

As an example take múng. The dál-farosh buys the unbroken grain at 22 seers a rupee. Two workmen, one employed to grind and the other to sift the grain, will prepare 40 rupees worth of dál in a day. As the grain is split by the dharéti, the small eye or shoot called nakwa is separated from the grain, and when sifted the dál and chunni fall apart, yielding $20\frac{3}{4}$ seers of the former and $1\frac{1}{4}$ of the latter in 22 seers. The dál-farosh sells the dal at 20 seers the rupee, and has $\frac{3}{4}$ seer dál and $1\frac{1}{4}$ seer chunni in the rupee's worth of grain to pay wages of labor and receive his own profit. The outturn is 40 rupees worth in a day or 880 seers of grain. This gives the trader 30 seers of dál and 50 seers of chunni in the day. Chunni sells at a rupee the maund, and dál at the price already stated. Thus the dealer realizes Rs. 2-12 on the Rs. 40 of grain which he purchased. He pays the two workmen 5 as. and thus clears Rs. 2-7. As a rule he is at no expense for carriage, because dál-faroshes reside in or on the skirts of large grain marts and beopáris deliver at their doors.

Arhar is either surkh, or bainjani. The latter is dearer by about 3 seers in the rupee than the former. Arhar dál is prepared in two ways. The arhar is broken with a dharéti, then crushed with a musal in an okhali (a large dish made of stone or wood), rubbed with oil and water, dried in the sun and again broken and crushed as before. The other method is similar except that the arhar is first parched by a bhurji, who receives Rs. 2 per 100 maunds. If the former method be adopted 25 seers arhar surkh which cost a rupee will yield 18 seers dál, 4 seers bhusi and 3 seers chunni. One workman will turn out 500 seers in 5 days and receive 3 as per diem wages. That is Rs. 23 worth of arhar is made into dál for 15 as. The yield will be :—

		Rs.	A.	P.
360 seers dál	at 19 seers per rupee, ...	18	14	1
80 „ bhusi	„ 15 as. per maund, ...	1	14	0
60 „ chunni	„ ½ anna „ seer, ...	1	6	6
	Total Rs.	22	2	7

Thus the trader makes Rs. 1-3-7 on Rs. 20-14.

It is not necessary to go into details regarding other classes of dál. Suffice it to say that the average rate of profit made by the dál-farosh is 6 per cent.

Dallal.—There are three classes of dallals. The first is the *pheríwálá*, who takes goods round as a pedlar and offers them for sale : the second is the *bázár gusht*, who lies in wait in the bázár, pounces on customers and guides them to shops : and the third is the dallál *tájiráná*, who executes wholesale commissions. With the two first every one is familiar. As a sample of the third take the case of a commission agent who negotiates wholesale lots of shoes. A merchant comes from, say Haidarábád and proposes to buy a large miscellaneous stock of shoes. He puts up at a sarai and summons a dallal well acquainted with the city. This dallál receives instructions and brings specimens and on their being approved gathers and delivers to the visiting merchant the required stock. He receives 2 as. per score of pairs of shoes purchased. This he realizes by charging the merchant full price and deducting the commission from the sum which he pays to the local shoemakers.

The following is a table showing all the rates which I have been able to ascertain :—

Goods.	Pheríwálá.	Bazár-gusht.	Tájiрána.
Government Promissory Notes,	...	1 an. per Rs. 100	...
Loans, ...	...	As agreed on	...
Gota kinárí, ...	...	½ an. per Re.	¼ an. per Re.
Shisha-álát, ...	...	1 do.	...
Silver bullion, ornaments, etc.,	...	¼ do.	3 as. per Rs.100
Gold do., ...	...	¼ an. per tola,	2 as. per tola,
Goldmohurs, ...	...	¼ an. per mohur	...
Precious stones, ...	...	1 an. to 2 as. ⅌ R.	2 per cent. *
Kiraya khilaat, ...	...	1 an. per Re.	...
Cotton piece goods, ...	1 an. per Re.	½ do.	3 pies per Re.
Chikan, ...	do.	do.	do.
Kámdání, ...	do.	do.	do.
Darí, qálín, etc., ...	do.	do.	do.
Dusútí, ...	do.	do.	do.
Topí, ...	do.	do.	do.
Second hand clothes, ...	do.	...	...
Pashmína, ...	...	2 per cent.	2 per cent.
Woollen piece goods, ...	...	do.	do.
Silk goods, ...	½ an. per Re	...	1 per cent.
Banarsí kapra, ...	do.	...	do.
Buffalos, cows, goats and sheep,	...	1 an. per Re.	...
Horses and elephants, ...	...	5 per cent.	...
Camels, ...	...	2 do.	...
Vegetables, ...	...	½ an. per Re.	...
Foreign fruits, ...	...	...	1¼ to 2 p. c.
Cow-skins, ...	...	1 an. per skin,	4 as. per score.
Goat and sheep-skins, ...	8 as, per 100 skins,	12 as. per 100 skins,	1 Re. per 100 skins.
Leather, ...	...	1 an. per Re.	½ an. per Re.
Shoes, of all kinds, ...	½ to 1 an. per Re.	2 as. per score,	2 as. per score.
Tallow, ...	...	½ an. per Re.	½ an. per Re.
Metals, other than bullion, ...	...	½ do.	...
Vessels (brass and copper) ...	½ an. per seer,	½ do.	½ an. per Re.
Bisátís goods, ...	1 an. per Re.	...	1 do.

* In this and in all cases it must be remembered that *haqq dallálí* and *haqq arhat* are quite distinct. For instance though the commission of a *dallál* on a *thok* of precious stones is 2 per cent the commission paid to an *arhatiyá* on sales of precious stones is 4 per cent.

Goods.	Pheríwálá.	Bazár-gusht.	Tájirána.
Oil, ...	1 an. per Re.	½ do.	paisa rupiya.
Books, ...	½ do.	...	
Paper, ...	...	½ do.	
Bhúsa, ...	...	½ do.	
Púla patawar, etc., ...	...	½ do.	
Bricks, ...	...	...	2 per cent.
Surkhi, ...	...	½ do.	
Lime, ...	...	½ an. to ¼ per Re.	
Building timber, ...	...	3 to 5 per cent.	
Bambus, ...	...	½ an. per Re.	

Dari-baf.—There are a good many weavers of darís in Lucknow, chiefly in the mohullas of Aishbagh, Berúníkhandaq, and Nayaganw, but none of these weave darís of first quality such as are manufactured in the Central Prison. It is their practice to mix old and new thread in equal parts. Were they to weave wholly with new thread they would not command a market for their goods. They turn out 3 classes of darís (1) bichauna, (2) farashí, (3) jaé namáz. The first of these will serve as a sample of all three. It is uniformly 2¼ yards long by 1½ yards wide and of very thin texture, weighing on the average 1¼ seer. The reason of the extreme lightness is that old thread is used and the thread is of the lightest description, frequently *sémal*. Two weavers sit at one loom (tanna) and weave from the middle, one at each end and complete a darí in a day. Their shuttle is made of bambu and is called *tahrí* as opposed to the iron shuttle of the Joláhá which is called *nár*. A master weaver calculates a bichhauna darí to cost as follows :—

	Rs.	As.	P.
Ten chittaks new thread, ...	0	7	3
Do. old ,, ...	0	5	0
Dyeing thread, per darí, ...	0	1	6
Two laborers at 0-1-6 each per diem,... ...	0	3	0
Total Rs. ...	1	0	9

This darí the master-weaver will sell for 19 annas if it be without flaw, or, if faulty for 18 as. He generally sells to shop-keepers, or, if not, consigns his darís at a slightly higher price to a broker, who holds them in árath and sells them for the weaver taking commission at 2 paisa per rupee. The shop-keeper who buys from weavers sells at a minimum advance of 2 as. per rupee on cost price.

Daryai-baf.—This is the only class of silk weaver left in Lucknow, and his business is rapidly dying out. Daryái is a silk fabric about 9 inches wide used for binding and for borders of doputtahs, paijámas, etc. There was great demand for this fabric under native rule as it was used extensively by Muhammadan females. The demand for a fabric for the same uses still exists but the English product sarcenet has almost entirely driven the native from the market.

The process of weaving daryái is the same as that described under the head joláha.

No daryái-báf is in the enjoyment of a business which would justify imposition of a License Tax.

Darzi.—A darzí who works alone on his own account can never pay tax. But there are master tailors in Lucknow who employ a number of journeymen and who are fair cases for taxation. The following are the usual charges for making native clothing :—

Angarkas from 3 as. to 8 as. according as the work is plain or more or less ornamented.

Mardána paijáma, 1½ as. to 2 as.

Kurta, 1½ as.

Saluka (made of chintz and without lining) 1¼ as.

    Do. with lining, 2 as.

* Paijáma zanána chúrídár, 2 as. per pair, no matter what the material.

    Do.   kalídár, 4 as. if made of calico and plain, if made of gulbadan or atlas 12 as. per pair.

Paijámas are the only articles of general female clothing made up by master-tailors, but the péshwáz, angiyás, and kurtís of dancing girls and other public women are also made up by master-tailors.

The wages of a journeyman tailor vary from 1½ as. to 3 as. per diem. The ordinary workman who gets 1½ as. per diem will make up 2 pairs of mardána paijáma in a day, and thus the master-tailor will pocket as much as he pays away in wages. Indeed, as far as I have been able to make out, it is a rule that the master-tailor daily earns by each journeyman a sum equal to the amount of wages he pays him. As the master-tailor supplies needles and thread the earnings of his personal labour may be allowed to cover the miscellaneous expenses of a shop. This is liberal. The daily income of a master-tailor may therefore be taken to be a sum equal to that which he pays in wages.

Dastar-band.—This is the person who makes the broad pagrís which khidmatgárs wear. He was an important man in the nawábi rule because every retainer and servant of the court and every one who went thither on any business

---

* *Churidar :* this denotes the tight trouser-like paijáma ordinarily worn by males and females : *kalidar* is the long, loose and flowing, paijáma worn chiefly by dancing women and servants. It is made of a number of long triangular pieces, the vertices meeting at the waist, and the flowing skirts are drawn through between the legs from behind and tucked into the waist at the front. Each component piece is called a kali.

was obliged to wear a pagrí. Now there is no rule or custom which prescribes styles of dress and the dastárbund is a poor man. He possesses dummies (qalib) made up of wood or rags and on these he folds into shape the tanzéb, malmal, or other stuff supplied to him by khidmatgárs, mahájans, and others who wear pagrís. The income of the dastárband is very small.

Dast-farosh, gudar.—These terms are used interchangeably though there is originally a difference in their meanings. *Dast farósh* is a person who buys up or takes on commission second-hand goods of any kind and sells at a stall by the road-side or walks about crying his goods. *Gúdar* is properly an old clothes-man. Both are extensive receivers of stolen property and their secret dealings are their chief source of income. They squat in Lucknow in Victoria Street, close to the Nakhkhas bridge where there is a Police Post. A very few squat in Aminabad. If one gives property to the dastfarósh or gúdar to sell he pays commission *taka rupiya*, but if the article sells for less than a rupee he pays one paisa only. It is impossible to lay down a rule as to the profit made by a dast-farósh on old wares and second-hand goods which he purchases speculatively to sell again. A mahá brahman who receives presents of clothes, shrouds, &c. on the death of jajmáns usually disposes of these to a gúdar.

Degwala.—This is a Muhammadan trader who keeps a stock of cooking utensils and lets them out on hire for festal assemblies in Muharram, in marriages, and on holidays, Shabrát, Bakr-íd, Id-ul-fitar, &c.; and also for cooking purposes on the fixed date when, as is often the custom, Muhammadans distribute cooked food as alms.

The vessels lent out are (1) *deg*, a pot often large enough to cook a maund of food at once; (2) *degcha*, a pot of smaller capacity; (3) *patila*, about half the size of a *degcha*; (4) *kathrah*, a wooden bowl in which dough is kneaded; (5) *lagan*, a similar vessel but made of copper; (6) *síní*, a copper tray used to serve out food on.

The rates paid for hire of these vessels is :—

Deg,	4 as. for each time it is used (fi táo).			
Degcha,	2 ,,	do.	do.	do.
Patíla,	1 an.	do.	do.	do.
Kathrah, } Lagan, }	1 an. per diem.			
Síní,	2 as.	do.		

The hirer of these vessels purchases mud ovens from kumhars.. Metal ovens are not let out on hire.

Lucknow is a Muhammadan city and degwálas have a thriving business. Their vessels are out on hire for about 3 days in every 5 all the year round.

It must be noted that degwálas do not lend their services as cooks at these rates with the vessels hired. If a degwála contract to cook he makes a separate charge for that service, viz: 4 as. per maund leavened bread (khamiri rotí), 8 as. per maund for shirmal roti (cooked in ghi and milk), 2 as. fi táo per deg and 2 paisa for every fraction of a maund per deg, 2 paisa fi táo per degcha and patíla.

Dhaliya, Dhalnewala.—This is the metal-worker who makes up hansalis, kharas, and tariyas from jasta, (zinc); channis, challas, panwas, and pachelas from ránga (pewter), and who moulds in lead models for other artisans. The moulds (sánchas) used by this class of founders are usually made of stone and come chiefly from Bahraich and Atraula where there are skilled stone cutters. There are, however, some stone cutters in Lucknow who make moulds but their work is not in much demand for it is less skilfully executed.

The goods made from zinc are not cast, but the metal is heated and worked with a hammer on an anvil. All pewter work is first cast and then finished with file and hammer. In either case two men work together, generally a master workman and a journeyman. The latter heats the metal and the former beats it out or casts it as the case may be. The labourer receives 1½ anna per diem. The present price of jasta (zinc) is Rs. 17-8 per maund of 48 seers. In one day 3 seers are worked up and this may be into hansalis and kharas. Suppose the latter. The outturn is 57 pairs. These the dhaliya delivers to shop-keepers at 24 to the rupee. That is, he receives Rs. 2-6. He has paid for metal 1 anna 6 pie; for charcoal 3 as. His total expenditure was Re. 1-6. Thus he has profit of Re. 1.

The price of ránga is Re. 1-5-6 per lambari seer and lead is Rs. 14 per maund. The dhaliya will make 3¾ seers weight of channis in a day. The metal is a compound of 3 seers of ránga and ¾ seer of lead. The cost of metal is Re. 1-14; wages of labourer 1 anna 6 pie; and charcoal 5 as. Total Rs. 2-4-6. The outturn is 45 pairs, sold to shop-keepers at 15 pair the rupee. Their profit is 11 as. 6 pies. Nothing is allowed for wear of moulds for they last for an indefinitely long period.

For retail dealing see *kasbhara*.

Dhoi-dar.—Is the person who keeps donkeys and mules and lets them out for carrying bricks, kankar, lime, rubbish, &c. The charges are 4 as. per diem for a mule and 3 as. for a donkey. One driver will take care of 8 mules or donkeys and will receive 1½ as. per diem. The latter out of the animals pays the driver. They are fed on a mixture of bhúsa, bhusi, and barley or other cheap-grain. It costs about 2 as. per diem to feed a mule and 1½ annas to feed a donkey. Grass is never cut for them as they have some opportunity of grazing when out or off work. Brick and lime carriers keep mules, and rubbish carriers who are generally sweepers by caste keep donkeys. A dhoídár is generally very far from poor.

Dhuniya *vide* **Rui-farosh.**

Dor Kankawwe-wala—Vendor of kites and cord. Kite flying is a wide-spread amusement in Lucknow; and persons often stake heavy wagers on two kites which are sent up together and the cords made to rub against each other in the air. He whose cord breaks and kite falls loses. The Nawabs of Lucknow are extremely addicted to this sport and bet very heavily. One wealthy Nawáb at least is said to have lost all his fortune on kites. This city has, as might be expected, grown famous for the manufacture of kite cord, and it is exported largely as far as Moradabad on the west and Calcutta in the east.

The cord manufacturer employs women who prepare the strands on a charkhí which revolves in the opposite way to that in which the ordinary spinning-wheel moves. The cord is made of from 3 to 13 strands (tár). The thread used is either English or country. But the cord used in flying for wagers is made of English thread and usually of 13 strands. This thread comes in bundles (gaddi), and is carefully opened out, steeped in water for two days and spun while damp. The strands are then twisted into cord by the hand. Finally a preparation of wheat starch and boiled rice is made and this is rubbed into the cord with a rag. This final process is called *har dená*.

English thread No. 80 costs Rs. 6-8 per gaddi which contains 2 seers nawábí, and by the time this is turned into cord (dor) the weight has increased to $2\frac{1}{4}$ seers nawábí. This is owing to the final process.

The wages of the women who spin the thread is as. 2-6 per seer, and the starch and rice in which there is a great waste may be set down as $\frac{1}{2}$ anna to the seer of thread. The total cost of production is Rs. 6-14 for $2\frac{1}{4}$ seers of dor of the very best quality; and this is sold at Rs. 4 per seer (trade-price) by the manufacturer. His profit is thus Rs. 2-2 on $2\frac{1}{4}$ seers nawábí. The shop-keeper who sells retail purchases at the nawábí weight and sells at lambarí weight, charging still Rs. 4 per seer, i. e., he has 5 chittaks dor left as a margin of profit when he has re-placed his outlay in purchase. This is equal to Re. 1-4. If the shop-keeper sells in fractions of a seer he still sells by lambarí weight but at the rate of Rs. 4-8 per seer. In this case his profit is still more.

Kites are made by *áráishwálás*, but no expenditure is lavished on them. They may be had for a paisa each, and though 2 as. will purchase the handsomest looking kite in Lucknow, it is the cheapest that are flown on wager. The shop-keeper buys kites wholesale at 4 as. per score, and as he sells at a paisa each his profit is one anna per score.

The reel on which the dor is wound and unwound by the kite-flyer is called *huchka, latái*, or *charkhí*. Those sold in the bazar are made by barhais from shisham or mango wood, and sell for about 4 as. each. Many people make up reels for themselves. These home-made huchkas are generally of bambu, and much ruder articles than the shisham charkhí.

Do-suti-baf.—Do-sútí is a coarse cotton fabric woven in two colors, used for floor cloth. Each piece is woven 5 yards long and is 11 girahs wide. This is the ordinary daily out-turn of one man. The weight of a piece (fard is

14

7 chittaks, of which 6 are thread and one is starch applied to the thread before weaving to strengthen it. The thread costs 4 as. and starch is but a trifle or, as the weaver says, " dhela fi fard " The coloring is about 5 paisa per piece, Total cost is 5 as. 4½ pies. The weaver delivers at 7½ as. per piece to shop-keepers, or sells direct at 8 as.

I have chosen the cheapest and lightest material as a sample, because it is largely woven by the poorer weavers of Lucknow and is much used in linings of purdahs and the like. Much more expensive do-súti is made to order, the length of web being as directed but the width is uniform.

Dudhwala or Shír-farosh.—Dairy men are usually ghosís or gwállas :—

(1) *Ghosís* have no other employment but the keeping of milch-cattle, chiefly buffalos of all kinds : and they breed buffalos. They sell milk to halwáis and make *khoyá*.

(2) *Gwállás*. These are generally Ahirs or Gadariyas and keep both buffalos and cows, and frequently cultivate some land. They seldom sell milk and khoyá to halwáis. They deliver nilk and butter to order and bring cows or buffalos and milk them at private houses.

(3) *Shír-farosh, Dúdhwálás.*—These are of no special caste but are generally Ahirs, Lodhs, Kurmis, Gadariyas, Halwáis or Brahmins. They buy up milk and vend it in large quantities to halwáis.

Buffalos of first quality (pachahin) which cost Rs. 70 or 80 give 12 to 16 seers milk per diem. This milk will yield one chittak butter per seer or 1½ chittaks ghí per seer. The ordinary buffalo (desi) which costs about Rs. 20 to Rs. 30 gives 7 to 12 seers per diem and the yield of butter or ghí is as before. The first quality cow (Nagauri) which costs Rs. 20 to Rs. 40 gives 8 to 14 seers milk per diem and the second class (desi) which costs Rs. 4 to Rs. 10 gives 2 seers to 5 seers per diem. The yield of ghi or butter is as before.

The first quality buffalo costs 10 as. per diem to keep.

    ,, second ,, ,, ,, 6 ,, ,,
    ,, first ,, cow ,, 8 ,, ,,
    ,, second ,, ,, ,, 3 ,, ,,

There is profit from dung of cattle (gobar) viz.,

1st. buffalo 6 pies per diem.
2nd. ,, 6 ,, ,, ,,
1st. cow 3 ,, ,, ,,
2nd. ,, 1½,, ,, ,,

Average quality milk fetches an average price of one rupe for 16 seers and ghi is sold by gwallas generally at 1¾ seers to the rupee. Butter is always one rupee per seer. There are few ghosis or gwallas honest in the sale of milk. They generally add 1 pau of pure milk to 3 seers of milk from which butter has been taken and vend the mixture as milk. Those who milk their cows etc. at private houses seldom give over 10 or 12 seers only to the rupee.

Ghosis and gwallahs calculate that a cow or buffalo is in milk for about 8 months in the 12 and buffalos give milk as much as 10 months in 12. That is, buffalos and cows give full milk for six months and then fall off one-third and then later on one-half. But sometimes cows and buffalos well cared for give milk up to within fifteen days of calving.

Thok-farosh shir-faroshes procure milk daily from places within 2 kos radius of the city and sell in large quantities to halwais. They purchase at 20 seers and sell at 16 seers the rupee.

The following account shows the profit, a good buffalo cow is worth to the owner.

	Six months 16 seers milk per diem.	Two months 10½ seers per diem.	Two months 7½ seers per diem.
	Rs. As. P	Rs. As. P.	Rs. As. P.
Butter	4 chittaks, 0 4 0	4 chittaks 0 4 0	4 chittaks 0 4 0
Milk from which butter has been taken.	3¾ seer ⎫	⎫ 10 seers 4 chittaks 0 10 3	⎫ 7 seers 4 chattaks 0 7 3
Pure milk. ...	12 seers ⎬ 0 15 9	⎬	⎬
Kanda.	0 0 6	0 0 6	0 0 6
	Rs. 1 4 3	0 14 9	0 11 9

For the remaining two months the only profit is from gobar 6 pies per diem. The Total income is Rs. 331-6-6 for a year and the cost of feeding at 10 annas per diem is Rs. 228-2-0. The net profit for the year is (excluding the calf) Rs. 103-4-6. In the same way a second class buffalo is worth Rs. 49-13-0. A first class cow Rs. 72-9-3 ; and a second class cow Rs. 58 per annum.

G.

Gadariya *vide* Galledar.
Gaddidar *vide* Abkar.
Gadhewala *vide* Dhoidar.

Galledar.—This is the name given to a dealer in sheep and goats. He sells the young to butchers, who fatten up and kill them, and he reserves a stock to breed from. He thus differs from the associations of five or more butchers (*vide* chikwa) who send some of their number out to remote places to buy up animals for slaughter.

Galledars are chiefly *gadariyas* and incline to keep sheep rather than goats. The reason is obvious. Sheep yield wool, a marketable article, and goats do not.

One *gadariya* will attend a flock of 100 sheep and goats, and is at no expense for fodder. He drives them out to graze on wild pasture. Goats and sheep drop young twice a year, and as many as four kids or lambs at a birth are not unusual. In a flock of one hundred sheep and goats let there be 60 sheep. It is the custom to cut the wool three times in the year, after the cold weather, the hot weather, and the rains. The idiom for shearing is *pairi karna*. The average is a quarter of a seer of wool at each *pairi*. Thus 60 sheep will yield 1 maund 5 seers of wool in a year. If the wool is sold, it will fetch about one rupee per 3 seers. But gadariyas frequently weave their wool into small blankets (kamli) of $1\frac{1}{2}$ seer each, which sell for one rupee each. But in this case they are at a cost of $\frac{1}{2}$ an. per kamli paid to a *behna* for carding the wool. Thus, from 60 sheep the gadariya may have either 45 seers of wool, value Rs. 15, or 30 kamlis to sell at Rs. 30. In the latter case he pays the behna Re. 1-6-6 and clears Rs. 28-9-6. The latter method of disposing of the wool is chosen by gadariyas who have grown sons or daughters, or wives without children, who weave.

The lowest estimate which any gadariya has given me of the lambs dropped by 60 sheep in one year is 90. These sell as lambs for 8 as. each, as one year olds for from Re. 1 to Re. 1-8, and as two year olds for Rs. 2. This is an average computation.

Gadariyas milk ewes but draw never more than $\frac{1}{4}$ seer per diem, for they have regard to the value of the lambs. Sheep's milk is sold to halwais at 1 an. per seer to make *khoa*. There will always be 12 sheep in 60 in milk and they thus bring 3 as. per diem by milk.

Sheep's manure is sold to dhobis for washing and Muraos purchase it as a high class manure for *dofasli* fields. It sells at Re. 1 per 5 mds. The pen where 60 sheep are kept at night will when swept in the morning give 10 seers.

Now take the 40 goats in the mixed flock of 100 sheep and goats. The estimate of kids from these is set at 90 in the year: and their milk 12 seers per diem. Goat's milk sells at 1 an. per seer. Kids are sold in the first year at from 12 as. to Re. 1 each and in the second year from Rs. 2 to Rs. 3 (if females) and Rs. 4 (if males). Goats when in milk are given bhusa: but 4 as. at most per diem is spent on 40.

Thus, a flock of 100 sheep and goats in the proportion taken above, is worth Rs. 405 per annum at the lowest computation, the sheep 157-8, the goats 247-8, after paying all expenses.

Gandhi.—The manufacturer of perfumes is properly called *gandhi*, but the tendency to supplant Hindustani by Persian words has given rise to the use of many other terms, itarfarosh, itarsáz, khushbúsáz, and attár (used in a perverted sense.) The process of manufacture is distillation as practised in abkari godowns; but the bhapka which is used in distilling perfumes is of peculiar construction. I can best describe it as a gigantic suráhi. It is made of copper. In this is placed what is termed the zámin or máwa of all itar, viz., sandal itar which is manufactured at Kanauj. The flowers from which the perfume is to be extracted are thrown into water in the cauldron on the fire and their perfume comes off in steam and passes through the worm into the copper bhapka and combines with the sandal itar. When the bhapka is removed the perfumed oil is separated from the water in the bhapka by skimming the surface with the hands.

The perfumer purchases sandal itar at nawábi rates and the perfume which results is measured by him in nawábi tolahs. He calculates up to time of sale at nawábi rates and he then sells at lambarí tolahs. He usually lays out his account to have profit of 2 as. in 10 as. on the produce of a still at nawabi weight thus :—He allows 4 as. for zámin; one anna for firewood and wages; 2 as. for profit; and the balance of three annas will regulate the amount of flowers which he will put into the deg.

Champa ka itar is not in much demand but it chanced that I came across a gandhi manufacturing it and he gave me his calculation in that case as a sample :—

	Rs.	As.	P.
4 as. zámin 100 tolahs *i. e.* 1 seer 4 chittaks nawábi			
Sandal ka itar @ Rs. 20 per seer, ...	25	0	0
1 a. firewood and labor, ...	6	4	0
2 as. for profit, ...	12	8	0
Total	43	12	0
3 as. margin for flowers, ...	18	12	0
Total.	62	8	6

Thus the profit is 25 per cent at nawábi weight; which is the weight between manufacturers; but the selling weight at which manufacturers sell wholesale to retailing shopkeepers is lambari.

The hundred tolahs nawábi will be 110 tolahs lambari. These at 10 as. per tolah will be Rs. 68-12-0.

Thus the manufacturer selling to wholesale dealers makes 25 per cent and if he sells to retailers he makes 37½ per cent. Once the perfume leaves the manufacturer's premises there is no rule which governs rate of profit. The retailer asks the highest price he can get for a perfume which suits the fancy of a purchaser, and that price depends on the rank and means of the purchaser.

The gandhi is supplied with flowers by málís who either go abroad and buy up flowers, or who take leases of gardens or have gardens of their own. There are, however, sometimes middle men called gulfaroshes, who buy up flowers from málís who have not large supplies, and thus forming thoks or dherhs sell in large quantities to gandhis. These are the traders who make sihrás and badhis (chaplets and garlands) for marriages. The rates at which flowers have been sold by thok to gandhis this year have been

Guláb (rose)	... 2,000 to 2,750 per rupee.
Motiya (Jasminum zambacum),	... Rs. 3 to Rs. 4 per maund.
Júhi (Jasminum Auriculatum),	... ,, 10 ,,
Chambeli (Jasminum grandiflorum),	... ,, 11 ,,
Champa (Michelia champaca),	... Rs. 10 to ,, 12 ,,
Maulsari (Mimusops), ...	... ,, 4 ,,
Hinna (Lawsonia inermis), ...	... ,, 5 ,,

The present prices of perfumes are :—

Hinnah,	1st quality,	... ...	Rs.	4 per tolah
Do.	2nd do.	... ...	,,	3 do.
Do.	3rd do.	... ...	,,	2 do.
Do.	4th do.	... ...	,,	1 do.
Chambeli	1st do.	... ...	,,	3 do.
Do.	2nd do.	... ...	,,	2 do.
Do.	3rd do.	... ...	,,	1 do.
Júhi,	... ...	... ...	,,	2 do.
Arús,	... ...	... ...	,,	2 do.
Barg i hinna,	...	... ...	,,	2 do.
Shahnáz,	... ...	... ...	,,	2 do.
Shamámat ul ambar,	...	...	,,	3 do.
Ruh i Khas, ...	...	... ...	,,	8 do.
Itar Keora, ...	...	... ...	,,	2 do.
Guláb 1st quality, ...	...	...	,,	5 do.
Do. 2nd do.	...	... ...	,,	2 do.
Do. 3rd do.	...	... ...	,,	1 do.
Subág,	... ...	...	As.	12 do.
Motiya 1st quality, ...	...	...	Rs.	2 do.
Do. 2nd do.	...	... ...	As.	12 do.
Ruh Pándari,	... ...	...	Rs.	4 do.

Gargarewala *vide* **Huqqewala.**

Ghalla-farosh *vide* **Arhat galla.**

Ghari-saz.—There are no watchmakers in Lucknow, but there are journeymen who have worked in English shops and who now practice as watch-menders and cleaners. They charge for cleaning a watch Re. 1, and for mending anything which is broken Rs. 2, exclusive of price of the metal or new part of the mechanism supplied. Thus, the charge for putting in a new spring is Rs. 2 exclusive of price of the spring. A prevailing practice with the ghari-sáz is to buy up old watches and take them to pieces and use the materials to repair watches entrusted to him. Among the ghari-sázes in Lucknow is one known as Nawáb ghari-sáz and he is certainly a very superior workman and has a very large business.

Ghiwala.—Ghi is imported to Lucknow from Cawnpore, Chandausi, Bans-Bareli, and the northern districts of Oudh. Jamnápárí ghi all comes through Cawnpore. The beopárí who imports and sells wholesale buys by local market weight (tháp), at Cawnpore 48 seers to the maund, Chandausi 50 seers, Bans-Bareli 52 seers, and so on. He delivers in Lucknow to wholesale dealers at two rates, in Saadatgunj 40¾ seers, in Rája Bazár and Amínábád at 41¼ seers. This is a matter of custom. In Saadatgunj the wholesale purchaser takes a chittak on each panseri for good weight and ¼ seer per maund, 'tari' or degs. In Rája Bazár and Amínabád custom further allows that the weighman should place a chittak with the panseri in weighing out the panseri and the purchaser thereafter takes as in Saadatgunj the chittak fi panseri and the pau man pichhe (tari).

To put the case of a beopari importing from Chandausi :—He brings the ghi in leather jars called kuppas, and pays the Railway Company carriage Rs. 49 per 100 maunds. His own railway fare from Lucknow to Chandausi and back is Rs. 3-15-0. His consignment is, say, 100 maunds. On arrival in Lucknow he takes four 2 bullock carts and conveys his goods, say, to Rája Bázár. The cart hire will amount to Rs. 2. He pays octroi duty at 12 as. per maund. This is an outlay of Rs. 75. He sells 41¼ seers to a maund at Rs. 27 per maund, (present price). He thus realizes Rs. 2,678-2. He pays brokerage 4 as. per maund and dalláli 2 as. per maund. These charges amount to Rs. 37-8. He purchased in Chandausi at 50 seers to the maund and the nirakh there was Rs. 28 the 50 seers. His 100 lambari maunds therefore cost him Rs. 2,240. Allow him the same charges for carriage to Railway Goods Shed there which he incurs in carting away at Lucknow. The total charges he has to set against the Rs. 2,678-2 realized in Lucknow amount to Rs. 2,409-7. He thus makes a clear profit of Rs. 268-11 on the 100 maunds or Rs. 2-11 per lambari maund.

Now take the case of the wholesale vendor in Rája Bázár. He has received 41¼ seers for Rs. 27 and he has also received 4 as. haqq i arath. He sells at lambari taul, and enters his purchase as 40 seers for Rs. 27. Thus his first profit is 1¼ seers (which are at this price equal to 13 as. 3 pies) and 4 as. arath. The average advance of price at which wholesale vendors sell to local shop-keepers is 8 as. per maund. Thus the profits of the wholesale ghi vendor may be taken at Re. 1-9-3 per lambari maund.

Now there is the shop-keeper selling by retail to be dealt with. His profit arises from two sources, legitimate profit from the difference between local wholesale and retail prices and fraudulent profit from adulteration. Retailers mix oil with ghi, til ka tel in the hot weather and mahua oil in the cold weather

Muhammadan retailers of ghi (mukheri) adulterate more freely than Hindus because they have no caste prejudices against fat and they therefore heat up suet of all kinds and mix it with ghi. Ghosis and others who make ghi in the neighbourhood and bring it to market do not sell as a rule to wholesale dealers but to shop-keepers and at private houses.

Ghosi *vide* **Dudhwala.**

Gilkhanafroz *vide* **Bhurji.**

Gota kinari farosh.—Gold and silver lace is one of the staple-manufactures of Lucknow. The process of manufacture is exceedingly interesting and yields employment to a large number of artisans. It will therefore be treated in detail.

The dealer in gold and silver lace calls a *kandila kash* and delivers to him Rs. 65-7-3 (present price of a kandila or bar of silver of the standard weight of 60 tolahs) in rupees for a *suféd* or *rupahli* (silver) kandila or a sum of rupees equivalent to $62\frac{1}{2}$ tolahs for a *sunahli* or *lál (i. e.* gold-coloured) kandila. He directs the kandila kash to prepare and deliver to him either a *rupahli* or *sunahli* kandila. If the latter is ordered the lace dealer orders the kandila kash to give so many máshás of gold, naming the amount, in the kandila. The proportion generally ordered is 8 máshás. The kandila kash then purchases from a sarraf the silver and gold required, and takes them to the kandila-kachahri. This is an institution maintained by the gotawálas as a body. It is in the Chauk. A darogha is appointed at Rs. 30 a month and he superintends the melting into bars of the silver brought. The kandila-kash records the name of his employers and the silver delivered. It is melted, and beaten into a standard bar of a cubit length which the kandila-kash carries to his workshop. This institution of a mint, if I may so call it, is intended to secure the guild against fraud of employés.

When the kandila-kash arrives at his workshop he beats the kandila and draws it through a succession of holes in an iron plate, each being smaller than preceding the one, till he produces a long wire of about $\frac{1}{12}$ inch thickness. If gold is to be added it is done by placing it at the plate and it adheres to the kandila as it is drawn through.

The process of wire drawing is rude. There is an axle placed over a hole in the ground and to this is attached a chain and clamp. The end of the kandila is beaten and pushed through a hole in the perforated iron plate and caught by the clamp. When it has been pulled sufficiently long it is released from the clamp and wound round the axle and pulled completely through the hole. This process is repeated until the wire is reduced to the required diameter. The axle is turned by a wheel. One workman holds the wire at the plate and another turns the wheel. The instrument used for wire pulling is called janta or jantri.

The kandila-kash pays 2 as. at the kachahri for melting and beating out of the kandila. He also loses 4 máshas (or 5 as. 4 pies) of metal in the 60 tolahs. The wages he receives for wire pulling are Rs. 1-3-6 per rupahli and Rs. 2 per sunahli kandila. His expenses are 4 as. charcoal and 3 as. laborer's wages per kandila. He thus makes 8 as. 2 pies per rupahli and Re. 1-12-8 per sunahli kandila.

The kandila-kash delivers the wire to his employer who sends for a tárkash. This workman takes the wire to his shop and drawing it from one charkha to another through an iron rest (a plate with holes in it called *jantri*) reduces it to the thickness of coarse thread and winds it finally on a reel. The wages of the tárkash are Rs. 3-12 per 100 tolahs.

The gotáwálá receives this thread and passes it on to a tárdabkaiya who beats it with a hammer into a flattened thread and winds it on a charkhi and finally arranges it in 32 lengths called lachchhis. This is the whole kandila now in the form of bádla. The wages of the tárdabkaiya are Rs. 2-12, for rasmi bádla, and Rs. 3 for mahín bádla per 100 tolahs. This workman ties each lachchhi with 2 ratis of thread. This is taken by the gotáwála and is counted by him with bádla in all weight that he delivers hereafter. Thus he has 60 tolahs and 8 mashas of bádla (*i. e.* for selling purposes) for Rs. 70-9. This he sells, at Rs. 1-4 per tolah, for Rs. 75-15. This gives a profit of Rs. 5-6 or Rs. 7-5 per cent rupees.

This will serve as a sample of the profit of manufacturing suféd or rupahli bádla.

Sunahli bádla stands as follows:—

				Rs.	As.	P.
62½ tolahs silver,	...	...	...	68	3	0
8 mashas gold,	...	...	...	13	5	4
Kandila kashi,	...	...	...	2	8	0
Tar kashí,	...	...	...	2	5	10½
Tárdabkai,	...	...	...	1	11	9
	Total Rs.	...		88	2	0

Allowing in this case as in the last for the thread on each lachchhi the gotáwála has, for selling purposes, 63 tolahs 10 mashas which he sells at Rs. 1-8 per tolah for Rs. 95-12. His profit is Rs. 7-10 or well over 8⅓ per cent.

When the gotáwála has thus prepared bádla he gives it out to gota báfs to weave. The gota-báf takes the bádla by weight and supplies the silk of which the warp is made. Gota báfs who have large factories usually buy silk in the rough state and prepare it for consumption in their factories. This gives them a profit; but now, to determine the gota-farosh's profit, let us take the cost of prepared silk, which is what he charges the gota-báf, when they make up accounts together. This price is Rs. 28 per seer of surkh resham, used in sunahli gota

15

(gold lace,) and Rs. 29 per seer suféd resham used for rupahli gota (silver lace.) I shall take the cheapest style of gota because it is that on which there is least profit and competition, if there be any, operates chiefly in the sale of this class to lower profits.

I.—Sunahli gotah sold at Re. 1-5 per tolah.

20 tolahs sunahlí bádla, ...	30	0	0
8 tolahs surkh resham at Rs. 28 per seer, ...	2	12	9
Wages of gotábáf ½ auna per tolah, ...	0	14	0

Total Rs. 33 10 9

These 28 tolahs sell for Rs. 36-12-0 trade price. The profit of the gotá-wálá is, therefore, at trade prices, Rs. 3-1-3, or Rs. 9-3-4 per cent.

II.—Rupahli gotah sold at Re. 1-12 per tolah.

20 tolahs bádla rupahli, ...	25	6	0
8 tolahs sufed resham, ...	2	14	5
Wages of gotábáf ½ anna per tolah, ...	0	14	0

Total Rs. 28 12 5

These 28 tolahs sell at Re. 1-2 per tolah for Rs. 31-8-0. The profit of the gotáwálá is therefore at trade prices Rs. 2-11 or Rs. 9-7-5 per cent.

From the foregoing it will be seen that the profits at trade prices between members of the guild of gotáwáls are:—

Bádla sunahli, ...	8	10	0 }	17	13	4	
Gotah do.,	9	3	4 }				
Badla rupahli, ...	7	10	0 } or 17	1	5		
Gotah do., ...	9	7	5 }				

per cent. where the one trader carries on all processes of manufacture.

That this is the rate of profit enjoyed by a wholesale manufacturer and vendor of gold and silver lace in Lucknow city, there can be no doubt. Such a trader, however, who exports (as many do) to Murshidabad and Bombay and other places incurs an extra charge of postage and commission charges and this cuts down his profit about a rupee per cent. The account books for the past 3 years of one of this class who resides in the Chauk, which were produced and examined, show a profit of 16 per cent. on manufacture and export of gold and silver lace.

The foregoing is an account at wholesale trade prices but some note must be made of the profit at retail prices. It is a rule that the gotáwálá charges arise of at least 1 anna per tolah on wholesale prices when he sells retail. This will give the rate of profit on retail sales by a manufacturer of gotá who buys bádla to give out to gotábáfs, Rs. 10-15-4 per cent. on sunahli and Rs. 11-3-5 per cent. on rupahli gotá.

The profit assumed on sales in this class in the assessment of gotáwálás in 1879-80 was an average rate of 10½ per cent.

The weaving of gotá, kinárí, lachka, patta and dáb is effected by laying the silk warp from a light beam (lapetan), stationed in front of a stool, at which the gotábáfs sits, to a charkha attached to the ceiling. The process is exactly the same as in weaving cotton fabrics except that the bádla which makes the wool is not put in a shuttle but is passed between the threads of the warp on a *nari* or bobbin. The width of a piece of lace is reckoned by *belas*. Bela is two threads of the silk warp. The gotáwálá directs a gotábáf to weave gotá, lachka, dáb or whatever it be, of so many belas width.

Some of the gold and silver lace, etc., woven by gotábáfs are subjected to a process of stamping which marks them with flower or water or other patterns. This is called *uttusazi*, and the dies used are called *thappas*. They are made of wood and the *uttusaz* impresses the die with blows of a hammer. The pay of the *uttusaz* is one paisa per tolah. He is purely a labourer and cannot pay license tax. The laces stamped in this way are lachká patta and dáb.

The gotáwálá though there is in this case an extra charge for labor, still makes a profit at the rate already noted.

Gotá is about a ½ inch wide and a variety of about half that width is called *dhanuk.*

Lachká is about 1½ inches wide.

Kinárí is 2 to 3 inches wide and beyond that up to 9 inches is pattá.

Gotá and dhanuk are used either as braiding or as binding. It is sometimes worked up with the fingers in forms called chutkí and gokhrú and sold at a slight advance in price for fancy trimmings. The workman who makes gotá and dhanuk into gokhrú and chutkí receives 7 paisa per 80 yards.

Gudar-farosh.—The term gúdar properly means old clothes and rags, but the gúdar-farosh deals also in old metal, glass, and other goods. He or his servant wanders from house to house with *chiura* (rice boiled, dried, and crushed,) and gives this in exchange for old clothes, rags, tattered daris, and the like, or for old brass, copper, iron, tin, &c., and odd articles of glass and crockery. The gúdar-farosh mends up any metal goods he gets that are worth mending. Other metal he disposes of to lohars, thatheras, &c. He sells the stout fragments of daris to Mochis, who sew them into the soles of shoes between two folds of leather. The other pieces of daris and rags in general are sold to Mashalchis. The gúdar-farosh is somewhat like the old clothes-man in English cities and has his familiar cry ' *lohá-chiúra* ! *lohá-chiúrawálá*' ! But the real old clothes-dealer of the east is the dast-farosh. The gúdar-farosh is a rag-man and his profits are unknown and subject to no rule. He is usually by caste a Jhamaiyá, and is certainly never poor.

Gul-farosh, *vide* **Gandhi.**

Gurwala.—Gur is an article of general consumption and is also largely exported. There is perhaps no article of food which is so profitable to the storer, but at the same time the storage is accompanied by great risks. There is great danger from wasps and hornets, and from the action of heat which would cause the gur to melt. To guard against these dangers the gur is buried in bhusá. Each párí (a large cake, average 1½ maunds weight) is placed in the sun, cut in two and dried, and again cut and dried so that each párí is made into four pieces. These pieces are laid in a store room on narkul matting spread over a layer of bhusá. The pieces are kept a little apart. Over them is thrown bhusá and the sides closed in with tát. Sometimes a large sheet of course cloth (chandni) is used to cover the heap.

The purchase of gur for storing begins in January and the bhadsár holds his stock until it suits him to sell. He may keep it for ten months and not sell until after Bhadon. In this case he makes a very great profit.

The following is the account furnished of a venture made in gur in 1879 :—

	Rs.	As.	P.
33 Maunds of gur bought in January at Rs. 3 per maund,	99	0	0
Gari-hire to store-room,	0	8	0
Carrying and cutting and drying,	0	8	0
Int. for 10 months on capital borrowed for purchase of the gur,	10	0	0
Bhusá,	2	0	0
Narkul matting,	0	8	0
Tát,	2	0	0
Cover (chándni.)	3	0	0
Tattar of bambu,	2	0	0
Rent of room at 6 as. per month for 8 months,	3	0	0
Loss of weight by drying at 2½ seers per maund,	6	3	0
Total	128	11	0

	Rs.	As.	P.
Sold at end of Bhadon 30 mds. 13½ seers at 7 seers 4 chittaks per rupee,	167	6	0
Profit.	38	11	0

This gives a shade over 80 per cent. profit to the trader who purchased with borrowed capital. The storer who purchased with his own capital would in the same venture have made Rs. 48 or Rs. 37¾ per cent. That this rate of profit was enjoyed by gurwálás (wholesale storers) in 1879 there can be no doubt. In this year 1880 gurwálás stored in January @ 12 seers the rupee and in March 10½ seers. Retail prices in May are already as high as 6½ seers.

Gwallah *vide* **Dudhfarosh.**

H.

Hakkak *vide* Almas-tarash.

Halwai.—There are two classes of Halwai (1) the confectioner proper who makes up sweetmeats and vends them at his shop either wholesale or retail, and (2) the khwáncha-farosh or tray man who buys from the confectioner and sells as he walks the streets or squatting at a booth. I have taken the five sweetmeats most approved and calculated the cost price and profit of one *táo*, the quantity usually made up at one time in a day by an average confectioner of the class who supply khwánchawálas. The *táo* costs in sugar, ghi, ata Rs. 19-11 and sells for an advance of Rs. 4-3-9 on cost price. There remains to deduct wages of three laborers or cooks from this. The head cook receives Rs. 7-8 per mensem plus ½ seer puri per diem; and the other two receive Rs. 3 each per mensem. Thus deduct 8 as 3 pies and the clear profit is Rs. 3-11-6 or Rs. 18 per cent. It is evident that a second táo on the same day will give the full profit of Rs. 4-3-9.

If the confectioner sell retail, his profit on a táo is Rs. 7-3-4 less the wages as before. This gives 6-11-6 or 33 per cent.

		Rs.	As.	P.	
Jalebí 10 seers.	Maida 2½ seers	0	4	0	For this sweet meat the shakkar used is the syrup left after the making of other sweet meats. This is cheaper of course than using new shakkar. Jalebi sells 2½ seers the rupee at large shops and traymen who walk about in the streets buy at this rate and sell at 2¼ seers. The confectioner makes 8 as. on 10 seers. and the trayman 7 as.
	Ghi 2 do.	1	5	3	
	Bási Shakkar 5 seers 10 ch.	1	13	6	
	Flavoring essence...	0	0	3	
	Fuel	0	1	0	
	Total Rs. ...	3	8	0	
		Rs.	As.	P.	
Bálu Shahi 10 seers	Maida 2½ seers	0	4	0	The confectioner sells at 2½ seers and the trayman at 2¼. The former has profit 7as. 9 pie and the latter 7 as.
	Ghi 3 do.	1	15	0	
	Sugar 2½ do.	1	4	0	
	Flavoring essence	0	0	3	
	Fuel	0	1	0	
	Total Rs. ...	3	8	3	
		Rs.	As.	P.	
Pera 11 seers.	Khoya 6¼ seers	2	3	0	The confectioner sells at 2 seers the rupee and the trayman at 1¾ seers. The former thus makes 10 as. 6 pies on 11 seers and the trayman makes 12 as. 6 pies.
	Shakkar 5 do.	2	8	0	
	Pista 2 chs.	0	1	6	
	Fuel	0	1	0	
	Total Rs. ...	4	13	6	
		Rs.	As.	P.	
Amarti 10 seers.	Dál Másh 2½ seers	0	4	0	The confectioner sells at 2 seers and his profit is Re. 1-8 on 10 seers. The tray-man sells 1¾ seers the rupee and make 11 as. 6 pies.
	Ghi 2 seers	1	5	3	
	Bási Shakkar 5 seers 10 chs.	1	13	6	
	Flavoring essence...	0	0	3	
	Fuel	0	1	0	
	Total Rs. ...	3	8	0	

Iaddú 12½ seers.		Rs.	As.	P.	The confectioner sells at 2½ seers and makes 13 as. 6 pies profit. The tray-men sell at 2¼ seers and make 8 as. 10 pies.
	Besan 4 seers	0	4	0	
	Ghï 3 seers 2 chs.	2	0	6	
	Sugar 2nd quality 5 seers...	1	9	0	
	Kishmish	0	4	0	
	Fuel	0	1	0	
	Total Rs. ...	4	2	6	

Púrí 1½ seers.		Rs.	As.	P.	The confectioner sells at 4½ as. per seer and makes 4 as. profit. The tray-man who sells at 5 as. per seer makes 9 as. profit.
	A'tá 14 chs.	0	1	0	
	Ghi 2½ chs.	0	1	2	
	Zira	0	0	1	
	Pickles and vegetables ...	0	0	3	
	Fuel	0	0	3	
	Total Rs. ...	0	2	9	

Huqqewala.—The variety of Huqqas is very great and it would occupy much space to give a detail of each. I shall merely give an account of the manufacture of the ordinary Huqqa made of a wooden stem (*gargara*) and cocoanut bowl, and I shall add a few remarks on other varieties. Gargarawalas are those who make the stems ordinarily attached to cocoanut shells for use as tobacco pipes. These stems are made of mango and shisham.

Mangowood purchased for this purpose costs Re. 1 per 2½ maunds, and 2½ maunds will yield on the average all round not less than 3 score gargaras. Shisham is purchased by measure at a varying price. Whether the wood be mango or shisham, the gargaras turned out are of 5 lengths: balishti, manjhola, pauna, hath-bhara, sawa-hatha: and one man will turn out 33 of the smallest, or 11 of the largest size in a day. Those who have gargara factories pay labourers:—

4 ans. per score	...	Hath-bhara.
4½ ,, ,, ,, ...	...	Sawa-hatha.
4 ans. per score and quarter,	...	Pauna.
4 ,, ,, ,, ...	...	Balishti.
4½ ,, ,, ,, ...	...	Manjhola.

Coloring costs ½ anna per score. The stuff used is lac. Each labourer is allowed one pie per diem *tasma* (*i. e.* for leather strap used to work kamáni and barmá.) Manufacturers sell these stems wholesale to naryalwálas who fit them to cocoanut shells. The wholesale prices are:—

Balishti Shisham,	4	score per Re.	1	0	Mango	6 score.			
Manjhola,	,,	2	,,	,,	Re.	1	0	,, 1 score for as. 3
Pauna,	,,	1	,,	,,	,,	0	11	,, 1 ,, ,, as. 4
Hath-bhara,		1	,,	,,	,,	0	14	,, 1 ,, ,, as. 5½
Sawa-hatha,		1 score	,,	,,	1	6		,, 1 ,, ,, as. 8

and in all cases they reckon 22 to the score.

Mahajans import náryals from Calcutta. Those which are intended for manufacture of huqqas are what are called ' Guaga náryal' (literally dumb) i.e.have no milk or kernel, and they generally come stripped already of the outer fibre. Importers vend these náryals in bags, some of which contain over 300 náryals and often 500. The purchasers of these bags (borahs) are the makers up of the naryals and the fitters to them of the gargaras purchased as described. They clean, polish and bore the shells.

There are seven kinds of náryals :—Jahází, Nakbhariyá, Kholí or Ratan-purí, Máldípa, Kallí, Márwár and Jasariya.

The importers vend these wholesale :—

Jahází,	@	Rs.	8	0	0 to Rs.	15	0	0 per %
Nakbhariya,	„	„	6	0	0 to „	10	9	0 „
Kholí, (Ratanpurí,)	„	„	3	0	0 to „	3	4	0 „
Máldípa,	„	„	1	4	0			
Kallí,	„	„	3	0	0 to „	5	0	0 „
Márwár,	„	„	1	10	0 to „	2	0	0 „
Jasariya,	„	„	3	0	0 to „	3	8	0 „

The rounder the náryal the cheaper, and the longer the dearer it is.

The naryal finisher who has bought a borah of cocoanuts and has fitted *gargaras* will sell them as follows :—

I.	Wholesale { Marwar or Maldípa, }	náryal with balishti mango gargara Rs. 3 per %
	Kalli, „	manjhola „ „ „ 5 „
	„ „	balishti „ „ „ 4 „
	„ „	manjhola shisham „ „ 8 „
	„ „	balishti „ „ „ 6 „
	{ Ratanpuri or Jasariya, } „	hathbhara mango „ „ 5 „
	„ „	manjhola „ „ „ 4 „
	„ „	{ manjhola to hathbha- ra shisham } „ 3 „

Jahazi and Nakbhariya cocoanut shells are the most expensive and are usually fitted with shisham gargaras and the price of made up articles vary as the price of the undressed náryal from Rs. 14 to Rs. 18 per hundred.

II. *Retail Sales.*—Obviously retail prices must vary much according to the place of sale and the demand, but in Lucknow a naryalwala will sell the cheapest kind of náryal with the cheapest gargara fitted to it, for 2 paisa, while he will sell the best Jahazi náryal fitted with best shisham gargara for 6 as.

The cost of cleaning and polishing náryals is :—

		Rs.	As.	P.	
Jahází,	...	1	8	0	per cent. wages and 4½ as. oil.
Nakbhariya, ...	...	1	4	0	,, ,, 4½ ,, ,,
Kholi (Ratanpuri),	...	1	0	0	,, ,, 4½ ,, ,,
Máldípa,	...	0	10	0	,, ,, 1¼ ,, ,,
Kalli,	...	1	0	0	,, ,, 2 ,, ,,
Márwár,	...	0	12	0	,, ,, 2 ,, ,,
Jasariya,	...	1	0	0	,, ,, 4½ ,, ,,

Seeing that (as above will show on calculation) a 2 as. náryal and gargara has cost the vendor under 1½ paisa, his profits are on the cheapest goods Rs. 33 per cent. and as the dearest which he sells at 6 as. has cost him less than 3 as. 9 pies his profits are on the dearest goods 60 per cent. The rate of profit is high but the daily sales are small.

The preceding account is of the huqqas in demand almost exclusively by Hindus. The following two descriptions of huqqa are those chiefly used by Muhammadans, but are also used by Hindus when moving about, when they need to purchase a cheap article for temporary use.

The Madariya huqqa is made up of an earthen vessel or stand (huqqa proper) to hold the water, instead of a cocoanut bowl, and of a double stem of narkul called naicha. One branch of the stem supports the chillam and the other is applied to the smoker's mouth. This huqqa is so called because the eathen part and the cloth used to cover the naicha are of the color of gerú, which is the color in favor with Madari Jogis. The vendors of these huqqas buy the earthen vessels from kumhars at 1 anna 3 pies per score of 22 and naichas from naiche-bands at 2 as. per score of 22. They also sell chilams, which they purchase at 3 pies per score of 22, with the foregoing so that the purchaser may have a complete pipe and the selling price is *paisa fi adad* that is, 5 as. 6 pies on an outlay of 3 as. 6 pies. Tobacco vendors usually sell these huqqas. The other class of cheap huqqa is the Azimullah-Khani, so called from the name of a cook of Wajid Ali Shah. It differs from the Madariya in that the branch of the naicha used for smoking is curved and the naicha is covered with various colors of cloth and bound with silk instead of cotton thread. In this case the chillams and huqqas are 25 to the score and together are purchased from kumhars at 5 as. 6 pies per score. The naichas are purchased for 3 as. 3 pie per score. The complete huqqa sells for *taka fi adad*. The profit 3 as. 9 pies per score.

Both the Madariya and Azimullah Khani Huqqa are largely exported from Lucknow.

I.

Ilaqeband.—Iláqeband is a Muhammadan who makes coloured cords of silk or cotton thread used to bind ornaments such as armlets (bázú) and to string together pearls, beads, etc., and also makes up braid, fringe, petticoat-strings, (nárá) and paijáma cords (izarband.) Patwa is a Hindu engaged in the same business but the Mussalman generally adds whip-making to his business which the Hindu does not.

Both iláqeband and patwa buy plain cotton and silk thread and they generally dye the thread themselves, not however as a rule using fast colours. The expense of dying is but trifling, not more than Re. 1-4 to Rs. 15 worth of silk or cotton. A stock of Rs. 15 will suffice for all demands on an ordinary iláqeband or patwa for a month, and he will sell his made-up goods for as much as double of that sum : but the latter is usually the less prosperous of the two. As a rule neither of them has an income of less than Rs. 10 per mensem.

There is a much more prosperous class of traders in Lucknow, chiefly in the Chauk, passing under these designations. They not only make up the ordinary goods of this class of shopkeeper, but they keep a stock of lachka, kalabattun, fíta, etc, and of false gems and beads, and they make up embroidery, *khilqats*, *hárs*, etc, and their income is most comfortable. A trader of this class will consume Rs. 50 of silk in a month. Such a trader can often pay Rs. 25 and there is at least one in Lucknow who pays Rs. 75. License Tax.

Intwala *vide* **Puzawewala.**

Itarfarosh *vide* **Gandhi.**

J.

Jariya *vide* **Murasa-kar.**

Jauhari.—Dealer in precious stones.

There are nine precious stones specially esteemed in the East above all others and termed *nauratan.* They are (1) Hira or almás, diamond, (2) panna or zamurrad, emerald, (3) yáqút, ruby, (4) nílam, sapphire, (5) pukhráj, topaz, (6) lahsaniya, cat's eye, (7) gomedak, a pale sherry-coloured stone resembling a ruby, (8) munga, coral, (9) moti, pearl. There are two other stones much esteemed, added to these in the jauhari's account books, making up eleven khátas, one for each class of precious stone. They are, (10) the lálri, an inferior ruby, and (11) firoza, turquoise.

I. Diamonds are made up by the diamond cutter in three forms. (1) *parab*, i. e. both upper and lower facet horizontal and the sides or edges cut or bevelled, (2) *polki*, a level facet below but cut above in facets (pankhari, pahal, tilakri,) six or more, (3) *kanwal*, cut in facets both above and below. There is one variety of old diamond cut in the *taura* form, as it is called, *i. e.* the uppermost facet is horizontal. This classification of the style in which diamonds and other precious stones are cut is called *bandish.* Diamonds when cut for earrings are either cut (1) *goshwára*, the shape of an elongated pigeon's egg or rather of a cone with a hemisphere on the base. (2) or *badámcha, i. e.* of the shape of an almond, like the last but somewhat flattened.

There are four classes of diamonds according to colour, called after the four classes of Hindus, the name of the class indicating the degree of esteem in which they are held. (1) *Brahman baran,* pure colourless crystal in appearance, (2) *kshatri baran,* red or rose colour (gulábí,) (3) *Bais* or *vaisya baran,* yellow (zard), (4) *Sudr baran,* soiled appearance (maila) or black.

A diamond has three grades of value when in the rough (kora). These are called *koraghát.* (1) *ashtank,* having eight sides, (2) *laddu* (moti chur,) round, (3) *bilki,* almond shaped. The first of these is the highest grade.

The diamond when cut has four grades, the first being the highest, (1) *kutbi,* cut in a rectangular shape, (2) * *athwás,* cut with eight corners ; (3) *girda,* cut with a round upper surface, (níbu ka phánk;) (4) *saro,* shaped like the cypress. Of the last there are three varieties, the *saro* proper, *pán* (betel leaf) and *tikoni,* triangular.

The foregoing are the terms and idioms and modes of cutting adopted for diamonds among natives of the East. European-cut diamonds are run into these classes as far as possible, being described thus : *battís pankhari polki walandesí, i. e.* a Dutch diamond with a level base and cut in 32 facets above. The tárif (expression used to express excellence) of a good diamond is ' *Sufed be aib muwáfiq biliaur ke.*

II. The *bandish* of the emerald is in three classes, in the following order, (1) *taura,* level above and below, with bevelled edges, (2) *mathaila,* level below and round upper surface, (3) *tilakridar,* level below and cut in facets above. The *gháts* are the same as those of the diamond, but an emerald in the rough is called *khar* or *khara* and the *tarif* of the best is ' *sabz be aib, kánch ka tukra.*' The *begri* who cuts an emerald is paid according to the *bandish* as given above (1) one rupee per rati, (2) and (3) eight annas per rati. This is the minimum rate but higher will be paid to ensure greater care in the case of exceptionally good stones.

III. In the case of the ruby the *bandish* is the same as that of the emerald and the *ghats* are as in the case of the diamond. It is called *khar* when in the rough. The *begri* is paid for cutting at the same rates as for the emerald. If a ruby be more than one rati in weight it is called *mánik,* if less, *chúni.* If either an emerald or a ruby of more than one rati be bored it is called *mani*' or if less than a rati, *kherki.* The tarif of a ruby is '*surkh be aib kabutar ki ánkh* (variatim, *atlas ka tukra).*

IV. Sapphires are as to ghát, bandish and cost of cutting, the same as emeralds and rubies. They are, however, made up as earrings similarly to diamonds, *goshwára* and *badámcha.* The tarif of a good sapphire is ' *alsi ka phul.*'

---

* *Kutbi* and ath̤wás refer to the number of corners which appear round the diamond when one looks at it from a ovo.

V. The topaz is in its classifications like the last three and the tárif of a superior topáz is 'Kundan ki dali,' lump of fine gold. This is a soft stone and is made by a nagina sá₹ as often as by a begri.

VI. The lahsaniya is made up only in the mathaila bandish and has two ghats, (1) girda, round, and (2) bádámi, almond shaped. The name given it in English, cat's eye, is taken from the current expression of what jauharis call its tarif, 'billi ki ánkh.' *

VII. The bandish of the gomedak is either (1) taura or (2) mathaila and the ghats are as in the case of diamonds.

VIII. Coral is imported in the rough in branches (shákh) and cut to make either beads (dána) or gems for setting (nagína). The begri who cuts the shákh receives Rs. 4 per tolah. There is no bandish of coral and there are no ghats except when it is cut for setting. The praise of good coral is that it is 'gulábi dáná'—a bead like a rosebud.

IX. The pearl is of four gháts (1) sira suráhidár, like the goshwára diamond; (2) gol, spherical; (3) kamar, a compressed sphere, like an orange; (4) páya (the foot, lowest kind), round above and almost level below. The flaws of a pearl are (1) lahar, undulating mark, (2) garaj, a cloudlike smudge, (3) choba, a wooden appearance; (4) geri, a circular mark round the surface. The tárif of the colour of a good pearl is 'dudh ka phena, shíshe ki khíl' froth of milk, inflated glass. Khíl is parched grain, inflated so as to have a frothy appearance.

X. The lálri is, if good, like a rose-leaf in colour, guláb ki patti. The bandish and ghát are the same as those of the emerald.

XI. Turquoise. The only bandish of this stone is mathaila and the ghats are the same as those of the lahsaniya. The colour of a good turquoise, is compared to 'níla thotha,' the colour of sulphate of copper.

The place from which precious stones are brought or rather where they are found is called the khet or field of the stone. Thus the lahsaniya has three khets, Kattak, Dhúm, and Shám (i. e. Persia) and the pearl three khets, Bombay, Basrah, and Ceylon.

All precious stones are sold by the rati, as standard weight, except very small pearls which are sold by number, and coral beads which are sold by the tolah. The rati is a small red berry with a black base. It is called rati when used as a weight but its proper name is ghungchi and it is gathered in jungles from a wild shrub (abrus precatorius).

The custom of a jauhari is to keep a separate kháta or account book for each of the eleven precious stones which I have detailed and he enters in these khatas his purchases and his sales. No jauhari has honestly produced a full account of his business as a dealer in precious stones until he has produced these eleven khatas. There will not be found in these books (as a rule) any account of balance of stock at the beginning or end of a year or term of years:

---

* The word lahsıniya is derived from lahsan, garlic, in allusion to the colour of the stone.

and thus it is impossible to throw the accounts into a schedule form to determine with absolute accuracy the jauharis profit's.

The system on which a jauhari proceeds in purchasing any precious stone is this. He carefully notes its baran, ghát and bandish. He calculates according to his experience the length of time the stone is likely to lie on his hands, for some precious stones and some classes of certain precious stones sell more rapidly or more slowly than others. He then makes up an account thus. 'I should sell this stone within such a term for so much. My capital will be sunk in it for that term. If I pay such and such a price now and sell for so much at the end of that term I shall repay myself my capital with interest at bazar rates on money lent on good security?' He then pays the price accordingly. Thus I have seen a jauhari buy an emerald at Rs. 215 which he has priced for future sale at Rs. 425 and he has explained that the emerald being large and having a flaw—and emeralds being rather at a discount among natives of India—he calculated that he might not sell it within five years and that therefore he paid Rs. 215 and priced at Rs. 425 so that he would not be at loss of interest (compound interest) on the money invested. He might sell, and would probably sell in a less term than he stated, for of course the jauhari takes the extreme limit so as to be on the safe side. This illustration is one of exceptionally long calculation but is taken for the reason that it all the better illustrates the principle. It serves to give a key to the profits of a jauhari. His business is open to few risks. His stock is equivalent to cash in hand and, even if he send stock to an arhatiya in another city for sale, the rule of trade demands that the arhatiya, if he sell on credit, should nevertheless pay the jauhari before he deliver the goods to the purchaser. The jauhari pays the arhatiya Rs. 4 per cent, the highest rate of arhat charged on any goods. The jauhari is thus free from risk. His profit in any year may be fairly though roughly determined by taking from the money realized by sales in that year a sum representing a percentage on capital lent on good security. As far as I can judge, the percentage is not less than Rs. 16.

Jila-saz.—This is the workman employed to give the final polish or gloss to gold and silver and plated goods. He receives payment at the rate of 8 as. per Rs. 100 value of the goods on which he is employed. It is said that a skilful *jilasáz* can earn 8 as. per diem though it may well be doubted. He is, however, only a journeyman labourer and is not liable to taxation.

Jildband.—Bookbinder. The work of the oriental bookbinder has not the durability or finish of English work. His appliances are rude, and consist of a wooden screw-press called *shikanja*, a long steel blade called *saifa* for cutting the edges, and a long coarse needle, ' *suja*,' for sewing. He usually makes pasteboard for his own use, from waste sheets of paper or buys them from daftris who make them up in the same way. These country-made boards sell at Rs. 4 a maund. One sheepskin (country leather) will suffice for 12 octavo books half bound, and for the same number of books one quire of marble paper (abri) is needed. The leather costs 5 annas, and the paper $5\frac{1}{4}$ annas. Boards for covers cost 4 annas.   Thread and paste will be about 9 pies.   Total cost 15 annas.   For binding a book of this kind the jildband receives 2 annas.   He has thus 9 annas on 12 books, and the time required for that number is 2 days. Clearly the jildband is not a case for taxation.

Jolaha.—This is the caste which devotes itself specially to weaving. There was some years ago a most extensive business in hand-loom weaving in Lucknow, but English goods are gradually pushing country fabrics out of the market, and joláhas are emigrating from the city or seeking other occupation.

The only cotton fabrics now woven are *malmal, tanzeb, addhi, dhótar, jabdi.* and *jómdáini.*

The joláha purchases cotton-thread from merchants who deal wholesale, *e. g.* Chedi, Thakur and Co. and employs a labourer at his *kirkhána* to open this thread on a spinning-wheel and wind it on small bobbins called *nari.* These bobbins are merely short pieces of reed, narkul generally.   They are used to insert in the shuttle (nár) to make the woof (banna) and are wetted before use. Besides these *naris* there are others much larger on which thread is wound. These are used for laying the *tanna* or warp.   The term is *tannai* or as the English idiom is 'warping.'   The process is this.   Narkul stalks are stuck upright in the ground at intervals and two large *naris* are fixed by wedges on the ends of long reeds and a person walking along round the uprights drops by a skilful movement of his hands the two threads one from each nari so as to lap on alternate uprights.   When the warp has been laid it is dressed with a paste of flour, and dried.   It is then taken to the loom, and each alternate thread is drawn through a hole in one *rachcha* (leaf of heddles) and the other threads drawn through the interstices of another *rachcha.*   Then all the threads are drawn through the interstices of the *hatha* (batten) and the ends are finally fastened to the beam or *lapetan.*   The other end of the *tanna* (warp) is attached to a hook or peg or other contrivance swung from, or fastened to, the ceiling.   There is but one beam in the loom.   The place of the second is taken by three reeds which are disposed so as to prevent the threads becoming confused behind the *rachchas.*   To the *rachchas* are attached treddles (*pansár*) and by their movement the ' shed' is produced through which the shuttle flies.

Take for a sample case of hand-loom weaving, cost of production, etc, *tanzeb.*   The warp is 40 yards long and there are woven from it four pieces of 10 yards each.   Suppose first that the fabric is of coarse texture, the weaver's wages are Re 1-8 for the 40 yards.   The warp is 5 polas of thread at 5 as. per pola and the woof 5½ polas at 5 as. per pola.   The thread is therefore Rs. 3-4-6.   The wages of warping are 1½ paisa per pola or for the whole warp 7½ paisa.   The charge for winding thread on bobbins is 1 paisa per pola or 10½ paisa the web.   Paste or starch is only one paisa, (a pau of átá.)   There is no charge of labour for dressing because this is done by weavers in a friendly way for one another without charge. The total cost therefore is Rs. 5-1-3.   The web is in 4 pieces of 10 yards each which sell for Rs. 1-8 each or Rs. 6 the whole web. Profit is therefore 14 as. 9 pies. Obviously if the jolaha be himself the operative his profit is Rs. 2-6-9.

Similarly a more expensive web of the same class will cost :—

		Rs.	As.	P.
Tanna { 3 polas fine,	... ...	1	8	0
3 do. course,	... ...	1	2	0
Banna 8 polas, ...	... ...	4	0	0
Warping, ...	... ...	0	2	3
Winding, ...	... ...	0	3	6
Dressing, ...	... ...	0	0	3
Weavers' wages, ...	.. ...	2	8	0
	Total	9	8	0

This web will sell in two pieces for Rs. 5-8 each. The profits of the master-weaver are therefore Re. 1-8, or if the weaver be an independant operator he will earn Rs. 4.

The tanzeb and malmal woven in Lucknow are the materials used for embroidery in chikan. The reason is that this class of fabric soft and easily worked by the native embroiderers who do not stretch the fabric worked on a frame.

Juria is a kori weaver *vide* **Kori.**

Jutafarosh.—Shoe-vendor. There are a great variety of shoes made up in Lucknow and they differ so much that an account of a number of specimens now before me must be given before a proper idea of shoemaking can be conveyed.

All shoes of whatever class are either *mardána* (terahwán, chaudahwán, pandrahwán, solahwán and occasionally athárahwan according to number of ungulis from heel to toe ;) *zanána* (bárahwán, igárahwán and terahwan ;) or *bachchakána* (satiya, athiya, nauwán and daswán.)

The first class of shoes is *zerpái* which are up only zanána and bachchakána. These are made with soles (*tali*) and fronts (*panjah*) only and a pad which lies under the heel of the foot. This pad is called *eri*. There is no heel (*khuri*), and no side (*addí or díwár*) to this class of shoe. I have four specimens before me. First, zanána terahwán badámí sádah. This has sole and eri of thick plain cowhide, no lining. The front is made of thin badámí cowhide and the binding is of lál m esha (red sheepskin). The shoemaker makes up this variety of zerpai, supplying all the materials, and sells to the shopkeeping shoe-vendor at the rate of twenty pairs for three rupees. The score embraces various lengths, is what is called pachmel, (ranging from bárahwán to terahwán). The average retail price is 4 as. per pair so that the shoe-vendor makes Rs. 2 on a score. The next kind before me is zanána makhmalí terahwán. In this case the front (panjah) is of yellow velvet, the eri covered with panni (brass foil), and the binding and sole as before, but the shoe is lined with red sheepskin. The shoemaker makes up these also wholly from his own materials, but does not sell them to the shoe-vendor. He sells them himself at 8 as. per pair. The total cost of manufacture is about 6½ as. per pair and the profit consequently 1½ as. The only case in which a jutafarosh buys these from the maker is when he has a large order from a dealer in a distant place and he then buys and despatches to order on commission. A third specimen is zanána bárahwán augidár. This variety has the front handsomely embroidered with kachcha salma, i. e. imitation gold embroidery. The rest is as in the last case. The embroidered front (augi) is purchased by the shoemaker from a zaidoz at 2½ as. per pair and the cost of other materials and manufacture is as before. The shoemaker sells this variety at 8 as. per pair to purchasers and has thus a profit of 2 as. per pair. The jutafarosh (shopkeeping boot-vendor) does not deal in this variety of shoe. The fourth specimen is zanána bárahwán jháridár. The front is embroidered in imitation silver work and is called jhári. The rest is as before. The jhari costs about 7 as. per pair and other items are as in last case. The selling price is 12 as. per pair. The profit to the maker is 1½ as. per pair. In this case also the maker vends direct and not to shopkeepers.

Another class is árám pái. I have one specimen. It is worn only by well-to-do women and is sold by shopkeepers at Rs. 3-8. It is made with a heel (khuri) and sides (addi) and a long curled up front. The whole upper is of imitation gold embroidery which has cost Re. 1-12. The shoemaker has been paid 8 as for his labour and the leather supplied by him. An ilaqeband has received 8 as. for his labour and for kiran (silver fringe) supplied by him and sewed on all round the seams of the uppers. The lining is of tulle and a small slip of velveteen which come to about two annas at most per pair. Thus the shoe-vendor has a profit of 10 as. per pair.

A third class is ghetla, a shoe with a long curled up front. It is made with an eri and the upper is in one piece with both front and sides. It is worn both by men and women. The specimens before me are two. The first is zanána makhmali terahwán selling at as. 4 per pair. The velvet is 3 giras to the pair and costs 4½ as. The leather and binding and making up cost 7½ as. The profit per pair is two annas. The second specimen is zanána augidar pur-zar terahwán. This is made exactly like the last except that the uppers are not velvet but márkin embroidered with imitation gold work. The uppers cost Re. 1·6 and leather and making up 8 as., lining, &c., 2 as., total cost Rs. 2. The shop price is Rs. 2-4 per pair.

Another class is the Salcmsháhi, a very long, pointed, shoe with a slight curve up from beneath the toes. This class is made of embroidered velveta in the uppers, the soles of cowhide, the back of the heel is overlaid with kharkin, and the tip of the toes with kimukht and the lining is of red sheepskin. The wives of the mochis who make up these shoes work the embroidery on the velvet uppers. The cost of making up a pair is :—velvet 6 as., embroidery 8 as. and leather and labour of mochi 14 as. Total Re. 1-12. The shopkeeper sells these at 2 Rs. per pair.

A fourth class is *charhauwán*. This is the description of shoe usually worn by men and need not be described in detail. There are two specimens before me. The first is a pandarahwán of yellow velvet in the upper and is tipped and backed with kharkin and kimukht. The sole is buffaloskin and the lining is red sheepskin velvet is allowed $1\frac{1}{4}$ yard to 8 pairs, *i. e.* Rs. 1-14 or, to the pair, $3\frac{3}{4}$ as. and the shoemaker makes up the shoes and supplies leather for 9 as, This shoe costs $12\frac{3}{4}$ as. and it sells for 14 as. the pair. The profit is $1\frac{1}{4}$ as per pair. This is a lower rate of profit than in other cases, but the reason is the great competition in production of this class of shoe. The other specimen of this class is a chandahwán made wholly of leather but the upper and back of heel (páu) are overlaid with háshíya (imitation silver work) and gokhru. These cost 6 as. and the leather and making up come to 8 as. Total 14 as. This shoe sells for one rupee per pair.

Another class is the *bút* (Anglicé boot). This includes all varieties of shoes and boots made on lasts. With those made for English customers I have nothing to do. Those made for the native market are chiefly two varieties, kámdár and jhári for native women and lúkdár (or patent leather) shoes for native men. I have three specimens of the former all terahwán. One is rupahili (or silver embroidered uppers). The next is sunahili (gold embroidered upper) and the third is jháridár (velvet uppers embroidered with flowers in salma sitára). The cost of the uppers in these cases is 10 as., one rupee, and 13 as. respectively. The cost of leather and wages of making up is uniformly 8 as. The selling price is in each case respectively Re. 1-4, 1-12, 1-8, and profit 2 as., 4 as., and 3 as. I have one specimen of patent leather shoes made for native market. This is a pandrahwán selling at Re. 1-4. The patent leather (luk) in the upper costs 4 as. and the soles, heels and lining, with wages of workmen, are calculated at 14 as. The profit is 2 as. per pair.

There is another class yet to notice the kafsh : but it is reserved for a separate note as it is made for a class and by a class, and is a speciality not exported.

A very large export trade is done in the shoe business in Lucknow and the places to which export is made are Agra, Mirat, Bareilly, Rampur, Murádábad, Cawnpore, Benares, Patna, Fatehpur and to Central India. The extensive export trade keeps local prices and profits on local sales low.

K.

Kabab farosh.—Every one who has walked through the native quarters of an oriental city must have noticed here and there a cook with his two upright iron rods and his 5 or 6 tiny spits resting on hooks attached to these uprights, each spit being run through a number of balls of meat roasting over charcoal fire : or with an iron or copper pan (máhí-tawá) over a charcoal fire in which are fizzing little round cutlets of crushed meat. This is the kabáb farosh. His dainties are of 3 kinds ; (1) *gólas*, balls which are small enough to admit of eight or a dozen to a spit of 18 inches length. In this case four or five spits are arranged over each other on upright iron-rods the fire being on the ground (2) *síkh ka kabáb* In this case there is but one spit and the meat is arranged in one mass, (3) *prasandá*. This is the name given to the small cutlet-like kabáb prepared in the frying-pan. The cook buys boneless beef at one anna the seer or beef with bone at 20 seers the rupee. He makes a compound of besan (gram flour onions, garlic, coriander seeds, pepper, and ginger, and salt. He adds $2\frac{1}{2}$ seers of this compound to 12 seers of meat. The meat has cost 12 as. and the spices cost 10 as. Half a seer of weight will be lost in cooking, and 5 seers of charcoal are required for cooking and cost $2\frac{1}{2}$ as. He sells his kabábs at 3 as. the seer or 2 Rs. 10 as. for the 14 seers. His profit is therefore Re. 1-1-6, or one and a half anna the seer.

Kabaria, *vide* Mewafarosh.

Kafshdoz.—The peculiar pattern of shoe called kafsh is not made up for sale at shops but is made up to order for private individuals.

It is broad at the toes, which are curled up in fantastic style, and is very narrow at the heel which is very high and protected by an iron tip round the rim. It is exceedingly difficult for one unaccustomed to walk with kafsh to move steadily while wearing them. They give that shaky movement to the wearer which is characteristic of old age. It may be for this reason that they are worn chiefly by sanctimonious maulvis carrying long walking sticks, as the movement necessitated is in keeping with the character of respectable and, venerable eld.

A pair of kafsh sells for Rs. 2, the kafshdoz employs workmen to sew while he cuts out the materials. One workman at 3 as. per diem will turn ou a pair in a day and the total cost is :—

Rúmí Makhmul $3\frac{1}{2}$ girahs @ 1-8 per gaz,		...		0	5	9
Leather,	...	...	...	0	10	0
Panni (brass foil leather,)	...	...	...	0	1	0
Thread and wax,	...	...	...	0	0	9
Iron heel tips,	...	...	...	0	1	6
				1	2	3

The profit is therefore 13 as. 9 pies per pair.

Kaghazi.—There is but little paper and that only of a coarse description now manufactured in Lucknow. Two descriptions have come under my notice as ordinarily manufactured. The first is *wasli*, or boards for book-binding. The kaghazi buys up refuse paper at from 12 as. to 1 rupee per maund nawábí.

He puts three *panseris* in nands and tramps them to pulp. He then takes this pulp to the river, washes it out, and again takes it home and throws it into a large *hauz* with 60 gharas of water. It lies for 20 days and is then in a pasty condition. The kaghazi then lifts out some on a chik spread on a large frame, presses it with his hands, drains and dries it. The produce of the 3 panseris of refuse paper is 10 seers of mill-boards 3 ft. by 2. ft. each which sell at Rs. 4 per maund. The profit therefore is 10 as.

The next kind ordinarily manufactured is *zard kaghaz*, a rough coarse paper, foolscap size, of a soiled white color and glazed. The waste paper bought up for this is about Rs. 3 per maund nawábí, and the process of manufacture is as before. The outturn from 3 panseris is one ream of 24 *dastahs*. This paper sells at 12 as. per gaddi of 10 dastahs, the outturn is worth Rs. 2-12-9 and the cost of material was Rs. 1-2. Profit is 10 as. 9 pies per ream.

Arwali was at one time extensively manufactured in Lucknow and was in great demand for M.S.S. The demand was all the greater in Lucknow owing to the cultivation of literature under the patronage of the Lucknow court which led to the collection of libraries. The demand for this class of paper has diminished under British rule as oriental learning has declined and the passion for large M.S.S. libraries no longer exists. Indeed the demand for *arwali* must soon be a thing of the past as cheap-printed books are quite supplanting the more expensive M. S.

Arwali paper is made of old tát (made of hemp,—*san*) which sells at Re. 1 per maund. Four maunds of this are steeped in a hauz with 20 seers sajji and 15 seers chúna. The mass is pounded with a dhékali and washed out. This process is performed some 30 times and is spread over 4 months.

The paper is finally prepared as in the case of zard kághaz. As the hauz is empty while the pulp is being washed, a second táo can be steeped and pounded in it. Thus two táos (batches) are prepared simultaneously.

There are six workmen required and they are paid 2 as. each per diem. The account of two táos would be :—

	Rs.	as.	p.
First táo 4 maunds of tát, ...	4	0	0
20 seers sajji, ...	0	5	4
15 seers chúna, ...	0	2	8
	4	8	0
Second táo, ...	4	8	0
Wages of labor, ...	90	0	0
Total Rs. ...	99	0	0

The produce of each táo is $2\frac{3}{4}$ maunds of paper of 12 gaddis of 10 dastahs each to the maund. The price is Rs. 3-8 per gaddi. The two táos will yield Rs. 231. The profit is therefore Rs. 132 per hauz in 4 months.

All other paper consumed in Lucknow is imported. Bambu paper comes from Naipal and is sold by weight at 8 as. per seer. Beoparis from Naipal import and sell wholesale to marwáris at Saadatganj. This paper is used chiefly for tying up parcels. Another use is in the business of the nyáriya for the straining of silver to separate it from tezáb (*vide* nyáriya). The price at which marwáris purchase this paper has not been disclosed. Badámí kághaz and sufed Serampuri (Srirampuri) the ordinary country writing papers, are brought to Lucknow from Bally near Calcutta.

Foolscap and colored papers and in fact all European papers generally are imported through Calcutta. I have not been able to fix any sample case of profit on this class of paper.

Kalabatun-farosh, *vide* **Zardoz.**

Kalwar, *vide* **Abkar.**

Kambal farosh.—Large blankets are not woven in Lucknow, but only small blankets called kamli. These are made by gadariyas who keep flocks of sheep (*vide* gallédár). They call in a behna who cards the wool and they then work the wool into thread on a dhiriya moved in the hand. This instrument consists of two cross sticks with an upright stick from the point of juncture. It is the same thing that one sees carried in the hands of kahars making sutli as they walk about. The gadariya weaves a kamli in the same way as a dari is woven. A reference to gallédár will shew that a gadariya weaving his own wool will clear 28-9-6 on 30 kamlis of 1½ seer each. If a kamli báf buys his wool his profit on the same number of kamlis will be Rs. 13-9-6. As sheep are sheared three times a year, there are three seasons when kamlis come to the market. Shopkeepers who purchase from gadariyas sell at an advance of one anna per rupee in the hot weather and 2 as. in the rains, and up to 4 as. in the cold weather.

Kamdaniwala.—Kámdání is often confounded with zardozi. The essential difference is that kámdání is work done with gold or silver thread (tár) and zardozi done with salma and sitára (*vide* zardoz). The thread used is flattened (dapka hua) and the employer delivers to the kámdání sáz a piece of cloth, usually tanzeb, malmal, chikan, jámdání, jáli, or other fabric of an open texture, such as net or crape. The cloth is stamped with the desired patterns and weighed before delivery. The gold or silver thread is delivered with it and the whole is weighed on return. The quantity of gold or silver is thus ascertained and wages are paid to the kámdání sáz at the rate of from 9 to 12 as. per tolah. The master or employer then totals up cost of material, stamping, and gold and silver thread, and adds 4 as. per rupee to the total for minimum rate of profit. The grand total determines his trade price.

Kandewala.—This word signifies a dealer in cowdung cakes (*kanda*). There are many such traders in Lucknow and in other large cities, and they purchase their stock from contractors who hold leases for the picking of the cowdung which falls in large grainmarts, camping grounds, sarais, and other places where cattle halt. Kandewalas sometimes take such leases themselves. The kandewala or the contractor, as the case may be, who holds the lease employs persons, chiefly children and women, to gather the cowdung which falls within the limits of the ground leased, make up the cakes and dry them. Besides this graziers, dairy men, and other persons in villages near cities bring to market large quantities of kandas in baskets, panniers, and carts.

It is obvious that there must be a great demand for fuel in a large city and sufficient fuel cannot be produced within the city limits. Wood is naturally the most convenient kind of fuel but it cannot be depended on alone to supply the demand. Kanda is brought into the market in the cold weather and continues coming until the rains. From Kuár to Asárh there is a great influx of carts bringing grain to gunjes in the city and deposit of cowdung is a considerable factor in the income of gunjes. Besides during that period of the year the weather being dry admits of the carriage of this class of fuel as an article of import. But with the commencement of the rainy season cattle cease to come with carts into the gunjes of the city and the rain is against the import of kanda. The price of kanda then rises and the kandewala (or bhadsár kanda as he is also called) sells at an enormous advance on cost price.

Kandas collected in guujes are sold by the collecting lessees to kandewalas according to size and quality and retailed in the rains by kandewalas at rates such as follow. There are seven classes :—

	Sold by lessee to kandewala.			retailed by kandewala.
1st	600 kanda per rupee,	...	4 kandas per paisa.
2nd	700	do.	...	5	do.
3rd	800	do.	...	7	do.
4th	900	do.	...	8	do.
5th	1,000	do.	...	9	do.
6th	1,100	do.	...	10	do.
7th	1,200	do.	...	12	do.

When the kandewala purchases stock from an importer, he pays but little for a head load or a pannier burden and he buys cart loads by guess at the average size and quality of the kandas, paying 12 as., Re. 1, or even Rs. 1-8 for the cart load. He does not in the case of kandas imported in loads purchase by tale.

It will be seen on comparing the prices given in detail above that the advance of retail price on cost price is enormous, over cent per cent., but this is not all profit. The greater part of the difference in the two prices represents interest in capital sunk in the stock for some months and insurance against risk. As the stock is liable to sudden destruction the risk is great and the interest necessarily high in proportion.

Kandila-saz, *vide* **Gotakinari-farosh.**

Kanghi-saz, Comb-makers.—Combs are made from ebony, hardawa, chicory, buffalo-horn, ivory, and mangowood. Ebony combs are not made in

Lucknow. They are imported. Ivory combs are only made to order from ivory supplied to the maker.

Buffalo-horns of the description used for combs are usually sold at Rs. 25 per hundred horns. If a horn be a seer in weight it will make 20 combs, *viz.*, 10 first class combs, which sell wholesale at Rs. 5 per hundred ; 5 second class combs, which sell wholesale at Rs. 3-8 per 100 ; and 5 third class combs, which sell wholesale at Rs. 2 per 100. A single horn may not be one seer in weight, but a seer of horn will generally yield as above detailed. Retail vendors sell these combs at 1 anna each, first quality ; 9 pies each, second quality ; 6 pies each, third quality. Hardawá, chicory, and mangowood are largely used in manufacture of combs. A block of wood 3 feet long by 1 foot 6 inches deep and 1 foot 6 inches wide will yield 1,500 combs, and such a block will cost from Rs. 2 to Rs. 2-8. A single workman cannot make over 50 combs in a day, and his wages are 4 as. per diem, if he be a hired laborer. Wholesale manufacturers vend to retail dealers these combs at 2½ as. or 3 as. per score, and they sell them at one paisá each.

All classes prefer ebony combs to others, but they are expensive. Of other kinds, women as a rule, use horn combs and men wooden co bs. This is so to such an extent that *zanána kanghis* (which are made with teeth on both sides) are made of horn exclusively, and *mardána kanghis* (made with teeth on one side only) are made of wood.

Karahiwala.—This title distinguishes a person who keeps a stock of iron *karáhís* to let out in the sugar-cane harvest for the cooking of *ras*. There are a few *karáhiwálas* in Lucknow, but they are more frequently met with in large villages. *Kalwárs* are those who most generally keep *karáhís* for this purpose and they let them out at a fixed charge per *karáhí* for the *fasl*. The charge ranges generally from Rs. 8 to Rs. 10 per *karáhí* for one *fasl*.

Kasbhara.—This is the vendor of ornaments made by *dhaliyas* and *bhariyas* from an amalgam of copper and zinc. *Kasbharas* do not manufacture. The articles they sell, and cost price and retail price, are :—-

	Manufacturer's price.	*Kasbhara's* price.
Jhanjh	... Rs. 9 0 per score.	Rs. 10 8 per score.
Pazeb	... „ 8 0 do.	„ 10 0 do.
Kharas	... „ 1 0 per seer nawab.i	„ 1 0 per seer lambari.
Gujaris	... „ 0 10 per seer.	„ 0 12 per seer.
Anwat } Bichiya }	... „ 1 2 do.	„ 1 4 do.
Ghunghrus...	„ 0 12 do.	„ 1 0 do.
Channis	... „ 1 2 do.	„ 1 4 do.
Palámi	... „ 1 8 do.	„ 1 10 do.
Majira	... „ 0 2 per pair.	„ 0 2¼ per pair.

When these articles are sold to a person who gives old goods of some class to the vendor as part of the price, the allowance made for old goods is 4 as. per seer of metal.

Of these, *dhaliyas* make only *karas* and *channis*. They cast in stone moulds. *Bhariyas*, who are a class of *sunars*, make the other ornaments named above, and they cast in clay moulds.

Kaserah *vide* Zaruf birinji o missi-farosh.
Kasgar *vide* Kumhar.
Kashiddar *vide* Abkar.
Kataiyā *vide* Almas-tarash.
Kathigar.—This is the maker of scabbards for swords. Since the

British have disarmed Oudh this trader's occupation is gone. He is now purely a hand to mouth laborer who for the paltry sum of 4 as. makes a scabbard, and is for that money expected to supply leather and wood, and subsist on the balance.

Khaiyat *vide* Darzi.
Kharadi.—The turner, works either as a day-labourer or as a shop-

keeper. In the former case he receives 3 as. per diem for rough work, such as turning boxes of wheels and legs of articles of furniture, and 6 as. for the finest work. In the latter case, *viz.*—when he is a shop-keeper, he works generally for native custom only, and his chief employment is making colored legs for charpoys. The best of these are made of *shisham*. It costs Rs. 3 to buy as much wood as will suffice for 8 sets. These sell at Re. 1 per set. One seer of coloring , which comes to about Rs. 3, will suffice for 8 pairs. It will thus be seen that the turner has only Rs. 2 left on 8 sets out of which to support himself and the laborer who pulls the *tasma* which moves his lathe.

Khatik, *vide* Mewa-farosh.
Khemadoz.—There are but few tent-makers in Lucknow and their

business has rapidly declined since the Muir and Elgin Mills were established at Cawnpore. There are, however, a few tent-makers who contract for the supply of tents, and a sample case will give a key to their profits such as they are. A raoti, let us suppose, is contracted for at Rs. 200. The cost of construction is :—

Coarse cloth (*gazi*) 25 webs,	...	...	...	25	0	0
Dusuti for interlining, 28 webs,		...	...	35	0	0
Khárwa, 22 webs,	...	...	...	33	0	0
			Carried over,	93	0	0

			Brought forword	93	0	0
Stamping and colouring gazi for inside of tent			...	6	8	0
Thread	...	...	...	...	...	2	12	0
Newar, 3 seers best quality, for staging		...	...	3	0	0
Newar, 9 seers inferior do, for eyelets		...	...	6	12	0
Ropes	...	...	...	...	...	11	0	0
Leather for binding	...	...	...	...	5	0	0
Wages of labourers (darzis)		...	...	...	32	0	0
Do. (mochis)	...	...	...	...	4	0	0
Iron hooks and spikes		...	...	...	2	10	0
Bamboo	...	...	...	...	...	2	0	0
Fringes over kanáats	...	...	...	...	0	14	0
Poles (prepared by kharádis)		...	...	...	12	8	0
Salita for bags	...	...	...	...	3	12	0
			Total Rs.	185	12	0

The profit is 14 Rs. 4 as. on an outlay of 185-120 when a master tent-maker employs other to work under him. It is of course higher where the khemadozes work in partnership. In this case, wages being added as profits, the total is 46 Rs. 4 as.

Khogirhoz.—saddle-maker. Khogír is the ancient packsaddle in use all over the East. It consists of a square pad called chár jáma and two takiyas (pillows) one before and one behind. The stuffing of the *chár jáma* and *takiyas* is felt (namdah) and the covering is usually the coarse red cotton cloth called *khárwa*. The khogirdoz generally makes felt for his own use. It is made of goat's hair, cleaned, carded by a behna, steeped in water, finally spread in layers on some broad surface (stone or wood). As each layer is spread it is damped with soap-water and an extract of linseed. The layers are pressed together while damp. They adhere. When the felt dries it becomes light but thick and springy.

Goats hair is sold 10 seers the rupee and when cleaned $8\frac{1}{2}$ seers remain, and this gives 9 seers felt. In two days the 10 seers of goats wool will be turned into 9 seers felt. The expenditure of soap and linseed is 3 as. This felt is sold at 4 seers the rupee. The use of the eastern packsaddle is dying out and English saddles are quite supplanting it. The result is that a Khogírdoz is a poor hand-to-mouth trader.

Khushbusaz *vide* **Gandhi.**

Khwanchafarosh, *vide* **Halwai,**

Kimukhtsaz *vide* **Chirmfarosh,**

Kirana *vide* **Pansori.**

Kirayah khwah-i-asas ul bait.—This is a large class of persons in great cities who can not be very satisfactorily taxed under the License Tax Act. They let out for hire daris, qálíns, shatranjis, jazims, palki covers, kahars' and barbers' clothing, tents, panj shakhas, shamadans, jhárs, kanwals, fánús, takhts, jhandis, masnad-takiyas, chándnis, doshalas, rumáls, cooking and drinking vessels, pankahs, chairs, tables, and every requisite for public meetings, processions, and entertainments, both furniture and clothing. These are chiefly supplied for baráts and jalsas and a native in his vain love for show will spare no expense to procure on hire a vast array of appointments to add to the lustre of a festive gathering. There are in Lucknow several persons who make a large income by letting out furniture and clothing and decorations for marriage feasts and dances. They can only be taxed however in the third class. The usual charges as hire are :—

Daris, 6 as. per 100 square yards per diem.

Qalins, 6 as. to Rs. 2 per qálín per diem according to the quality of the article.

Shatranjis, same as daris.

Jazims and chandnis, same as daris.

Palki covers, 2 as. per cover per diem.

Kahars' and náís' clothing, 8 as. per diem for each palki, four kahars and one nái going to each palki.

Tents, 4 as. to Rs. 2 per diem according to style of tent.

Jhárs, one anna per batti without lights and 2 as. per batti lights included.

Kanwals, fanús, and shamadáns, same as jhárs.

Glasses, i. e. tél páni in tumbler like glass, Rs. 3 to Rs. 5 per 100 glasses per night including lighting.

Panj shakhas (a kind of torch) Rs. 5 per hundred per night, lighting and bearing included.

Takhts, 2 as. each per diem.

Jhandis, Rs. 5 per hundred per diem, including bearers.

Chobs, ásás, 2 as. per chob (plated), 4 as. per chob, (silver) per diem including bearer.

Khwán ma khwán-posh, Rs. 2 to Rs. 5 per hundred per diem.

Masnad-takiyas, 10 as. to Rs. 4 per diem according to the quality supplied.

Doshálas and rumáls, from 4 as. to any amount per diem on each article according to quality.

Khilat poshak (for bridegroom) Re. 1-40 to Rs. 10 per suit per diem.

Zanána jora (for mussalman women and dancing women,) Re. 1 to Rs. 10 per diem.

Zewar, Rs. 2 per Rs. 100 worth silver, and Rs. 4 per Rs. 100 worth gold ornaments.

Cooking utensils, 1 a. to 4 as. per vessel per diem according to size of vessel.

Beds and chairs with silvered legs Re. 1 to Rs. 5 per bed, and ¼ as. to Re. 1-4 per chair.

Changer-dáns, itar-dáns, gulabpashes, Re. 1-4 per set per diem.

Aráish, to any amount according to style supplied.

The foregoing is a complete and carefully prepared list of the articles usually hired out among natives and the rates given are those prevailing in Lucknow.

Kirkinsaz, *vide* **Chirmfarosh**.

Kishtiwala, *vide* **Mallah**.

Kitab-farosh, *vide* **Chhape-khana**.

Koela-farosh.—Charcoal burners buy tamarind, dhak, mahua, bábúl, sákhu, and mango trees, cut them and burn them where they fall and transport the charcoal for sale. They buy the trees standing from the zamindar and tender payment *ba-hisáb kut*, by guess or calculation of probable outturn.

The proportion of charcoal which remains when wood is burnt varies according to the firmness and closeness of the timber. The average is given :—

33	maunds	tamarind charcoal to 100 maunds wood.			
25	,,	dhák,	do.	do.	do.
25	,,	mahua,	do.	do.	do.
25	,,	bábúl,	do.	do.	do.
37½	,,	sakhu,	do.	do.	do.
25	,,	mango,	do.	do.	do.

Tamarind, mahua, and bábúl are most in demand by workers in metalsd. Sákhu is in greatest demand by iron-founders, mango among qalaigars and dhobis : dhak for huqqas and fire places.

As a sample of the business of a charcoal burner, I give the following taken from the lips of an extensive charcoal burner, retaining his quaint metaphor :—' I burn dhák charcoal in the jungles of the Rája of Bilehra ' at Bhatiamau. I cut down the dhák trees and build a '*shewála*' of the wood. I ' then cover it over with wet mud and set fire on the top. At the end of a month ' it is all alight. I then begin to put water on it and to take out charcoal as I find ' it ready. From 500 to 700 maunds of wood go to one ' *shewála*' and 25 p. c. of ' the weight comes out charcoal. My expense is about Rs. 40 per ' *shewála*' ex-' clusive of the original cost of the wood. The jungal where I burn charcoal ' is 16 kos from Lucknow and there is no road properly so called leading to it. ' I pay Rs. 25 carriage per 100 maunds to Lucknow and carriage is by 4 bul-' lock carts. A four bullock cart carries 25 maunds. The carriage is very expen-' sive, for gáriwáns object to carry charcoal at ordinary rates because the gárís ' and their clothes become soiled. The cost of carriage varies according to dis-' tance and condition of road ; I deal by the pakka maund until I get to Luck-' now and I then sell by panseris. I pay octroi duty Re. 1 per 4 bullock cart and ' I pay 5 as. per gári to a wazankash ; This trader's account is therefore :—

18

700 maunds wood,	...	14	0	0	Sells at Lucknow the 175		
Cost of cutting & burning,		40	0	0	nawábi mounds (*i. e.* 1400		
Carriage to Lucknow of					panseris) at 10 panseris		
the out turn 175 pakka					per rupee,	...	140 0 0
maunds charcoal,	...	43	12	0			
Octroi duty,	...	7	0	0			
Tauláí,	...	2	3	0			
Total Rs.	...	106	15	0	Total Rs.		140 0 0

This profit is therefore Rs. 33-1 or something over 30 p. c. This is not an extraordinary profit considering the risks attaching to the business.

The city wholesale dealer buys from a trader like the foregoing and stores. He pays for carriage to his coal yard, carriers who charge from Re. 1-4 to Re. 2-8 per 100 maunds according to distance. He there sells at ' lambari taul'. Take the 175 maunds nawábi which have been calculated before. The city wholesale dealer has purchased 175 nawábi maunds for Rs. 140. He has paid, say, the dearest charges, 2-8 per 100 maunds, for carriage to his coal yards, *i. e.*, 4 Rs. 6 as. Total cost 144 Rs. 6 as. He sells the lot by the English seer at 10 panseris for 161 Rs. His profit is 16 Rs. 10 as. Suppose, however, that he does not sell at once but keeps his stock till the rain falls and charcoal is no longer imported, he then raises the price to 9 panseris and this gives Rs. 34-8-2 profit. Towards the end of the rains the *nirakh* falls to 8 and 7 seers. There can be no doubt that a charcoal dealer who buys from importing burners and stores to sell at high prices makes enormous profit.

Kori —There are two classes of koris, the kori proper who weaves gárhas and lahngas only and the juria kori who weave gárha, dhotar, dhoti, etc.

Four lahngas are woven in one web and the amount of thread set apart for a web is 2 seers. The thread is first dyed—and generally the only colours chosen are black and red. The kori employs a rangréz to dye black and pays him 4 as. per seer for dyeing: but he dyes red himself with al, sajji, castor oil and alum, in which case he is at 2 as. 10 pies expense per seer. The thread is next opened on a comical revolving frame called charkhi and then by means of a spinning wheel wound on bobbins (called by koris *chuchi*.) Then the warp is laid and drssed as jolahás dress their warp. After this the warp is applied to the loom and the weaver begins his work.

He receives 3 pies per cubit which he weaves. One addah or web of 4 lahngas can be easily woven in three days. The account will stand:—

Thread 2 seers,	...	...	1	10	0
Dye ½ seer black,	...	...	0	2	0
Dye ½ „ red,	...	...	0	1	5
Starch for dressing,	...	...	0	1	0
		Carried forward	1	14	5

			Brought over	1	14	5
Wages of dressing,	...	...		0	2	0
Fuel for preparing starch,		...		0	0	3
Laying warp in loom,	...	...		0	1	0
Weaving,	...	...		0	5	0
		Total Rs.		2	6	8
Web of 4 lahngas sells for, ...				4	0	0
		Profit Rs.		1	9	4

If the kori's family perform all operations his expense is 1-8-8, and his profit is 2-7-4. The price of Re. 1 per lahnga is, is in either case, the price for which the kori sells his lahngas to shop keepers. The standard length of a lahnga is 5 yards and width one yard.

The juria weaves dhotis in the same way, four to a web, but a dhoti is $1\frac{1}{8}$ yard wide and $4\frac{1}{2}$ yards long. His account is almost as above:—

			Rs.	as.	p.
Thread 2 seers,	...	...	1	10	0
Opening and winding thread,		...	0	1	6
Starch,	...	...	0	0	3
Wages of dressing,	...	...	0	2	0
Fuel,	...	...	0	0	3
Laying warp in loom,	...	...	0	1	0
Weaving,	...	...	0	9	0
		Total Rs.	2	8	0
Four dhotis sold at 14 as. per piece,		...	3	8	0
		Profit Re.	1	0	0

If the juria perform all operations through members of his own household his profit will be 1-13-6.

Kumhar.—The processes of pottery are familiar and need not be here described. It is enough to say that there are three methods of manufacture of earthen vessels, by wheel, by mould, and by hand. It would be uninteresting to detail for all kinds of earthen vessel the cost of production, but I give the result of calculations made with care, arranging the ware according to the process of manufacture:—

Wheel made—In Rs. 14 realized by sale of	Gamlas,	Rs. 5	1	is profit.
,, ,, 4 ,,	Gharas,	,, 1	6	,,
,, ,, 2 as. 4 ,,	Handis,	,, 0	14	,,

Moulded.	In Rs. 12	,,	Ghunghis, Nals and Tiles Rs.	4 4 is profit.
	,, ,, 27	,,	Bricks ,,	8 8 ,,
	,, ,, 37 as. 2	,,	* Kothi cháb,	8 10 ,,
Hand made.	In Rs. 8 as. 6	,,	Milk, Pans, Nands, &c. ,,	3 6 ,,

Kasgar is the name given to the particular class of kumbhar who makes suráhis, cups, plates, madari huqqás, chillams, &c. He makes all his wares on a wheel and his profit is Rs. 2-2 on every Rs. 6-14 of goods which he vends.

There is a growing demand for glazed pottery in Lucknow. The process is as yet rude and a variety of color cannot as yet be imparted to glazed wares.

Kundan Saz—This workman buys the first quality of gold, melts it into the shape of a lead pencil, and then draws it through a jantr, (a piece of iron perforated with holes of various sizes) until he has reduced its thickness to somewhat less than the twenty-fourth part of an inch. He then heats the wire and beats it out on an anvil until it becomes a tape about quarter of an inch wide. This is kundan, and is used by jariyas and others in setting precious stones, &c. The kundansáz prepares a tolah weight in 2 days, and at present prices his profit on a tolah of gold will be as follows :—

Gold (one tolah),	Rs. 20 8 0	11 Mashas 6 rati of Kundan	
Charcoal,	,, 0 1 0	at Rs. 22-8 per tolah, Rs.	22 0 6
Acid, salt, &c.,	,, 0 0 6		
Wages of servants, 2 days,	0 8 0		
Loss in melting, 2 rutis ,,	0 6 10		
Total Rs.	21 8 4	Total Rs.	22 0 6

The profit is 8 as. 2 pies.

There are two kundan factories in Lucknow : one at Taksal, and another at Sabzi Mandi.

Kunjara, *vide* **Mewafarosh.**

Kuppesaz.—Maker of leather jars. The large kuppas in which ghi and oil are carried in the east are familiar to every one who has once passed through an Indian bazaar : but the tiny leather phials (called phuleli) made like kuppas and used to hold scented oils are a much more remarkable product of the skilful hand of the **kuppesáz.** These may be seen hung in lines in the *gandhis'* shop and are often of but one tola capacity.

The kuppesaz buys up the clippings (katran) of undressed hides and skins from hide-exporters, tanners, kimukhtsazes, &c., and from the last named he buys up the *gudar* or *chilan* (*i. e.* scrapings) of half finished skins (*vide* kimukhtsáz). He pays for katran 1-8 per saikra (including dallálí, &c.,) *i. e.*, for the clippings of 100 hides or skins. He buys *gudar* by weight, 1 Re. per 2

---

* The term kothi cháh means 30 rows of bricks of the curved description used in building wells. each row is called a *patti.*

maunds. These clippings and parings he brings home, scrapes them and thins them and steeps them in water till they become soft and pulpy. He prepares hollow mould of unbaked earth of the size and shape required and on this he spreads the pieces of soft leather which adhere and unite so as to present the appearance of one piece. He covers this mould with from 5 to 8 layers. (tah). He then takes a ring of earth and lays it on the neck and works over it the edges of the layers from the body of the mould. He dries the kuppa in the sun : taps it with a stick till the mould breaks and then inverts the kuppa and the earth tumbles out. The ring which has been completely covered with leather is preserved unbroken to give shape and solidity to the mouth of the kuppa.

" Do saikra katran" is the estimate of the leather required for one kuppa to hold 4 maunds. These clippings have to be steeped, cleaned, thinned with a *ránpi* (scraper), and steeped again. Each successive layer has to be dried on the mould before another is applied. In addition to the *katran* 10 seers of *gudar* will be required. This is mixed with *khali*, steeped in water, pounded into pulp and applied to the middle of the kuppa in the girth after the second layer of katran to give firmness and is also applied over joinings. In this class of kuppa the full number of layers (8) is required. One kuppesaz cannot prepare a 4 maund kuppa in less than a month. He will sell it for 7 Rs. He has paid 3 Rs. for *katran*, 2 as. for *gudar*, a paisa for khali, and nothing for his mould. This had been made by his wife or children. His profit is 3-14-9.

Phulelis are made of only one layer and are made up pachmel (unassorted) varying from a tolah to 2 chitaks in capacity. They are sold by the kuppesáz at 1½ as. per score to gandhis. They are very rapidly made and the *katran* of one hide suffice to make a score.

The income of a kuppesaz is, however, largely augmented by the manufacture of *saresh*, a business carried on almost exclusively by his class. (*Vide* Sareshsáz).

L.

Lakrihara, *vide* **Talwala.**

Lakriwala also called **Chob'i marat farosh** is the timber merchant. Two classes of timber are imported. The first is the superior class of wood used for Government buildings and well built houses. This timber costs about Rs. 93-12 per 50 cubic feet at Bahramghat. Carriage to Lucknow and octroi duty bring the cost up to as near as may be Rs. 100. These logs are sawn in Lucknow. About half is sold as first class at Rs. 4 per cubic foot and re-coups the timber merchant the whole cost of import. The remaining half of the timber is his margin for profit and can never bring less than Rs. 12-8, after paying sawyers.

The second class log is much more extensively imported and is purchased at Bahramghat for Re. 1-4 per cubic foot, i. e., Rs. 62-8 for 50 cubic foot. The expenses of carriage and octroi charge are as before. The total cost may therefore be laid at Rs. 68-12 for 50 cubic feet. The importer can sell this timber uncut for Re. 1-8 per cubic foot, i. e., Rs. 75 for 50 cubic feet. His profit is Rs. 6-8 or a shade over Rs. 9 per cent.

There is a very large business done in Lucknow in the sale of timber taken from old buildings. Some of this wood is so well seasoned that it may be reckoned far superior to new timber. Persons who deal in this class of timber generally buy up houses by deed and at auction sales domolish them and sell the bricks, tiles, &c , as well as the timber. The profits of this class of business are subject to no rule, but can be ascertained by referring to the account books which arei nvariably kept by persons carrying on the business.

Luhiya.—Iron Monger.—There are two classes of iron imported into Lucknow :—desi, and wiláyati. Both are brought from Cawnpore where desi is sold wholesale by the nawábi gon (3 maunds nawábi) and wiláyati by the nawábi maund. This maund is 46 seers lambari. Desi iron is brought to Lucknow generally in karánchis and waláyati usually by rail. The octroi duty is Re. 1-8 per 100 rupees worth. Wholesale transactions are all done in Lucknow in nawábi maunds, but retail in lambari seers. The charge for carriage from Cawnpore to Lucknow by karánchi, including octroi and tolls, is covered by 4 as. per maund. The Railway Company charge Rs. 12 per 100 lambari maunds for carriage and the importer is at a further expense for carriage to and from Railway Station, half in Cawnpore and half in Lucknow, but in this case also the cost of carriage is about 4 as. per maund. The following table shows profits on wholesale dealing in iron at Lucknow at present :—

	Price in Cawnpore.	Carriage plus octroi.		Total cost to Importer.			Wholesale value at Lucknow.			Profit.		
DESI.	Rs.											
Gadra tawá, ...	18 per gon.	12	as.	18	12	0	21	0	0	2	4	0
Danda, ...	12 do.	12	„	12	12	0	15	0	0	2	4	0
Chandiya, ...	18 do.	12	„	18	12	0	21	0	0	2	4	0
Chir, ...	15 do.	12	„	15	12	0	18	0	0	2	4	0
Chandiya 2nd class, ...	9-15 do.	12	„	10	11	0	12	0	0	1	5	0
WILAYATI.												
Chaddar, {	6-12 per md.	4	„	7	0	0	7	8	0	0	8	0
{	8-12 do.	4	„	9	0	0	9	12	0	0	12	0
Steel (kamani.) ...	8 do.	4	„	8	4	0	8	12	0	0	12	0
Steel (sang tarash,) ...	9-12 do.	4	„	10	0	0	10	10	0	0	10	0
Pattiya ...	6-6 do.	4	„	6	4	0	7	0	0	0	8	0
Patti, ...	5-4 do.	4	„	5	4	0	5	12	0	0	8	0
Sikh (thin,) ...	6-8 do.	4	„	6	12	0	7	0	0	0	4	0
Sikh (thick,) ...	6-12 do.	4	„	7	0	0	7	4	0	0	4	0

The foregoing shows that the average profit on *desi* iron sold by wholesale is 10 as. and on *wiláyati* 7 as. 9 pies per maund.

The profit on wholesale vend of iron is not so great as on the manufacture of iron goods. The articles made up are chiefly these :—

From *Chaddar* —Karábis, dols, tawas, dolchis, angethis, and the like.
  ,,   *Sikh.*—Chains, hinges, gratings, &c.
  ,,   *Steel.*—Carriage,-springs, cheni, hathauris, khurpás, kudárs, &c.
  ,,   *Pattiya.*—Tires of wheels.
  ,,   *Patti.*—Cages, chimtás, &c.

To give an idea of the profit as manufacture of these goods take the much-in-demand dol, as competition in the manufacture between Lucknow iron masters enters into determination of profit to lower the rate. Further the local manufacturer has to compete with goods imported from Bahraich, where dols of great repute are manufactured. One maund of chaddar costs the importing manufacturer Rs 7. It is 46 seers. From this are cut 13 dols of 3 seers each, and the clippings (7 seers) are either used in working up rivets, &c., or sold at Rs. 2 per maund. 2 seers are used up in the latter way. Two lohárs employed one at 4 as. and one at 2 as., make up two dols in a day. The dols sell at 14 as. each.

One maund iron...	7	0	0	13 dols @14 as. each...	11	6	0
Wages of labor ...	2	7	0	5 seers clippings ...	0	4	0
Total Rs.	9	7	0	Total Rs.	11	10	0

The profit is Re. 2-3 to the manufacturer who is also importer. If the manufacturer buy metal from importers his profit is Re. 1-10. These rates prevail as a minimum on all made up iron goods.

There is one very profitable business in which some lohárs engage. It is the manufacture of horse-shoes. The na'lband who shoes horses does not like an English farrier make up shoes but furnishes them made up and purchased from lohárs. The smith who makes these purchases old iron rails, clippings from forges, etc., and mixes old and new iron. The metal he uses costs thus about Rs. 3 per maund nawábi. He makes from this with the aid of 3 laborers in $2\frac{1}{4}$ days 36 seers of horse-shoes. Ten seers of iron go to waste. The charcoal expended is $22\frac{1}{2}$ seers. The cost of charcoal is 9 as. and the wages of laborers Re. 1-2. The total cost of production is Rs. 5-3. The shoes are of sizes and kinds but sell alike at 4 seers the rupee. The amount thus realized is Rs. 9 and the profit is Rs. 3-13. There are five large horse shoe factories in Lucknow. One is in Husenganj and the others are in Rikabganj.

Luksaz *vide* Chirmfarosh.

M.

Madakwala.—Madak is prepared from the syrup of opium made in the same way as detailed in the article *chanduwálá :* but *insi* is not mixed with it. The syrup is mixed with chopped pán leaf or paper, or babul leaf, cardamum husks or chopped cocoanut fibre. Whatever be the ingredient of admixture *(jásu),* it is chopped and parched before it is added to the syrup : and the proportion observed is 3 tolahs of *jásu* to one tolah of syrup of opium.

Madak is made up in golis of about 6 raties each sold at 1 paisa per *goli :* but the madak made with cardamum husk is dearer, being sold at 2 paisa per goli.

Chandu is smoked in a *nigáli* but madak is smoked in a chillam called *mahru* placed on a huqqah. Smokers purchase by the goli but generally break the goli up into fragments called *chítah* and smoke them in successive chillams.

The madakwálá supplies lights and water to his customers and his other expenses are fees paid to the drug farmer, and costs of opium and of the materials for *jásu,* and rent of shop.

There are fewer madak shops than chandu shops in Lucknow, but the profits of both businesses are about equal.

The effect of madak varies with the temperament of the smoker. Visit the famous madak shop at Pulgáman about 8 P. M., and you will see a small square shop where the madakwálá sits with a few of his more privileged customers. On the opposite side of the street is a long shed where other smokers are gathered. They sit in a long line with their backs to the wall and their knees drawn up to their chests. They are a very medley group in clothing and their faces are a study for the physiognomist. Each has a mudáriya huqqa before him and he draws a long draught from the huqqa inhaling the whole chítah at one breath. The effect varies strangely with the temperament of the smoker. One bursts into loud guffaws of laughter as if the long hidden point of some joke had dawned on him, another sings a sentimental ballad ; a third is moved to valorous gesticulation ; a fourth weeps uncontrollably ; while another poses in a gravely meditative mood : and so on, the whole forming a medley group of harmless irrationality and helpless intoxication.

Mahajan.—This term is used very loosely in describing the employment of traders and it is often uncertain whether it is meant to describe a moneylender or merely a trader in other ways on a large scale. In the latter sense it is frequently used interchangeably with *thokfarosh,* or wholesale merchant, dealing in, it may be, cloth (thokfarosh párcha). In this sense also the word *kothiwal* is frequently used and if it be used, the same dealer would be described as *kothiwál bazzáz* whatever be the business in which a wholesale dealer engages the reader is referred for an account of it to the heading which covers that business elsewhere in this dictionary. I shall in this note deal only with transactions in money and precious metals and the system of account-keeping practised.

Moneylending is either by bond or on *bahi* or in pawnbroking. Where money is lent by bond it is a matter of little difficulty to estimate the profits of loans. A moneylender will not as a rule, however, produce all his bonds, and there is little help for the License Tax officer. In the case of registered documents he always has the Registrar to fall back upon and a reference to him will show the amount of money lent on registered deeds and the interest falling due thereon. But as to non-registered deeds, there is in their case no hold on the moneylender. It is true that many, in fact, I may say, all money lenders who keep account-books enter in their books a note of money lent on bonds and the payment of interest or principal made from time to time, but I have found in practice that *all* such loans and payments are *not* entered, and that the knowledge by moneylenders that they might be called on to produce their account books in evidence in License Tax cases, has led them to omit from their books the entry of loans secured by deed and payments of interest on account of these loans. Once a money lender does produce bonds I take it to be only fair to tabulate those loans and to set down in a column opposite each loan the amount of interest falling due in the year for which the assessment of License Tax is being made. The total of this may fairly be taken as profits on money lent at interest and secured by deed. There are some money lenders who object to produce bonds as the names of their borrowers become known. I have contrived to meet this objection by the following table :—

No.	Name of borrower.	No.	Date of loan.	Amount of loan.	Nature of deed.	Rate of interest.	Amount of interest falling due in year of assessment, 1879.		
1	Ahmadullah, ...	1	1st June 1878,	1,000 0 0		24 per cent. ...	240	0	0
2	Dayál Rai, ...	2	3th July 1878,	500 0 0		18 per cent. ...	90	0	0
3	Sundar Dass, ...	3	26th Feby. 1879,	375 0 0		12 per cent. ...	17	8	0
4	Nawab Ján, ...	4	1st April 1879,	200 0 0		24 per cent. ..	36	0	0
4		4		2075 0 0			483	8	0

The table being filled in, it is torn in two down the dotted line and the left half is handed to the trader with his bonds and the right half is filed with the record. The officer assessing is the only person who need know the names of the debtors and the use of the corresponding numbers secures the Government a record useful for all its purposes and yet sufficient to prevent the trader from fudging in case other deeds be brought to light, the trader being in that case bound to produce the left half of the table for comparison. The table gives the detail of the nature of the deed, registered bond, unregistered

19

bond, mortgage deed, &c. Mortgages of revenue paying land are, of course, when possession is given, not liable to come into the table.

Loans on bahi are kept up as a regularly running account made up and balanced from time to time. This is called *hisáb fahmi* or *lekh* Loans are entered on the right of the page and payments on the left. A *munim* employed to examine accounts can readily tabulate the totals and state the amount of money lent and interest realized. It frequently happens that a money-lender whose business is large, a banker in fact, receives money in deposit. In that case he pays interest on the deposits. To decide a case of this class the two items of interest should be set—the interest received as *jama*, and the interest paid as *nám*—one against the other, and the excess of *jama* over *nám* is net profit.

There are two special classes of money lending by bahi, practised chiefly by Rastogis, *augáhi* and *rozahi*. *Augáhi* is lending of money to be repaid with interest at 20 per cent. in monthly instalments. Thus, if a Rastogi lends on the 1st January 10 rupees, he receives one rupee on the first of each month for twelve months and thereby realizes Rs. 12 rupees, of which Rs. 2 are interest. A Rastogi's *augáhi bahi* is a curiosity. It is ruled like a chessboard but has twelve columns. As each month's instalment is realized it is entered in a square until the twelve squares are filled. He generally keeps also a separate bahi in which the principal is noted when lent. It may, however, be noted in the margin of his check-pattern account. *Rozahi* is money lent to be realized in daily instalments with interest at 25 per cent. Thus, if a rupee be lent, one-half anna (taka roz) will be realized daily. The account of this money is kept in a similar way but the account book will be ruled in lines of 40 squares. A Rastogi keeps his accounts by locality ; that is, he has several *khets* as he calls them ; one, say, is Saadatganj, another Hasanganj, a third Deori Agha Mir, and so on. Debtors are called *asámis* and the amount to be collected is called *lagán*. A separate set of account-books is kept for each *khet*, and a servant (generally a Brahmin on Rs. 3 per mensem) is employed to collect each *khet*. There is a check on *augahi* and *rozahi* lenders in this way. If, as I have found, a Rastogi represents that he has but one set of books and that set of books shows Rs. 383 profits, and he states he has paid Rs. 72 wages of collection, it is at once known that he has two *khets* and has produced the accounts of one only.

Money lending by pawnbroking, if there be direct dealing, is regulated by the following rules :—The pawnbroker gives only 4-5th of the value of the article pawned. Thus, on a pair of gold kharas worth Rs. 100 he will lend Rs. 80. The charge of interest is either 10 as., 12 as., or Re. 1 per mensem per cent. rupees lent, and the rate is determined by the credit of the pawnor. Thus a baniya or other well-to-do-man can pawn his wife's ornaments at 10 as., but a person with bad credit will be charged the Re. 1 rate. If the article pawned be of small value and the loan trivial, the rate is not less than *paisa rupiya mahwari*, or 18¾ per cent. per annum. Petty *sarráfs* engage in this last class of pawnbroking and when they get together a large lot of miscellaneous articles they go to a pawnbroker who does business on a large scale and re-pledge with him, paying the light rate of interest 10 as. per cent. rupees per mensem, and obtaining cash to carry on further business. A sarraf who does this is said to do pawnbroking *dusre ke pet men.*

A pawnbroker carries his business on in either of two ways or in both. The first is to simply number goods and enter them in a bahi under the pawnor's name and keep the account in the bahi as if it were an ordinary bahi loan. The other is by *chittas, i. e.,* to tie a slip of paper with a note of the loan to the goods pawned and to keep up the account on the slip. In the former case account books are easily examined for license tax purposes, but in the latter it is impossible to make up an account unless the pawnbroker brings his goods and chittas into Court. It is, however, palpable that a pawnbroker who does his business with *chittas* is necessarily an independent pawnbroker working with his own capital and not repawning.

All traders, moneylenders and others, keep *chittas, i. e.,* slips on which items are noted first and then copied into the *Roznámcha* or day-book. Then all the items are entered in a *Lekha* or ledger in which accounts are kept under the names of customers. As a key to this the trader keeps an alphabetical index—*fihrist radifwár*—of his customers' names. Every trader pretending to keep account books by rule of business should produce all these.

There are few traders who engage in one business only and where a trader is engaged in more trades than one, though he may have but one *roznámcha,* he will have his *lekha bahi* divided into as many *khátas* as he has trades. The following are the khátas usually found :—

Biyáj	Khátá,	(Interest received and paid.)
Batte	,,	(*Vide* **bazzaz.**)
Hundiáwan	,,	(Bills of Exchange.)
Nafa	,,	
Sona	,,	
Chandi,	,,	
Jawáhirat	,,	(*Vide* **jauhari** for sub-divisions.)
Girwi, giron	,,	
Currency Note	,,	
Govt. Prom. Note	,,	
Mál	,,	
Kapra	,,	
Pashmina	,,	
Kiráya	,,	(Of houses let.)
Kasarát	,,	(*Vide* **bazzaz.**)
Makán	,,	(Houses bought for demolition and sale of
Kharch	,,	materials.)
Gáyál	,,	

All these but the last two contain both *jama* and *nám* and the excess of the former over the latter is profit. Kharch kháta is purely *nám, i. e.,* payment, and covers all payments in the way of shop expenses, rent of shop, salary of *gomashtas*, &c. and it is to be observed, that some traders very slyly slip into this payments of money made for their private domestic expenses. These items should not be set off against profit.

Gayál khúta is the head under which bad debts are written off. It is an absorbing whirlpool and is used to deceive the License Tax officer. I have found a highly esteemed banker lump into this khâta for the year under assessment all his bad debts for the past seventeen years. The only thing to be done in a case like this is to cut out all items which had become barred at law at any date previous to the year for which the assessment is being made.

One class of money lending must not pass without notice, the lending to wasiqadars and political pensioners. Government has exempted these annuities from attachment in execution of decree. A wasiqadár or political pensioner needs money. He goes to a special class of money lender who deals with such persons. He obtains a loan and gives a bond. He also executes a power of attorney in favor of the money lender empowering him to draw his monthly instalment of wasiqa or pension, and gives him his seal with which to sign the receipt for the money. The money lender receives not less than Re. 1 per mensem for drawing the money. He gets all the wasiqadar's or pensioner's pension into his hands. Then begins a fight. The money lender proceeds to plunder and the pensioner goes deeper and deeper into debt till the moneylender will do no more for him. The moneylender has not lost but he still claims something. The moneylender sues the debtors. The debtor cancels the power of attorney, gets his old seal back or makes a new one turns over to another moneylender, and sits at home with shut doors while the former creditor besets his house with process servers, flaunting a decree like a red rag before the self-immured wasiqadár, who is possibly all the while peeping over a wall at the frustrated Jew below, and laughing at his vain efforts to obtain an execution. The present state of things between moneylenders and wasiqadárs and pensioners in Lucknow is a matter for grave consideration on the part of Government. The kindness, well-meant of course, which exempts wasiqas and pensions from attachment in execution of decree, has driven the recipients of these stipends into improvidence and a probably-now-irretrievable distress.

Maidafarosh, *vide* **Chakki wala.**

Mali, *vide* **Gandhi.**

Mallah.—Much of the trading of Lucknow with other places is done by boat and there are some boatowners who derive a considerable income from hiring out their boats. There are five kinds or sizes of boats :—

1.—*Kalan.*—120 feet long by 30 feet wide, called also *dasmariya* because the number of cross planks running from edge to edge of the boat is ten. This boat is so large that it is used generally in the rains only and for carriage of charcoal and the like cargoes which are light weights in large space. The tonnage of this boat is said to be as much as 7,000 maunds.

2.—*Addha.*—The tonnage of this is set down at 4,000 maunds in the rains and 3,000 in dry weather. It is used in all seasons : and is most used for carrying wood, bamboos, grain, patáwar, &c.

3.—*Chauthaiya.*—Tonnage 1,200 maunds. This is the size of vessel most in use and carries bhúsa, charcoal, wood, grain, kanda, sentha, patáwar, &c. Season and lowness of rivers do not affect this size of boat. It draws but little water. Hence it is the most profitable boat to the owner.

4.—*Malhni.*—This boat is always 66 feet long and is either chaugazi (four yards wide) or tigazi (three yards wide.) It is used for all carriage without restriction, carrying even prepared lime. Tonnage ranges from 400 to 600 maunds.

5.—*Dungiya.*—This is a small boat carrying 70 or 80 maunds and is used only in carrying lime and the like between one ghát and another in the city.

The charge made for boat hire by the owners is determined by two factors, weight loaded and distance traversed. There are all along the Gumti ghâts which are at well known distances from Lucknow. The rate charged is so much per 100 maunds to a given ghât. For instance there is Kechghát 25 kos down the river. The charges for coming up stream to Lucknow from that ghât are :—

Wood,	Rs. 10	per 100	maunds.
Charcoal.	,, 12	,,	
Grain,	,, 13	,,	
Bhúsa,	,, 9	,,	

and going down stream from Lucknow to Kechhghát the charges are one half. It is calculated by boatmen that the time required to come up stream is to the time required to go down stream, in the rains as 3 is to 1 ; and in the cold weather as 2 to 1 ; and in the hot weather 3 to 2.

The owner of the boat is of course at some expense in paying boatmen. This is done in either of two ways. The *mánjhi* or helmsman sometimes manages *in toto* for the owner. In this case he gets half receipts and out of this pays the boatmen and secures his own remuneration. Otherwise the boat owner pays the boatmen and the *mánjhi* monthly wages. For instance, the manjhi will receive Rs. 5 or 4 per mensem according to the size of the boat ; and *gunyas* (towers) and *khewats* (paddlers) receive Rs. 3. It is a safe rule to say that half the hire of the boat is clear profit and I am assured that a chauthaiya brings Rs. 500 a year to the owner.

Manihar.—There are two classes of manihárs, (1) *kachéra* (maker of glass churis,) and (2) *lakhéra,* (maker of churis from lákh). Glass churis are manufactured at Firozabad, Agra and other places in the N.-W. A beopari who imports these to Lucknow sends for a dallál and calls a number of manihárs together. These form themselves into a committee or panchayat and buy up the beopari's thok in shares. The usual prices paid are :—

        Plain uncolored glass,   1 Re. per 1000 churis.
        Plain but colored glass,   2 ,,   do.
        Scolloped and colored glass, 3 ,,   do.

These are then made up into sets, and 50 usually go to a set; i. e. 25 for each wrist.

Take a case at random among the manihárs at Amínabad. I find a set of this number made up as follows, selling for 2 as. 6 pies.

        Plain colored glass, ... 9 for each hand.
        Covered with panni (foil,) ... ... 12 do.
        Studded with beads and glass naginas, 4 do.

                      Total. 25 for each hand.

The panni, beads (pot) and naginas are fixed on the glass churis by means of a layer of lakh. Lac of the quality used is purchased @ Re. 1 per seer, and one tolah is required to make up $2\frac{1}{2}$ sets of churis. Panni is bought for 4 taós or sheets the paisa, and one taó suffices for 30 churis. Beads are Rs. 2 the seer, but manihárs buy by the *guchhi* (or string of beads), 5 *guchhis* for 9 pies. One *guchhi* is ample for a set of churis. Naginas are 2 paisa per tolah and a tolah does for 12 churis.

The account for this set is therefore :—

    18 churis @ Rs. 2 per 1000 }
    32 churis @ Re. 1 per 1000 } 0 1 1
    Panni for 24 churis, ... 0 0 0·6
    Lakh, ... 0 0 4·8
    Beads, ... 0 0 1·8
    Naginas, ... 0 0 0·25
    Charcoal @ Re. 1 per 100 sets of churis, ... 0 0 1·92

                    Tota 10 1 10·37

This gives a profit of $6\frac{5}{8}$ pies per set of churis selling for $2\frac{1}{2}$ as.

The lakherá's case I take in the same way. I find lakh churis such as Murao and Kachi women wear selling for 4 as. per set. These are made of kachcha lakh and earth mixed in proportion of 3 to 1. They are coated with chapra and colored. The colors used are shingarf, hartál, and níl.

The cost of making 2 sets is :—

	Rs.	As.	P.
Lakh 6 chittaks, ...	0	4	0
Chapra, ...	0	0	9
Colors, etc., ...	0	0	6
Charcoal (for heating purposes), ...	0	0	4
Total	0	5	7

This gives 2 as. 5 pies profits on two sets.

Mashak saz.—Mashaks are made of *hallali* goat skins, and *murda* skins are absolutely forbidden. The reason is obvious. Twenty skins make a *táo* or batch. They are purchased undressed at from 12 as. to Re. 1-8 each small size; and Rs. 2 to Rs. 2-8 each the largest. These skins are sprinkled with *khári namak* (unrefined salt,) ⅛ a seer to a skin and they lie thus for a day. Then they are thrown into a *nundolá* (earthenware tub) with 20 seers of *chúná* (lime), and the vessel filled with water. Twelve days they lie thus. Then they are taken out and the hair removed with a *khurpi*. They are then steeped in water in a *nandóla* and the water changed each day for three successive days. They are then for four days steeped in water in which is infused 3 seers of wheat-flour-paste. This process is then repeated, but to the paste is added 2½ seers of *khári namak*. This being done the skin is finally tanned in an infusion of babúl bark.—20 seers to the score of skins. They are steeped in this for eight days and again for 4 days in a fresh infusion. They are after this cleaned of all loose nap and again steeped for two successive periods of 3 days each in fresh infusions of babúl-bark. They are then sprinkled with *khári namak* and dried and sewn up. The skin of the hind legs is cut off, but the skin of the fore-feet is retained. The charge for sewing up is 1 anna and the sewing, thread, etc., are 1 anna per *mashak*.

Mashaks are of 4 sizes :—do ghara, tín ghara, chár ghara, and pánch ghara : and the respective prices at present are Re. 1-8, Rs. 2-4, Rs. 3-4, and Rs. 4.

Suppose a case of a score of mashaks, 5 do gharas, 10 tín gharas, 4 chár gharas, and 1 panch ghara-wálá.

				Rs.	As.	P.
Cost of skins,	...	...	...	29	12	0
Khári namak,	...	...	...	1	4	0
Chúna, ...	...	...	...	0	1	6
Babúl-bark,	...	...	...	1	8	0
Sewing and thongs, etc.,	...	...	2	8	0
Wheat-flour paste and cooking,...	...	0	7	0
		Total Rs.	35	8	6

These mashaks will sell at prices noted above for Rs. 48-4. The profit is Rs 12-11-6.

.There are only five mashak-sazes in the vast city of Lucknow and as a mashak does not last over a year it is obvious they must have a most profitable business.

Mewa-farosh.—For the sake of convenience a note may be made under this head of all dealers in vegetables and fruits. The castes who usually deal in country vegetables and fruits are Kunjaras, Kabariyas and Khatiks. These persons buy vegetables daily in the mandis to which they are brought by Muraos, Kachis and others, who are occupied in market gardening. They buy country fruit in the various seasons in the same way. Greengrocers who deal only in this limited way are not cases for taxation. There are, however, other dealers in vegetables and fruits who can fairly be taxed at Rs. 5, or Rs. 10. I allude to those Kunjaras, Bhatiyaras and other castes already named who buy up produce of fields, sugarcane, potatoes, onions, yams, ghoyán and other vegetables by *kút*, store onions, potatoes and other tubers for seed and for sale when the market is dear. These traders are to be found in Huseinabad and Amínabad. They often take speculative leases of the produce of groves and gardens and not unfrequently store tobacco. Local enquiry is the only means of deciding the ability of such a trader to pay a license tax.

A very large business is done in Lucknow in the sale of foreign fruits. The largest dealers in these goods are to be found in Sarai Bich between the Chauk Khass and Naya Sarak. Their business is of two classes (1) They buy fresh fruit, pomegranates, grapes, apples, pistachios, etc., from Kabulís, and (2) dry fruit, dates, almonds, walnuts, chuhára and dry fruits generally from brokers at Saadatganj. They also deal in tea, miscellaneous goods from the hills, wool, horns and yak tails, mishk, zafaran, and they likewise make up jellies, chatnis, pickles, preserves, and sharbat. Some dealers of this class pay Rs. 25 license tax, although owing to the Cabul war the supplies of fruit in that quarter are in great measure cut off. All their purchases are made by the nawabi maund. Their sales by thok are made by the same weight and a profit is secured merely by an advance in price. Sales by retail are all made by the lambari maund and also at an advance price. In the latter case the source of profit is therefore two fold.

The *haqq dallálí* is invariably in sales of all classes of fruit, vegetables and nuts, ' *taka fí rupiya.*' It is a curious fact that sales of country vegetables and fruits imported to mandis take place by auction and the Kunjaras' chaudhari is the auctioneer. He receives an anna per rupee.

Mina-saz.—Enameller.—The business of enamelling is not carried on by sunars only but persons of the mochi caste have of late years begun to practice this art in Lucknow. The substance used (mína) is imported in a prepared state and the mína-sáz merely cuts or engraves letters, figures, pictures, and so forth on gold and silver goods supplied by a sunár and lays the *mína* or enamel in the furrows which he has cut and places the goods in a *bhatta* and the enamel spreads and fixes itself in the required places. When the goods have cooled the *mína-sáz* cleans off the superfluous enamel with a file (sohan) and steeps them in *khatái* (acid) of tamarind or lemon.

The *mína-sáz* receives in the case of jewellery, for enamelling lines at least Re. 1 per tolah weight of gold or silver in the goods sent him, and he receives as much as Rs. 5 per tolah when the enamelling is of some elaborate design of flowers or animals. The mína-sáz receives the gold and silver which he cuts out in engraving the designs he enamels, and in the case of silver goods he also receives the price of the enamel which he has expended, but in the case of gold goods he does not receive the price of the enamel because gold and enamel are approximately of equal weight.

The most expensive enamelling cannot be executed more rapidly than at the rate of a tolah of gold or silver per diem and it may be said that a mína-sáz earns Re. 1 per diem exclusive of the gold and silver cuttings which he takes as a perquisite of his trade, and which more than pay the cost of the *mína* which he expends. For the enamelling of sword hilts and large vessels the rate paid is much lower than for ornaments, being only 5 as. per tolah, and the mína-sáz does not receive the price of the mína expended. The reason alleged is that the patterns worked are large and free and the scope for cutting away in engraving is greater than in the case of ornaments.

The necessary expenses of a mína-sáz are price of wood and pay of a bellows-blower, but these are needed only when the goods are in the bhatta, and that is but a short time as compared with the time spent in engraving. The average expenditure would be about 2 as. per diem and thus the mína-sáz would earn about 14 as. of every rupee paid him as wages, while his cuttings of gold and silver more than recoup his expenditure on mína and tools.

The tool used by the mína-sáz to engrave with is a steel pencil or chisel, *fauládí qalam*, much resembling a barber's nail-knife or *nihanni*.

Mochi, *vide* Juta-farosh.

Muhar-kan.—There are two methods of seal engraving adopted by native artificers. The first is that by lathe. The seal engraver squats before a small lathe placed on a tipahi and applies the substance to be engraved to a tiny wheel like a button (steel tired with copper) which is attached to the tip of a *barmi*. This *barmi* is the axle of the lathe and the lathe is moved by the ordinary contrivance of *tasma* and *kamani*. The stone in the engraver's hand is wetted with a solution of *kurand* (corandum-stone). In this way are engraved words and figures on seals, amulets, etc., of glass, mother of pearl, agate, crystal, and precious stones. When a precious stone is to be engraved, the letters, etc., are first traced on it with a diamond pencil of steel.

The other method of seal engraving is by a steel pencil (fauladi qalam) worked with the hand.

In neither case is a muhar-kan a subject for taxation.

Mulammasaz or Mulamchi.—The latter is a corrupt and vulgar term, a bazar word, used ignorantly for the former.

The Mulammasáz is a gold and silver plater. *Mulamma* either is *thanda* or *garm*. The former is electro-plating and is not much resorted to by native traders. *Garm mulamma* is, however, very common and most sunars practise the art, both with gold and silver. The process with gold is this. The article to be plated is overlaid with a compound of *pára* (quick-silver) and gold and heated. Gold leaf is then applied *ad libitum* and pressed with a cotton pad. The process with silver differs. The surface of the vessel to be plated is roughened with a steel chisel (*fauládi nihanni*) and covered with silver leaf. The vessel is then heated and the leaf rubbed in. The plater (mulam-masáz) is purely a day labourer receiving as a rule six annas per diem and works with materials supplied to him by sunars. There is no master-plater in Lucknow.

Murghi-andewala.—There are few persons in Lucknow who keep poultry-yards for breeding purposes to supply the market. There are, however, a few persons in Chiriya Bazar Nakhk'has, and one or two in Aminabad, who buy fowl in villages, fatten them in the city and sell them, and also breed fowl, ducks, pigeons, quails, etc. The market is, however, chiefly supplied by persons who go out from Lucknow and import poultry and eggs from. Kursi, Mulliabad, Kakori, and Zaidpur, in the Lucknow District, and from Sandila, Bahraich and Bareilly. They purchase as cheap as 12 fowls of sizes per rupee, and these they distribute into three lots and they sell (1) 4 fowls per rupee, (2) 6 per rupee, (3) 8 per rupee. In a large lot a few fowls will be found which are sold at 7 or 8 as. each.

Those who bring in fowls to the city also bring eggs from the same places. They are said to purchase hen-eggs as cheap as a rupee per hundred, and they certainly sell as dear as $3\frac{1}{2}$ as. per dozen. But the chief source of supply of eggs is in the city itself. There are a great number of poor Muhammadans who keep laying-hens and sell the eggs. These are the people who chiefly supply the market with pigeons. There is no necessity for calculating the rate of profit enjoyed by traders of this class, for it is only in a very exceptional case that a License Tax would be found justifiable.

Murassakar.—This workman is employed to set precious stones. He is called in Hindi *jariya* and *pachchiwála*. There is some difference in the terms. *Jaraó* is the setting of precious stones with *kundan*. *Pachchi* is setting by turning over a portion of the ornament to hold the stone. The latter method of setting is little resorted to in the East. The former is the traditional oriental method of setting. It is performed thus. A goldsmith or *jauhari* hands to the murassakár a made up gold or silver ornament and the precious stones to be set. The setter places lac in the place which is to receive the stone and over it *dánk* (silver foil) which is colored to match the stone. The stone is then placed in its bed and the crevice round it is filled in with *kundan* (gold rolled out much like a piece of tape) and this is pressed home with a steel tool called *salai*, much resembling a barber's *nihanni* or nail-parer. The murassakár is paid by agreement on an estimate formed of the amount and class of work involved. If however, the work involve the expenditure of a tolah of *kundan* the murassakár will receive Rs. 2-8 wages. Such a case would be the setting of an armlet called *nauratan gir*. This is an ornament with the nine conventional precious stones set in a square centre piece, with two side pieces or wings set with pearls and diamonds. This will be completed in about 3 days ; so that, if a murassakár has constant employment, his wages may be taken at, say, 13 annas per diem or as he supplies the *dánk*, say 12 as. per diem. In all cases his employer supplies the *kundan*.

The murassakár or jariya is seldom honest. He cuts away and scrapes out precious metal from the insides of ornaments, and appropriates part of the *kundan* given him for setting. As he uses surmai lác, which is heavy, and not chapra, it is not possible to detect fraud by weight. Trade custom rules that, if the employer of a murassakár open the ornament to try the weight, the murassakár is to be held a fair dealer if only $10\frac{1}{2}$ mashas in 12 of *kundan* delivered to him are found to have been used in the setting. If a less proportion be found the murassakár is held to have cheated. In the former case the employer must pay the employé for resetting and in the latter the employé must bear the expense.

N.

Naichaband.—This is the maker of stems or tubes (naiche) for huqqas. The cheapest of these are those which will be found referred to in connection with the Madariya and Azim-ullah-khani huqqa in the article **huqqewala.** The profits on these is trivial and no account of them need be taken. There are, however, naichas made somewhat similar to them, that is, without a *qulfi* or metal joint and which sell at 3 paisa each. These are made of narkul which poor naichebands who cannot lay in a large stock, buy at 3 stalks the paisa. These suffice for two naichas. Old cloth purchased from a gudar farosh is tied with thread round the narkul and four light brass rings (challas) or bands of wire are used to secure the ends of the narkul. A piece of *panni* is used for ornamentation. One damri is the amount which the naicheband calculates the *panni* of each naicha to cost him and the challas one damri. The old cloth and thread cost not more than one paisa. Thus the naicheband makes about a paisa on each naicha of this kind.

Another naicha is made of three pieces of narkul. Two of these are tied together at the ends where they are fixed into the huqqa. On the other end of one the chillam is placed and to the other end of the second the third piece of narkul is attached by a qulfi. The naicheband buys qulfis from qulfigars (*vide sub verb.*) A naicha of this class is bound with silk and kalabatun and sells for about 4 as. in which one anna is profit. A naicheband making up this style of goods buys narkul reeds by the hundred and lays in stock. Qulfidár naichas are of two kinds *ulti chin* and *gandedár*. The distinction is in the pattern according to which the silk is bound round the narkul.

The naicheband is also the person who makes the coiled snake—like tubes used in smoking, and these are of two kinds, (1) *satak*, a short coil used with the huqqa called *bidar farshi* and (2) *pechwán*, the long and heavy coil used with a large *gargari*. Both are made in the same way. The workman takes a long, round, thin slip of wood, winds round it spirally a thick cord or fine rope and then over this he coils zinc wire. Outside this he binds the bark of a tree called *Bhoj pattar* and over this again cloth, and he finally secures all with silk, kalabatun, and fine wire. A satak sells for from 8 as. to 5 Rs. and a pechwan for from Rs. 2 to Rs. 10. The cheapest of these, the satak sold for 8 as., is made in one day by one man and his profit, which is purely wages of labour, is 4 as. Each more expensive article requires a proportionately longer time and greater amount of labour for manufacture.

Naginasaz, *vide* Almastarash.

Najjar, *vide* Barhai.

Nalband, Farrier.—The tools used by the farrier are a hammer, *zambúr* (pincers), *nihai* (anvil), *sumtarásh* (hoof-cutter), *poz mál* (curved-knife), and *sohan* (file). These he carries in a tobra (leather nose bag) slung across his shoulders. He buys made up shoes from blacksmiths at Re. 1 per 100 pachmel (unassorted) and he supplies these shoes and is paid @ 4 as. to 8 as. each for shoeing and supplying shoes for small ponies and 12 as. to Re. 1 each for large animals. In all cases six nails are driven through each shoe. It is the right of the farrier by custom to take the old shoes removed from horses of casual customers but the old shoes are the due of the sáis in livery stables.

The farrier buys shoes from the blacksmith pachmel (unassorted) @ Re. 1 per 100, and nails are at 2 as. per 100. He pays the sáis half a pie per pony and one anna per horse '*haqq dallali.*' The nálband has over 2 as. profit in 4 as. and as much as 14 as. in a rupee; but this is really wages of his labour and the custom which one farrier receives is not so great as to afford a profit justifying taxation unless he has a contract on a large scale for shoeing Government cattle or the like.

Nanbai, Baker.—The baker in large cities bakes *khamíri roti, shírmál, kulche, sálan, kabáb, dál roti, nihari*, &c., and exposes them for sale. If he buy átá at 16 seers the rupee, he will sell his roti at 2 as. per seer. One batch of chittak rolls is 40 in number. The cost of flour is $2\frac{1}{2}$ as. There is a lotah of khamir (barm) used and the oven is heated with a fire of straw and karbi refuse. The barm and firing cannot be more than 3 pies. Thus the baker has $2\frac{1}{4}$ as. profit on $2\frac{1}{2}$ seers of bread. This is not, however, his sole business. He takes in flour, &c., sent by private individuals to him and cooks, charging dhélá fí seer for *khamiri roti* ; paisa fí seer for *roghani roti*, (*i. e.*, bread of flour and ghi or milk) and taka fí seer for *parátah* (a kind of roll made flour and ghi). The baker finds that this pays him because once the oven is hot it is not difficult to keep up the heat.

A nanbai seldom makes over 8 as. per diem, but there are in Lucknow two extensive bakers, Mahamdu of Parchawála gali Chauk, and Din Muhammad Kabábí, of Nakhkhas.

Naryal farosh, *vide* Huqqewala.

Naryal saz, *vide* Huqqewala.

Newar-baf.—The weaving of newár is a steady business in Lucknow. Only new thread is used, purchased at one seer 6 chittaks per rupee or Rs. 29-1-6 per maund. The newár-báf gives this to a charkhazan who converts this into thread for Rs. 2 per maund. The wages of the weaver are Rs. 4 per maund. The thread used is rubbed with paste which strengthens the woof, and the method of weaving is similar to that of tát patti. The use of paste increases weight so that a maund of thread gives close on 43 seers of newár, say 42⅔ seers.

The account of one maund country cotton turned into newar will be:—

1 maund country thread,	...	...	29	1	6
Charkhazani, &c.,	...	...	2	0	0
Paste for thread,	...	...	0	1	6
Weaving,	...	...	4	0	0
Total Rs.			35	3	0

The product 42⅔ seers of newar will be sold to shopkeepers at 15 as. per seer, *i. e.*, for Rs. 40. Shopkeeper's sell retail at Re. 1 per seer. The profit of the newár-báf is Rs. 4-13 and the shopkeeper's is Rs. 2-10-8.

The vendors of newár also sell suti rassi—ropes made of cotton thread used for pankhas, tents, &c. These ropes are either khális, wholly of new thread, or gilafi, made partly of old and partly of new thread. The ropes are made by Koris who purchase thread themselves and make ropes with their own hands. They sell to shopkeepers khalis rassi at Rs. 30 per maund and giláfi at Rs. 14 per maund. The shopkeeper sells the former at 14 as. per seer and the latter at 10 as. per seer. There are only some three or four rassi saz in Lucknow.

Nilaksaz, *vide* Chirmfarosh.

Nimak farosh.—There are two kinds of salt imported into Lucknow for consumption in food and each must be noted separately.

Sambhar comes to Lucknow through Cawnpore in sacks, called gon, containing 3 maunds nawábi each. There are three qualities now selling in Cawnpore, at Rs. 12, Rs. 13 and Rs. 14 per maund. The Railway freight is the same for all. Suppose an importer brings 3 gons one of each class to Lucknow his account would be:—

3 Gons, 9 maunds nawabi or 10 mauuds 14 seers lambari,	...	39	0	0
Railway freight,	...	0	9	6
Cart hire in two places,	...	0	6	0
Arath at Cawnpore 3 paisa per gon, ...		0	2	3
Total Rs.		40	1	9

In Lucknow the importer sells by the lambari seer 32 seers of his consignment will be *reg*, bad salt which sells at 16 seers per rupee. The rest sells at an average price of 10 seers the rupee. The total amount realised is Rs. 44-3-3, and the profit is 4-1-6. This is the account of wholesale dealing. The pansari who buys at 10 seers sells at 8 retail.

Lahauri.—This also comes through Cawnpore and is generally imported by retailing pansáris, and not by wholesale dealers.
The account for a maund imported would be:—

1 maund nawábi, *i. e.*, 46 seers lambari,	... ...	9	0	0
Railway freight, &c.,	... ...	0	2	0
Total Rs.		9	2	0

This is sold in Lucknow at 4 seers the rupee and the importer thus makes Rs. 2-6 profit.

Nyariya.—This is the refiner of precious metals, who washes the sweepings of goldsmith's shops and extracts gold and silver filings, and who melts down clippings of gold and silver received from sarrafs, zardozes, and others, and then separates the gold from the silver. The acid used in this process is nitrous acid (aqua fortis) and this is made by the nyáriya for his own use by distillation. The ingredients used are *shora* and *kasis* in equal quantities of 5 seers each. The price of the former is Rs. 8 and of the latter Rs. 6 per maund. Two seers of *tezáb* (aqua fortis) are distilled from the ten seers shora and kasis. This quantity suffices for Rs. 100 of *rawá* (melted mixture of gold and silver filings or clippings). The firewood used for the nyáriyá's still is dry wood sold at $2\frac{1}{2}$ maunds per rupee ; and each tao distilled requires $1\frac{1}{2}$ maunds fire-wood. The cost therefore to the nayariya is 2-5-7 for production of two seers of aqua fortis.

Having his aqua fortis ready, the nyariya takes *rawá* and melts it in a crucible (ghariya) and when it is in a liquid state he pours it from a height into a vessel containing water. This fall into water makes each large drop of liquid metal remain separate. Then all these pieces of metal are put into an *átashi-shishi* or glass phial prepared to resist the action of fire. These phials are like balloons covered with a coating of mud so as to leave only a circular portion of the glass exposed at one side for the use of the operator watching the action of the acid. The narrow neck of the balloon is of course turned up vertically to prevent the contents from spilling and it is not closed up in any way. The mud used to cover the glass is called *pili matti*. Having placed 100 tolahs of rawá drops in the phial the nyáriya pours on it 200 tolahs tezáb. He then places the phial on a charcoal fire of 8 chittaks charcoal to a phial. When the action of the *aqua fortis* and fire has become complete, the liquid is poured off. The gold lies in the bottom of the phial, and the silver passes off with the acid, which is poured into a mud vessel in which there are pieces of copper. The silver adheres to the copper and is scraped off and thrown again with the tezáb into another mud vessel in which there is no copper. The nyáriya then places a cloth strainer over an empty mud vessel and lays over the cloth a sheet of bamboo paper. He pours the silver and tezáb into this strainer and the silver, settles on the paper, the tezáb passing through the cloth into the vessel below. In this process $\frac{1}{2}$ a masha per tolah of silver is lost. The silver is then further cleared by burning in a *chhari* (an earthen ware pan) containing cold charcoal ashes ground to powder. In these ashes a lead is made about the size of the hollow of one's hand. The silver is laid in this hollow with a piece of lead and covered over; charcoal fire is laid above the ashes and blown with a bellows. This clears the silver completely. The only labourers whom the nyáriya employs are two, one on 2 as., and one on 1½ as., per diem. He receives Rs. 7 for every Rs. 100 of rawá he purifies and his whole expenses on that amount are not over Rs. 3.

Old ornaments are also melted down by the nyáriya for sarráfs and sunárs. The only process required is melting in the chhári. For this the nyáriya receives 4 as., per Rs. 100 of metal melted. It is known that nyáriyas employed by sarráfs who buy stolen property receive haqq chaháram as hush money.

The nyáriya makes crucibles for his own use and the substance used is a compound of khariya matti and paper reduced to a soft pulp.

P.

Palledar.—This is, properly speaking, a porter or carrier. He is generally a hanger on at gunjes who gets jobs from purchasers, parchúnwálas and also private individuals, to carry a maund or so of grain from the ganj to a shop or house and he receives one paisa or two paisas per rupee of grain on the value he carries according to distance. The palledár sometimes buys grain at one ganj and sells it at another. Thus it is a favorite speculation of the palledar to buy a maund or two of grain in a ganj north of the Gumti where grain is generally a seer the rupee cheaper than in other ganjes and carry it to a ganj on the south of the river and sell it at the dearer rate. Even on the south of the river retail price is always a seer in the rupee higher than wholesale rates on tfie same side. This gives a key to the profits of a parchunwálá vending grain, who does not store speculatively but buys from day to day in the cheapest market. It is two seers the rupee minus two paisas on a maund of grain. Thus, when wheat is 18 seers the rupee at ganjes north of the Gumti the profit of retail vending of grain by parchunwálás is 3 as. 6 pies in 2 Rs. 4 as. which he realizs by sales.

Many persons who have a large business as chakkiwálas have tried to pass off as palledárs because they employ palla laborers to bring grain to their premises for grinding.

Panfarosh, *vide* Tamboli.

Pannisaz.—Panni is very thin leather covered with a metallic coating, resembling gold (sunahli) or silver (rupahli). The former is not made in Lucknow but comes from Delhi. The latter is extensively made in Lucknow and the process of manufacture is as follows :—

The pannisaz takes a sheep's skin which has been cured and dressed but not colored (khudrang mesha), cuts out six pieces of about 10 by 9 inches each, steeps them in water. He takes a piece, when thoroughly damped pares it with a scraper until it is somewhat thinner than parchment or about the thickness of stout vellum paper. He then coats the surface with gum, dries it in the sun. He then paints the surface over with a mixture of ránga and glue, and when it is dry, the surface is rubbed with a glass much resembling the bottom of a bottle. This glass is called *muhra.* The brush used by the panni sáz is made of goat's hair. Panni is sold for one anna the takhta and one workman will turn out 24 takhtas in one day but the profit of this employment and the demand for the product are not such as to justify taxation.

Another panni is the tin foil used to put at the back of looking-glasses. This is called kachchi panni. It is made in the following way :—

Ránga is melted in an iron ladle called kalchcha It is then poured out on a stone which has long ducts cut in it. These ducts are about $\frac{1}{2}$ yard long, and an inch wide, and half an inch deep. The ránga flows into these ducts, and the workman takes one of these bars and beats it out to about three times the length and double its width. He then covers it with oil and folds it up length wise. He repeats this process three or four times, until it is about 4 inches in width. He then cuts it into small pieces, the length being about double of the width, and operates on each of the pieces separately. The sheets turned out are 10 × 8 inches. One hundred sheets weigh a seer and are beaten out in two days by one man.

There remains pakki panni. This is of two kinds (1) sunahli, and (2) rupahli. The former is extensively manufactured in Mullihabad and is said to be quite equal to the similar European article. Pakki rupahli panni is made in Lucknow as well as in Mullihabad. The metal is a mixture of 78 tolahs ranga and 2 tolahs copper. The process of manufacture is the same as in the last case. It is turned out in sheets as thin as note-paper and each sheet is 6 × 5 inches. 2,000 sheets go to a *gánth* or ream. The difference in thickness of the sheets makes 3 qualities and the *gánth* is accordingly either 1½, 2, or 2½ seers in weight. The precision of the manufacturer is such that the workman melts the weight required for a specific *gánth* and produces from it the 2,000 sheets of the standard size. Though some owners of panni factories were charged with License Tax in 1879, it is doubtful whether any are proper cases for taxation under the Act as revised by VI. 1880.

Pansari —The pansári is the trader who deals in kiránah, a term which includes all spices, drugs and chemicals, and also gur, ghi, oil and salt, either by wholesale or retail. For the rate of profit and method of dealing in gur, ghi, salt and oil, the reader is referred to the separate heads relating to these goods. As to the other stock of the pansári it is very difficult to lay down a rule regarding the profit which he enjoys: but I have found from accounts examined in cases of objection to tax that wholesale dealers who supply retail shops make about 7½ per cent. profit. The profits of the retailer are, however, subject to no rule and retailers do not keep accounts of cash transactions but only of credit sales.

Parchunwala.—This is a vendor of grain, gur, ghi, oil, salt, flour and wood by retail. He supplies all customers who buy daily these necessaries of life, and he usually has a steady daily demand from established customers. A parchunwála who sells all the foregoing goods in a fairly well populated mohulla can without hardship pay at least Rs. 5 tax. Some idea of the profits which such a dealer makes on grain will be learned on referring to the article **Palledar**. If he has chakkis to supply his shop with flour, profit derived from this source will be known on looking up the head **Chakkiwala**. It may safely be presumed that the profit on oil and ghi is not less than 1 anna per rupee. Gur frequently yields much more. When firewood is sold by talwálas at 3 maunds a rupee, the parchunwála retails at 1½ seers per paisa. His business is therefore highly profitable.

Some parchun wálas sell only for cash, others sell on credit as well as for cash and keep account books. In the latter case when a customer gets deeply into the shopkeeper's debt his copper and brass vessels are seized and held in pawn by the shopkeeper who takes them at half their value and sells them remorselessly after a month or so.

Patwa, *vide* **Ilaqeband.**

Pharya, *vide* **Arhatghalla.**

Pirachiya.—This is the dealer in pieces of cloth, remnants, cuttings, etc. If a person purchase velvet, silk, or other expensive material to make clothes he sells the cuttings to a piráchiya. These pieces are re-sold by the piráchiya to topiwálas and zardozes, and if any one need a piece of cloth of a particular pattern to mend a garment he will seek it at a piráchiyá's store. The piráchiya also buys up old clothes in which there is woven or worked gold or silver and also old gota, kinari, etc., and he unravels these, and sells the gold and silver, and the thread and silk of which they are made.

There is no possibility of determining a rate of profit on such a business. The illicit profits of piráchiyas are considerable for they deal in stolen goods.

Pule-patawarwala.—Tin and patáwar used for thatching purposes are imported by boat and are brought very long distances from jungles on the bank of the Gumti.

The dealer goes to the jungle and estimates the outturn of a patch of land. These jungles are generally marked in lots of 100 bigahs. The average outturn of this area is 5,00,000 púlás of tin or 4,00,000 of putáwar. The purchaser employs laborers to cut and tie these by contract and each big handful is tied up as it is cut and is called a púlá. The charges are all clearly fixed, and I take the case of 100 bigahs of each in known jungles as sample cases :—

Tin from Itaunja.

	Rs.	As.	P.
Purchase 100 of bigahs (produce is 5,00,000 púlás,)	50	0	0
Cutting and tying of púlás, ...	50	0	0
Carrying to boat, ...	5	0	0
Hire of boat, ...	25	0	0
Carrying from boat, ...	5	0	0
Octroi duty, ...	10	0	0
Total Rs.	145	0	0

These púlás are assorted when brought to Lucknow and fall into three lots and a refuse heap :—

	Rs.	As.	P.
1,50,000 @ 600 per rupee, ...	250	0	0
1,50,000 @ 800 do. ...	187	8	0
1,50,000 @ 1,000 do ...	150	0	0
50,000 @ 1 anna. per bundle of 250, ...	12	8	0
Total	600	0	0
The profit is Rs.	455	0	0

Patáwar from Naurangabad.

			Rs.	As.	P.
Purchase of 100 bigahs (produce is 4,00,000 púlás,)			50	0	0
Cutting and tying of púlás,	...	...	60	0	0
Carrying to boat,	...	...	12	0	0
Hire of boat, ...	...	...	80	0	0
Carrying from boat,	...	...	12	0	0
Octroi duty,	...	...	20	0	0
	Total Rs.		234	0	0

These púlás are assorted and fall into four lots :—

			Rs.	As.	P.
1,00,000 @ 200 per rupee,	...	...	500	0	0
1,00,000 @ 300 do.	...	...	333	5	4
1,00,000 @ 400 do.	...	...	250	0	0
1,00,000 @ 500 do.	...	...	200	0	0
	Total Rs.		1,283	5	4
	The profit is		1,049	5	4.

There is one difference between the purchase of tin and patáwar The latter yields sentha and this is first pulled and collected apart. It is separately tied up and stored and generally sent into the city before the patáwar is cut. Take the average yield of the plot at Naurangábád, of which the patáwar has already been calculated.

Sentha 2,000 bundles.

			Rs.	As.	P.
Pulling and tying,	...	...	40	0	0
Carrying to boat,	...	...	5	0	0
Boat-hire, ...	...	...	40	0	0
Carrying from boat,	...	...	5	0	0
Octroi duty,	...	...	8	12	0
	Total Rs.		98	12	0
These sell at 10 bundles the rupee,		...	200	0	0
	Profits Rs.		101	4	0

The profit on this business is exceedingly high but the risks are exceptionally great and this sufficiently explains the apparently abnormal rate of profits.

Puzawewala.—The brick manufacturer buys the field from which he digs the earth required for brick making, and the price ranges from Rs. 50 to Rs. 100 per bigah according to the depth of earth suitable for brick making which it is estimated the field would give. He then gives out to Lúnias by contract the moulding of bricks at 12 annas per 1,000 bricks. The Lúnias dig the earth, moisten it, mould the bricks, dry them and heap them at the skirt of the brick field. Then the brickmaker employs coolies or more generally dhoidárs to carry the bricks to the brick field. A contract for laying the bricks in the kiln is given to a Kumhar at Rs. 20 per 100,000 bricks. Rubbish and sweepings are brought to spread in layers over the bricks at certain intervals. The brick maker usually procures these sweepings, etc., from a dhoidár to whom he pays Rs. 4 per 100 sacks carried by mules. The fuel used for firing the kiln is wood and kanda. 400 maunds of fuel will burn a kiln of eight lacs. It is impossible to tell accurately what the profits of a brickmaker are. The outturn of a kiln consists of bricks, khangar, nausádar and rora. Good bricks of the size used in Government buildings are sold by the puzawewala at Rs. 7 per 1,000. Condemned bricks, which have come out imperfectly burnt are called *tharra* and sell at Rs. 4 per 1,000. Rora is of two kinds *pakka*, the well burnt fragment, and *zard*, the imperfectly burnt fragment. The former sells at Rs. 3 per 1,000 cubic feet and the latter at Rs. 3-12. Rákh or ashes of the brick kiln sell at Rs. 4 per 100 maunds and khangar at Rs. 4 per 100 sacks carried by mules. Naushádar sells at Rs. 2-8 per maund.

Q.

Qal'aigar.—Copper vessels used for drinking and cooking purposes are always coated with tin and as they are very widely used, no Muhammadan or Christian house being without them, there is an extensive employment given to tinners (qal'aigars). Vessels of this kind, to be safely free from poisonous accretions, must be tinned at least once a month. Vessels which are tinned for the first time are boiled in phitkari (alum), zangár (verdigris), tútiya (sulphate of copper), and naushádar (salammoniac). The naushádar used in this case is a very impure kind, 4 maunds the rupee, procured at brick kilns. Thereafter and at all subsequent coatings they are merely covered with tin (qal'ai). The old qalai is removed as far as possible by scrubbing the vessel with ground kankar. The ground naushádar (1st quality, 11 as. the seer) is taken up on cotton and by means of it the qalai is rubbed into the vessel. The vessel is heated on a charcoal fire to prepare it for receiving the naushádar and qal'ai, and the fire is blown up to a brisk heat by a *khál*, as qal'aigars call it. This bellows is the same as the lohár's *dhaunkni.* The charges for tinning are 20 as. per score of pots in European use; and 5 as. per score in native use. The charges are double for first time of tinning. The profit of this business is 4½ as. on 5½ as. materials used, but there are so many in the business that no one is well off except perhaps the holder of a contract from the commissariat or for vessels or pots in a large public institution.

Qalinbaf.—Qálín denotes either a small rug used to spread on a charpoy or a floor to lie on, or a larger rug like a pile carpet. The latter are extensively made in Mirzapur of wool, and in Lucknow Central Jail of cotton. The ordinary qálín-báf of Lucknow now weaves only small rugs of cotton. The warp is altogether new thread and the woof is old and new thread mixed together in the proportion of 5 to 3. The pile (called *bod*) is of new thread and is made by tying and knotting pieces of thread on the warp after each successive passage of the shuttle.

The loom and process and implements of weaving are the same as in dari weaving.

Two colors of thread are generally used and dyeing costs Re. 1 per 3 seers. The ordinary charpoy-qálín is 2 seers weight and the cost of production is :—

	Rs.	As.	P.
New thread 10 chittaks,	0	8	0
Old thread 17 do.,	0	6	6
Thread for bod 5 do.,	0	4	0
Dying do.,	0	0	9
Wages, chár nafar at 4 as. per seer,	0	8	0
Wages of charkha-zani,	0	0	9
Total Re.	1	12	0

This qálín is sold by the qálín-báf to shopkeepers for Rs. 2-4 and shopkeepers sell at Rs. 2-8.

This trade has been seriously damaged in Lucknow by the Central Jail Factory.

Qandsiyah-farosh, *vide* Gurwala.

Qassab.—This word has come to denote the beef-butcher as opposed to chikwa the goat and sheep butcher. Generally two or more qassábs join together, keep a hátah in the city and buy cattle from surrounding districts and drive them into the hátah. They graze the cattle by day in the neighbourhood of Aishbagh and keep them in their pen at night. The market is also supplied by Kanjars and others who drive in flocks of cattle for sale, both buffalos and bullocks.

There are two classes of *qassábs*, *kamíladár* and *ghair kamíládár*. The former are slaughtermen who sell wholesale and the latter are retailers of meat who buy from them and sell at shops. The former always count the hide their profit and the latter sell at a fixed charge of 1 anna per seer for meat with bone and

1¼ anna per seer for boneless meat. Whatever be the profit this gives, it is what the retailer of beef makes. Obviously his interest does not lie in buying the very best meat.

Qulfigar.—Qulfi is the joint of the stem of a huqqa and is made *jalébidár*, (curled), *kuhnidár* (having a joint like the elbow), *khamdár* (curved), *derhkhami* (shaped like the letter S), and *sulfedár* (bent at an obtuse angle.) These are made from sheets of copper. The qulfigar cuts a slip of the metal and rolls it into a tube, places it in the fire, and joins it with a solder composed of brass filings and *sohágá*. He then fills the tube with *rángá* and taking a block of wood with a groove of the required shape cut in it, beats the tube with a hammer into the groove. He then places it again in the fire and takes out the *rángá*. There is no finish or polish beyond a slight filing given to the qulfí because it is covered by the naicheband with cloth or tinsel. One seer of copper will suffice for 11 qulfis which sell at 2½ as. per chittak for Rs. 2-8. The cost of making these up is :—

				Rs.	As.	P.
Copper 1 seer,	...	...	...	1	1	0
* Rángá 1 chittak,	...	...	...	0	1	3
Charcoal,	...	...	...	0	1	0
Solder,	...	...	...	0	1	0
		Total Rs.	...	1	4	3

His profit is Re. 1-3-9. A qulfigar can turn out 11 qulfis in a day but the demand for them is not so great as to make it likely that any qulfigar is constantly in employment, or enjoys this daily income when in employment.

R.

Rafugar.—This workman is properly one who repairs rents and holes eaten by insects in Cashmere shawls, Rampore chaddars, pashmina and other textile fabrics made of wool. He does not execute repairs by laying on patches (paiwand) but he darns the hole so skilfully that no trace of a joining remains which can be detected by an unpractised eye. He also embroiders shawls and adds borders (báshiá) to dóshalas and chaddars. As might be expected in the case of a skilled workman, his pay is high, but he is only a day laborer, and so not liable to taxation. Care must, however, be taken to prevent the escape of pashmina and shawl brokers under the misdescription of rafúgars. Many of these brokers employ rafúgars, and sometimes rafúɀars do shawl broking ; and the exact

---

* NOTE.—A seer of rángá is needed for 11 qulfis, but as the rángá is used over and over again the waste in 11 qulfis only is estimated.

extent of the business of either must be known before it can be said whether the case is *primá facie* one for taxation.

The work of the rafúgar is sometimes called *sozan kári*, that is needle work.

Rangia Charsa, *vide* Chirmfarosh.

Rangbhara.—These are the casters of pewter ornaments in stone moulds. They manufacture in this way tariyas, hánslis, pauwas, angúthís, challas, and so on. They have a profit of but a few annas per diem, and the only profit worth speaking of on this class of goods is made by kasbhara shop-keepers and bisatis who add these goods to other stock.

Rangrez.—The Indian dyer reckons six simple or principal colors from which he treats all others as being compounded. These are :—

I.—Blue (nila.) Of this there are various shades (1) nila surmai, (2) nila ábi, (3) nila dudhiya ábi, or ásmáni.

II.—Yellow (zard.) The lighter shade of this color is called basanti.

III.—Red (surkh.) There are four shades of this color (1) gulnár, (2) qirmichi, (3) shuftálu, (4) gulábi.

VI.—Black (siyah). Under this head is placed siyah bhura or dark brown.

V.—Agrai. There are three lighter shades of this (1) badámi, (2) khashkháshi (3) mahua.

VI.—Kháki. There are four other shades of this color, (1) fákhta, (2) shutari, (3) gahra, (4) dudhiya.

All other colors are treated as compounds of the first three and they are as follows:—

I.—Compounds of blue and yellow, (1) máshi, (2) zamurradi, (3) mungiya, (4) ábi, (5) dháni, (6) pistai.

II.—Compounds of blue and red, (1) kokai, (2) kákreza, (kochki,) (3) (unnábi), (4) uda, (5) bainjani, (6) nafarmáni, (7) kásni, (8) kanjai.

III.—Compounds of yellow and red, (1) naranji, (2) sunahra, (3) champai, (4) gendai.

The colors above detailed are applied both to cotton and woollen fabrics, but the method of preparation and mode of dyeing differs much. I shall first treat of the former and then of wool dyeing, giving in all notes the proportions for a seer of cotton yarn or of wool :—

COTTON.

Blue—This color is given by the use of indigo and is prepared thus : An earthen vessel called *mát* is placed in the ground. Into it are thrown 25 gharas of water and 3 seers of lime and stirred 4 times a day for about an hour each time. At the end of 12 or 15 days 2 gharas of *tali nil* (drugs remaining in an old *mát* which has been disused) are thrown into the *mát* and stirred up. After a few days the lime and refuse are taken out of the water and replaced by 1 seer fresh lime and 2 gharas of *tali nil*. After about six days the lime and refuse are taken out of the water. If the water is tinged with red it is ready. If it is uncolored, 2 gharas of *tali nil*, 1 seer lime and $\frac{1}{4}$ seer *shira* are infused in it and the water assumes the required shade in about six days more. The extraneous substances are then removed from the water, and into the *mát* are thrown $\frac{1}{2}$ seer indigo, $\frac{1}{2}$ seer lime, 2 chittaks *shira* and two gharas of *tali nil* taken from another *mát* which is in working. The contents of this *mát* are stirred with a stick some four times a day for about six days; the mouth of the *mát* is then closed air tight. The *mát* is opened after a few days and if there be a reddish black froth on the water and if the water and drugs be yellow the *mát* is in a fit state for use. Then a seer of indigo, a seer of lime and one chittak of *shira* are thrown in and the last process is repeated. When the froth, water, and drugs present the same appearance as described in the last process the color is ready for use. It is a fast color. In preparing this color, if a west wind prevail more *shira* and less lime is infused; if an east wind prevail more lime and less *shira*. Cotton may be dyed in this *mát* for 2 days, but on the third day it is advisable to add to the water 4 chittaks lime and 1 chittak *shira*; if the color grow weak 1 seer *lime* 1 seer indigo and 1 chittak *shira* should be added. No articles should be dyed on the day when anything is added to the *mát*. If the water becomes low, fresh water may be thrown in. It is very much better, however, to have a second *mát* filled with water buried in the ground beside that in which the color is prepared and to throw into it the lime and *tali* which are taken from the latter. The water of this adjacent *mát* is preferable for renewing the supply in the *mát* containing the dye.

There are 2 kinds of indigo in use, *khurja* and *tathiya*. The former costs Rs. 27 and the latter Rs. 20 per panseri. The dearer stuff is the more profitable as it is the more powerful dye of the two. The difference in shade of blue depends on the amount of indigo infused. If one seer be infused and the strength of the color regulated by the addition of water the following is the weight of the cotton which may be dyed in each of the shades.

Níla, 16 to 18 seers.
Surmai, 10 to 11 ,,
Abi, 25 ,,
Asmáni, 30 to 32 ,,

Indigo is sold in Lucknow by nawabi rate. The panseri is therefore $5\frac{3}{4}$ seers lambari.

Yellow.—Yellow color may be obtained from *haldi*, *harsingár*, *tun* seeds and from the flowers of the *tesu* or of the *genda*. If one seer of cotton be dyed, the quantity of these needed to produce a bright yellow color is $\frac{1}{4}$ seer in the case of the first three, and in the case of *tesu* flower 1 seer, and of *genda* flowers $\frac{1}{2}$ seer. The lighter shade called *basanti* may be imparted with half the quantity. *Haldi* and *genda* are ground and steeped in water; *tun* and *harsingár* are boiled; *tesu* flowers are steeped in water and crushed in the hands. In any case the quantity of water must be only just sufficient to cover the quantity of material to be dyed, which in this case is 1 seer of thread. After the dyes have been imparted, it is in all cases necessary to draw the cotton through a solution of alum. Half a chattak suffices for a seer of thread. All these colors are fleeting. A permanent yellow color is obtainable by dyeing first in *haldi* and subsequently in *aqqal bir*. This is a vegetable product brought from Cashmere and is probably the shot-plant (*canna indica*).

Red.—This color is obtained from *kusum, patang, ál* and *manjít*. Colors imported with the first two are fleeting and those imparted with the last two are permanent. An account of each follows :—

(1) *Kusum* is placed in water, trodden and rubbed with the hands. With a seer of this prepared *kusum* the dyer mixes either a chittak *sajji* or 2 chittaks *khar* (ashes obtained by burning stalks of the tobacco plant). These are mixed in water and strained off through a cloth spread on a wooden frame. The first color which comes is yellow and is called *paiwar*. The dye stuff which remains in the cloth is again rubbed with the hands, placed in water, and strained as before. The color then obtained is the best red. The stuff which remains in the cloth will bear two more infusions but each successive color will be weaker than the preceding one. The color called *gulnár* is imparted by steeping cotton first in *haldi* and afterwards in the three several shades of red obtained from *kusum*, beginning with the last. *Kathai* is used with these shades of red to impart brightness to the color. *Qirmichi* is produced in the same way, only that the stage of *haldi* is omitted. *Shaftálu* is imparted in the same way as *qirmichi*, but the colors are reduced to half the strength. *Gulábi* is also produced in the same way but the strength of the dye is again reduced by one half. *Gulábi* is of 3 shades, *gahra gulábi*. (2) *phul gulábi*, and (3) *piází gulábi*.

(2.) *Patang* or *Baqam*—This is sappan wood, and it is only used for the colors *gulnár* and *qirmichi*. Two seers of cotton yarn are dyed with one seer of the wood. It is first cut into very small pieces and boiled in 3 gharas of water until only $\frac{1}{4}$ of the water remains. The wood is taken out and again boiled in the same way. This is repeated a third time. The thread is first steeped in water in which have been infused 2 chittaks *dál hara* and $\frac{1}{2}$ chittak *haldi*. It is then cleaned out in a solution of alum, 4 tolas to the seer of water, and being now ready to receive the dye, it is steeped in the three successive infusions of *patang* already described, beginning with the last.

(3.) *Al.*—Take one seer of cotton yarn, place it in a vessel with 6 chittaks of *sajji* and as much water as will suffice to cover the yarn, and press the yarn so that the *sajji* will mix well with the thread. After 12 hours throw out the *sajji* but keep the water; mix with it 3 chittaks linseed or castor oil; then steep the thread in it; take it out and dry it; then take 4 tolas of camel or sheep's manure, steep the yarn in it, in the same way as it was steeped in the *sajji*; wring it out and dry it; then wash the yarn once a day and dry it daily for ten days. Now take half a chittak of alum and $\frac{1}{2}$ seer *ál*, mix them with as much water as will fully cover the thread

22

and place the thread in this infusion out in the sun for a day ; then wring it out and dry it. Repeat the process and the result will be a luminous red.

(4.) *Manjít*—*Manjít* is little used by dyers ; it is much more used by chhipis. It is ground very fine and 6 chittaks are needed for coloring one seer of yarn. Yarn is first steeped in an infusion of *sakki* (the bark of a tree) for one day and is then dried ; it is then boiled in a mixture of sweet oil and the water from which it was previously taken ; it is then washed and dried. The *manjít* is then made into two equal parts for two infusions and the yarn is dyed in one and dried and then dyed in the second.

Black—To produce a permanent black dye, it is first necessary to give the blue color already described : then boil half a seer of *dál hara* in 2½seers of water until only 1½ seer remain. The thread to be dyed must be steeped in this 4 or 5 times until the liquid is exhausted. Then grind 2 chittaks *kasís* and 1 chittak iron filings; mix them with 1½seer water and steep the thread as before until the solution is exhausted. Wash out the thread and dry. Next take 1 seer *khali*, steep in five seers of water, and wash the thread in this preparation until it is clear of ill odours. For this purpose it is well to add ½ chittak mustard oil to the water.

Siyáh bhura—Is a very deep brown and is produced in the same manner as *siyáh*. The preparatory coloring in blue is omitted.

Agrai.—This color is produced with *katha*. Take 2 chittaks *katha*, grind them and mix in water with 1 chittak lime. When the water assumes a red tinge it is ready for use and imparts a fleeting color. To render this color permanent take 4 chittaks *babul* bark, or 4 chittaks *jáman* bark, cut them in small pieces and boil them in water until one-fourth of the quantity of water is left : steep in this the material which has already received the fleeting color and the result is a permanent dye. To produce *ágrai bádámi*, the quantity of *katha* is ½ chittak to one paisa weight of lime. This color is fleeting and to render it permanent 4 chittaks of *pipal* and 4 chittaks *jáman* bark are used with water in the manner already described. *Agrai khashkháshi* is produced with 1¼ paisa weight of *katha* and 6 mashas lime. This color is fleeting. No method is known of rendering it permanent.

Agrai mahua is produced in the same manner as *agrai* but requires half as much again of each ingredient.

Khaki.—The deep (*gahra kháki*) color is produced with 2 chittaks of *dál hara*, either boiled or ground and steeped in water. After this color in *kasís*. Ordinary *khàki* is produced in the same way but requires only half the quantity of the dye stuff.

Fákhta kháki is produced in like manner, the stuffs being reduced by one-half, and *kháki dudhiyai* similarly, the dyes being reduced again by one-half. To produce the color called *khaki shutari*, dye the stuff first in one-and-half paisa weight *geru* and proceed thereafter as for ordinary *kháki*.

Máshi.—Suppose one seer of thread is to be colored, first dye blue, then color in 6 chittaks haldi, then in *kusum paiwar ;* dry and finish with a solution of 1 chittak alum.

Zamurradi.—Dye first a *níla ábi gahra,* then proceed as in *máshi,* taking however 4 chittaks instead of 6 chittaks *haldi.*

Mungiya.—Color *ábi níla ;* then proceed as in *máshi* using only 3 chittaks *haldi.*

Káhi.—First impart a light *ábi* color, then proceed as in *máshi,* using only 2 chittaks *haldi.*

Dháni.—First color *dudhiya ábi,* the rest as in *káhi.*

Pistai.—First give a light *dudhiya ábi* color, then proceed as in *máshi,* using only 1½ chittaks *haldi.*

The foregoing compound colors are fleeting. The following process will render them permanent:

Take 4 chittaks *aqqal bír,* grind and mix in one ghara of water, add 1½ chittaks alum; place this mixture in the sun for one day; pour off the water and color in it. Another process is this. Take 2 or 3 seers *rusa* leaves, 1½ seer *tesu* flowers, and 8 to 12 chittaks *náspál ;* mix these together; boil them in water; place the decoction in the sun for a week, pour off the water and use it as in the last case.

Kokai.—Dye in *ál* or *manjít,* then in indigo. This color is permanent. Dye in *kusum* or *patang* and then in indigo. This color is fleeting.

Kákreza.—Color as for *kokai* using less indigo.

Unnábi.—Dye a light red and then a light blue.

Uda, bainjani, nafarmíni and kásni are all progessively lighter shades of red and blue imparted as for *unnábi.*

Kanjai.—This color is produced by dying red as for *kásni* and blue as for *baijani.*

Náranji.—Color first in 4 chittaks *haldi,* then in 4 chittaks of the three shades of *kusum* and finally in 4 chittaks *khathai.*

Sunahra.—Dye first in 4 chittaks *haldi,* then 8 chittaks *kusum* of each shade and finally 8 chittaks *khatai.*

Ohampai.—Color in 2 chittaks *haldi,* then 4 chittaks *kusum* and lastly 2 chittaks *khatai.*

Gendai.—First 2 chittaks *haldi,* next 2 chittaks *kusum,* lastly 1 chittak *khatai.* For this color *genda* flowers may be used instead of *haldi.*

WOOL.

Blue.—*Nila sumair*—Boil 4 chittaks alum and 4 chittaks *murabba nil* in water ; dye the wool in this; then draw through cool water in which 2 chittaks *tezáb* have been dissolved; wash well. *Nil*—This color is imparted in the same way as the last but only one half the quantity of *murabba nil* is used. *Níla ábi* is produced similarily, using only 1 chittak *nil. Dudhiya ábi nil,* also called *ferozai,* is produced by using half a chittak *murabba nil,* 2 chittaks alum, 2 chittaks *tezáb.* The process is as before.

Yellow.—This is produced in two ways. Dye first in *desi haldi* 4 chittaks, then in 4 chittaks *aqqal bir* dissolved in water; wash out in 1 chittak alum. The other process is to dye first in *amba haldi*, then in an infusion of the bark of the *riri* mango-tree. *zárd surkhi máil*,—boil the wool for 2 hours in one seer *kamíla* and as much water as will cover the wool, then wash out and dry. (2.) *Basanti*, this color is produced in the same manner as *zard* (yellow) by using half the dye stuffs.

Red.—(1) *Gulnár.*—Take 2 chittaks of *kírmdána*, 10 chittaks *khatai ám*, 2 chittaks *haldi* and 4 chittaks *tezáb*; pound these and mix them together ; put them in water with the wool; boil up; take out; wash and dry. Another process is by using *kachchi lákh* 2 seers, instead of *kirmdána*, and other ingredients unchanged. *Qirmichi.*—The process is the same as in the last case only that *haldi* is totally omitted. *Gulábi.*—Take ½ chittak *kírmdána*; 4 chittaks *tezáb* and 8 chittaks *khathai* ; proceed as for *gulnar*. The three shades of *gulábi* are produced by lessening by degrees the quantities of *kírmdána*.

It is to be noted that where *kachchi lákh* is used as a dye, it is not thrown into the water with the other ingredients but its color is separately extracted thus :—Mix 2 seers dried *kachchi lákh* in water; rub it well with the hands until the water assumes a red color; put this water aside ; pour on other water and repeat the process. This may be repeated until all the coloring property has been extracted from the *lákh*. If this water be used with *khatai*, *haldi* and *tezáb*, *kirmdána* is not needed.

The colors *gulnár* and *qirmichi* are produced by another method in Mirzapur. Steep 2 chittaks *sajji* in water for a whole night. In the morning heat the water on the fire but so that it may not come to boiling point. Wash the wool in this. Next take a ghara of the extracted color of *lakh* prepared as before mentioned. Mix in this 4 chittaks of flour paste. Keep this until it ferments. This requires about a week in hot weather and 2 weeks in cold weather. Steep the wool in this for 3 days, turning it frequently. Then dye in *khathai ám*, *haldi* and *tezáb* boiled up in water, using the same proportions for *gulnár* and *qirmichi* respectively as already stated. This is called *mót ka rang.*

Black.—Only wool which is naturally black is dyed black, and it is never dyed *siyáh bhura*, but only *siyáh gahra.* Boil 8 chittaks *dál hara* in water, cool it and rub in 4 chittaks *kasís* to the *dál hara* with the hands, put in the wool, boil again for 5 or 6 hours, cool, wash out and dry.

Agrai.—To produce *agrai* proper take 1 or 1½ seers *dhák* flowers; steep them in water; put the wool in this water for 2 or 3 hours; take out the wool; mix from 4 to 6 chittaks *khathai* in the same way, boil the wool in this again; and when it has taken the color, wash it out and dry it. *Agrai bádámi.*—Same as in the last case, using half the dye stuffs. *Agrai khashkháshi*—as before, reducing again by one-half. *Agrai mahua.*—First proceed as for *agrai*, using one and a half seers *dhák* flowers, half a seer *katha*, but add to the infusion of *katha* a decoction of half a seer *babul* bark.

Kháki.—All *kháki* colors are imparted to wools in the same way as to cotton.

Máshi.—First dye with 6 chittaks *haldi*, then boil in water with 3 chittaks *murabba níl* and 4 chittaks alum. The *haldi* used in the first stage is steeped in the extract of *aqqal bír* (half seer) prepared as described before.

Zamurradi.—This color is imparted in the same way as *máshi*, but the proportions of the stuffs used are : *haldi* 4 chittak, *murabba níl* 2 chittaks, alum 4 chittaks, *aqqal bír* 6 chittaks.

Mungiya.—As before, using only 1½ chittaks of *murabba níl.*

Kahi.—As before, using 1 chittak of ditto.

Dháni.—As before, using ½ ,, ditto.

Pistai.—Use half the ingredients prescribed for *dháni.*

Kokai.—Color *qirmichi* with *lákh* or *kirmdána* and then in *níl mát* as used for cotton.

Kákreza, unnábi, uda, bainjani, nafarmáni, are colored in the same way, but each receives a less degree of blue than the one preceding.

Kásni and Kanjai.—Color *gulábi* and then impart a very faint shade of blue, lighter than in the preceding cases.

Sunahra.—Use *kirmdána* 1 chittak, *haldi* 4 chittaks, *tezáb* 4 chittaks, and *khatai khali* 1 chittak, in the same way as used for coloring wool *gulnár.*

Náranji.—As before, using only ¾ chittak *kirmdána.*

Champai.—Proceed as before, using *kirmdána* 1½ tolah, *haldi* 3 chittaks, *tezáb* 2 chittaks, *khatai khli* 4 to 6 chittaks.

Gendai.—As in *champai*, using only 1 tolah *kirmdána.*

The foregoing directions for dyeing will be interesting to all persons who admire the many brilliant colors which are every day to be seen in the clothing of the people in the East, and who may wish to know how these colors are produced. It is, however, simply impossible to give any certain data by which to estimate the profits of a *rangrez.* There are some famous dyers in Lucknow in the mohullas round the Chauk who were undoubted cases for at least Rs. 5 License Tax, but there are no dyers of whom it can be said with certainty that they should come into II. class, 3rd grade for taxation.

Rangsaz.—The only occupation for painters now remaining in Lucknow is on *pálkí gárís.* Palankins do not afford the same employment which they did in days when there was no railway and when street arrangements were so bad as to render *palkí* travelling preferable to *gárís.*

The painting of a *gárí* involves the removal of the old paint, the softening of the surface of the timber with *sajjí*, sand-papering, *astar* (color-washing), a second sand-papering, a first coat, a second coat, a rubbing for smoothness‘ and then painting proper. After this comes picking out with lines and so forth. This is the orthodox method of painting *á l'orientale.*

One carriage can be painted in 25 days, or two in one month, as a carriage lies to dry for a day now and then in the course of the many operations it undergoes. Two pálkí gárís are painted for Rs. 44 and the master painter has to meet the following charges per gárí :—

Workmen, *chális nafar fi gárí* at 3 as. *fi nafar*,				7	8	0
Color washing,	...	...	...	...	0	15	9
First and second coat,	...	...	...	1	7	0
Painting proper,	...	...	...	...	2	7	0
Painter who paints the lines,		...	...	1	0	0
Varnisher, ...	...	...	...	...	1	0	0
Miscellaneous, sand paper, &c.	...	...	0	10	3
			Total Rs.	15	0	0

This gives Rs. 14 profit on two garís. This is after all but little when it is remembered that the master painter himself works and the burden of superintendence in a matter of such delicacy as carriage painting is not light.

Rassibat, *vide* Banfarosh.

Reshamfarosh.—Two kinds of silk are imported in to Lucknow *sangal* and *bának*.

Sangal comes from Balkh and Bukhára through Amritsar and is of two colors, white (*suféd*) and yellow (*zard*). The difference of color in no way affects price. This silk comes in *bandis* or skeins varying from 3 páu to a seer in weight, and the present price for the undressed article is 20 Rs. per nawábi seer of 92 English rupees: and it sells by the English seer of 80 English rupees.

The silk is put on a large framework reel called *charkhi*, attached to the ceiling, and a man sits on the ground below and winds the silk off the large *charkhi* to another framework reel called *liauti*, and then from it to other frame work reels, one after another, called *khali*, held in his hand on a staff, made either of shisham or of bamboo. If made of the former it is called *distah* and if of the latter *nigáh*. He winds the silk off in five threads, the first is called *agári* and the next *dúsra*, *tisra*, and *chautha* down to the fifth, called *kachar*, which is a very rough and hard thread. The proportion of each in a seer of *kachcha sangal* is :—

Agari, 1 chittak nawábi, sold @ Rs. 26 per seer English,					1	13	10
Dusra, 4¼ chittaks,	do ,	...	„ 25	...	do,	3	1	4
Tisra, 4½ chittaks,	do.,	...	„ 25	...	do.,	8	1	4
Chautha, 4 chittaks,	do.,	...	„ 25	...	do.,	7	2	9
Kachar, 2 chittaks,	do.,	...	„ 10	...	do.,	1	2	0
					Total Rs.	26	10	3

The original cost was Rs. 20 per seer of Rs. 96 nawábi weight and wages of labour is Rs. 2 per seer. The selling price Rs. 26-10-3 gives a profit of Rs. 4-10-3.

Sangal is not twisted for sewing but is used as wound off the reels for the warp in weaving *gota*.

The other kind of silk is *bának*, which comes from districts in Lower Bengal near Calcutta. It comes in *bandis* of 4 or 5 tolahs each, is opened on a *gol charkh* but wound off in the same way as *sangal* on a *liauti* and *khali*. It gives four kinds of thread, *agári*, *dusra*, *tisra*, and *kachar*, in the following proportion per seer :—

Agári,	6	chittaks.
Dusra,	4½	chittaks.
Tisra,	5	chittaks.
Kachar,	½	chittaks.

Agári, *dusra*, and *tisra*, are sold untwisted at 5 as. per tolah : but the three are generally twisted into one thread irrespective of quality and sold at Rs. 26 per English seer of 80 rupees. This silk thread is called *maktúl*. The wages of winding off are Rs. 4 per seer and for twisting into thread Rs. 2-8. and dyeing Rs. 2 per seer. The cost of this silk in the raw state is Rs. 16 per seer nawabi of 92 rupees English. The cost of a nawábi seer of colored silk thread is therefore Rs. 24-8, and this at Rs. 26 per English seer sells for Rs. 29-14-5. The profit is therefore Rs. 5-6-5 per seer.

Roghan siyah farosh, *vide* Teli.

Roghan zard farosh, *vide* Ghiwala.

Rudegar, sometimes called *tántiya*, is the maker of catgut. Lucknow has been always celebrated for its catgut and the facilities for manufacture are great owing to the abundance of material. The gut of goats and sheep is used and as the number of these animals killed each day in this great Muhammedan city is necessarily vast, the catgut maker enjoys the advantages of procuring abundant materials for manufacture on the spot.

The guts of sheep and goats are steeped in water and cleaned with a *sipí* (shell). They are each 16 cubits long and each is split down into two strips. They are then stretched round two poles fixed perpendicularly in the ground and dried. They are then steeped in a vessel containing an infusion of *dudh madár* (juice of the (*asclepias gigantea*) and other ingredients, which these traders will not disclose, and 5 guts are then opened carefully and four are twisted together on a *phirauna*. The remaining one is used to work in and extend the length of the guts to 20 cubits. Each piece of catgut turned out is of 20 cubits standard length.

The cost of guts of animals in the undressed state in which the rúdegar purchases them from the chikwa or butcher is 7 score per rupee. A seer of *dudh madár* is sufficient for 10 score guts and the other drugs used cannot be expensive for rúdegars say that the whole does not amount to more than one anna per rupee of undressed gut. If the rúdegar buy 7 score of guts, his outturn will be 56 standard lengths of catgut which sell, at 3 as. per length, for Rs. 10-8.

His expenses have been only Re. 1 for guts and Re. 1 for drugs used in cleaning. He is at no expense for labor as he and his family perform all the processes of manufacture. He is looked down on by other classes of Mussulmans in this country where even Muhammedans are affected by caste prejudices. This in a manner accounts for the high profits enjoyed; for others are detained from taking up the trade and competing. The business is a monopoly enjoyed by three brothers and the members of their families in muhálla Nawábganj.

Ruifarosh.—Raw cotton is not imported into Lucknow from any place of production for purposes of export. It is brought into Lucknow for local consumption in stuffing bedding and clothing, and a very small quantity is spun for a few exceptional cases of local manufacture of textile fabrics still lingering in the market. It is imported chiefly from Cawnpore. The weight by which cotton is sold in that market is fixed by custom at 48½ seers to the maund. The weight at which sales are made in Lucknow is the standard maund of 40 seers. Cotton which costs Rs. 21-8 per maund in Cawnpore sells in Lucknow @ Rs. 19. Allowing for difference in weight and deducting cost of carriage, the profit is 12 annas per maund. The only extensive cotton dealers in Lucknow city are at Saádatganj, Maulviganj, Yahiyaganj and Amínabad. The *behna* and *dhuniya* are only labourers and their remuneration is either by weight or task. A *lihát* is a heavy counterpane interlined with cotton, average 4 seers. In this case the *behna* is paid 4 annas, *i. e.*, 1 anna per seer. If the same *behna* be called in to prepare cotton for a *razai*, and if the cotton given him is only 3 quarters of a seer, he will receive as much as 4 annas. The reason of this is that the labour in both cases is equal and were he paid in both cases by weight the remuneration would be unequal.

S.

Sabunfarosh.—Ordinary ' *desi sábun*' (country soap) is made in large quantities by manufacturers in Lucknow who supply the local market and export to other parts of Oudh. The process of manufacture is simple. Two reservoirs are made, the upper large and with its bottom on a level with the edge of the lower which is much smaller. In the upper are thrown 3 maunds *chúna* (lime), imported from Kalinjar and Banda, and 6 maunds *sajji* (impure carbonate of soda). Water is added and percolates slowly through a hole in the reservoir into the lower basin. Two days are required for the whole to pass. This fluid is then placed with *charbi* (bullock and buffalo fat) and *tel*, (either castor or linseed oil) in a large iron pan (*karáhi*) and boiled for about two days over a strong fire and stirred with a bambu potstick (*khúríyá*) to prevent the rising of froth. When it reaches the consistency of syrup, the fire is extinguished. Three labourers are needed for the first four of the seven days.

The account of one karáhi for one week is as follows :—

Chuna,	3	maunds,	...	Rs.	2 0 0
Sajji,	6	,,	...	,,	8 0 0
Charbi,	3	,,	...	,,	9 0 0
Oil (castor)	35	seers,	...	,,	10 0 0
Firewood,	25	maunds,	...	,,	6 0 0
Wages of labour,			...	,,	1 8 0
			Total Rs.		66 8 0

The produce is twelve maunds of soap which sell at Rs. 7-8 per maund (wholesale trade price) for Rs. 90 The manufacturer's profit is Rs. 23-8.

The manufacturer keeps all his accounts and sells by nawábi weight. Retailers who purchase from him sell at *lambari taul* and their present *nirakh* is 5¼ English seers to the rupee. Dhobis allege that 2¼ seers of soap are expended in washing 100 pieces for *sáhib log* and for native customers 1 seer per 100 pieces. When the population of Lucknow both native and European is considered (2,81,000) in conjunction with this estimate, it will be seen there must be a large demand for soap. There is also an export trade of considerable extent but not yet determined. The manufacture must, however, be undoubtedly extensive.

There are two well known manufacturers of soap in Lucknow, one in Hasanganj, the other in Beruni Khandaq, and many others less known.

Sadakar, *vide* Sunar.

Saiqalgar.—Polisher of steel armour and weapons. The sword or whatever it be, which is to be polished, is first rubbed with a *kurand* (corundum stone) ; then all signs of scratches and scrapes are removed by oiling and rubbing with a piece of cowhorn, and finally the weapon is polished up with a steel called *misqal*.

The occupation of a *saiqal-gar* has now dwindled to a trifle, and he is a poor man.

Salme Sitarewala, *vide* Zardoz.

Sang-tarash.—There are no stone-cutters in Lucknow who enjoy a business which would justify imposition of a License Tax. Those that are in the city may be counted on one hand and make only *chakkís* and *silbattás*. There are none who make stone images of worship or cut building stone, but some there are who can cut inscriptions in the vernacular on stones, for setting in the door-ways of mosques.

Saqin, called also **Bhangerin**.—This female is an important feature in bázárs in the East. She chooses a prominent place in a thoroughfare and has a gay array of huqqahs on her counter, and has as her assistants young women, pretty and well dressed, called *neauchis* and 'she sitteth at the door of her house on a seat in the high places of the city to call passengers.' The dissolute idler and lascivious gossip drop in and pay for the huqqah which is handed to them. The conversation is free, and the smoke exhilarating and the visitor perchance retires with the engaging *neauchi*, or perchance with the *náika* (mistress) herself if she be not unbearably *passée*.

The huqqahs are always ready and, as a visitor drops in, a *chillam* is filled and passed on a huqqah to him. In the *chillam* is placed a mixture of one másha of *charas* and two máshas of tobacco and the smoker pays from one paisa to any greater amount he pleases, and the vain spendthrift will fling down a rupee for the pleasure of a chillam in the jovial company of the *sáqiu*. If he retires with a *neauchi* he pays more freely, but whatever his gift be, it passes into the *sáqin's* hands. The *sáqin* takes all the receipts of the shop and of her *neauchis* and she clothes and feeds the latter in return.

Tobacco such as the *sáqin* sells costs 1 Re. for four seers and *charas* may be as cheap as 16 Rs. and as dear as 40 Rs. per seer. The custom as to clothing is, that the *sáqin* gives her *neauchi* four suits in a year and some ornaments, and as the *neauchi* is the attraction of the shop, the *sáqin* is liberal in feeding, clothing, and supplying ornaments and the usual *pándáan khassdán* and other appurtenances of the public lady in the East.

A *sáqin* with two pretty *neauchis* should after paying all expenses, clear much money in a year: but on the principle that ill-got goods are soon spent, such a woman will seldom be found with 50 Rs. to the good.

There are men who keep shops for the sale of *charas*, but there is no immorality connected with these houses. The profits are very much the same in the case of a *Charasfarosh* as in the cases of the Chandufarosh and Madakwála. (*vide-sub verb.*)

Sarangisaz *vide* Sitarsaz.

Sareshsaz.—The manufacture of *saresh* (glue) is carried on in the cold weather by *kuppesazes*. They collect the scrapings and hair of hides and skins from tanners, *rangaiyas, chikwas, luksázes, kimukhtsazes* and others. They pay a merely nominal price for these things, which are more a refuse to be removed than goods to be stored for sale. They go round periodically and clean up the premises on which these substances are to be got and pay a paisa or so for the privilege of the service. When a *kuppesáz* has collected a lot of this refuse he puts it with water in a burnt earthen pot and boils it all night long, until the water has evaporated leaving a syrup-like mass behind. It is then removed from the fire and the *saresh* which is above is poured off and the sediment and refuse pieces of leather are thrown away. The *saresh* which is poured off is kept in a *kundah*, open earthen vessel, till it begins to harden. It is then cut out in pieces with an instrument called *hathwa*.

Twenty seers of refuse leather and hair are put into a pot at once. They have cost perhaps 2 as., certainly not more. Two annas worth of fuel will be spent in boiling. Three seers of *saresh* will be the result and the price is 4 annas per seer. The profit is 8 as. per pot or *matka* boiled. The figures given are all *muqarrari, i. e.*, the proportion of refuse per pot boiled and the yield do not vary and the price does not fluctuate. 20 seers are always boiled in a pot.

Sarraf.—This term properly means a money-changer, but the business of a sarráf is much wider than the word denotes, and includes pawnbroking, purchase and sale of precious metals, and of gold and silver ornaments, &c.

The following are useful bazár tables ordinarily current by which the sarráf trades:—

Money.

2½	gandas of cowries ...	...	equal	1 addhi
2	addhis	...	...	,,	1 damri
2	damris	...	...	,,	1 dhela
2	dhelas = 3 pies	...	...	,,	1 English paisa
4	paisa	...	...	,,	1 anna
16	annas	...	...	,,	1 rupee

Weight.

8	ratis	...	...	,,	1 másha
3	máshas	...	...	,,	1 tánk
4	tánks	...	...	,,	1 tola
11½	máshas	...	...	,,	1 English rupee
11	,,	...	...	,,	1 nawábi ,,
4 to 9 m. 4 rati	...	...	,,	1 English chittak
5 to 6 máshas	...	...	,,	1 nawábi chittak
16	chittaks	...	...	,,	1 seer
40	seers	...	...	,,	1 man

The sarráf buys up cowries at 20½ gandas to the paisa (English) and he sells at the rate given in the table. This gives him ½ ganda profit in the paisa. A ganda is four units. He buys paisa from banks and treasuries at 16 annas and from shopkeepers at 16¼ annas for the rupee. He sells at 15¾ annas to the rupee: and sometimes he sells as near par as 15⅞ annas.

Pawnbroking is practised by most sarráfs. They receive in pawn gold and silver goods, clothing, copper, brass and other metal goods. A reference to **Mahajan** will give a view of this business.

The purchase of silver is regulated by rule. If the silver be of the quality of a Nawabi rupee or an ornament made of pure Nawábi silver the sarráf gives 15½ annas for the English rupee's weight, and if it be of the quality of an English rupee or an ornament made of silver equal to English rupee silver, the sarráf gives 15 annas for the English rupee's weight. If the silver tendered to the sarráf be not of the quality of the silver of an English or Nawabi rupee, or if it be silver made up and having joinings, the money given ranges from 12 annas to less than 15 annas for each English rupee's weight. The sarráf purchases old gold and silver lace and *kamdani* for the sake of the precious metal. When he has accumulated a stock of gold and silver in these various ways he hands it over to a *nyárya* (*vide sub-verb*) who melts and refines the metal and the sarráf sells the refined gold or silver at the prevailing bazár *nirakh*. The net profits on this business are certaining not less than 10 p. c.

The tricks and artifices of a sarráf are many. If he buy a tolerably new gold or silver ornament he often gets a sunár to furbish it up and he sells it for new. This is sharp practice but what can be said of a sarráf who weighs short weight and takes long weight and depreciates the quality of precious metal when he buys from ignorant persons. Such tricks are common. Besides this, the sarráf is usually a dealer in stolen goods and as he must quickly melt stolen gold and silver he generally has some confidential nyárya to whom he gives such property and he pays him one-fourth of his illicit gains as hushmoney.

Most vendors of jewellery made for the English market are not sunars but really sarráfs who employ sunars to make up goods for them.

Shalbaf —There are a few Kashmiris in Muhallas Golaganj and Bansmandi, in Lucknow city, who have tried to introduce shawl weaving into Lucknow, but the industry has not taken deep root.

The warp and woof are wool and the loom is in all respects like the *julahas*, but is raised from the ground like the British handloom. The woof is not woven into the warp with a shuttle but with a number of bobbins (called *tili*) laid on the web along the roller immediatly in front of the weaver and on these bobbins there are wound woollen threads of various colors. These bobbins are made of *kákraunda* (? *karaunda*,) which is much like boxwood, and in size and shape they resemble thick but short porcupine quills. I have reckoned over 500 *tilis* on a web of a rumál only $2\frac{1}{2}$ yards wide. There were four weavers working at this loom and they were all guided by hieroglyphics marked in lines on pages of a MS. book. These hieroglyphics are understood by all workmen who have learned in the one school of weaving and the M. S. I saw, could be read and understood by some workmen in the Punjab and by other weavers in Lucknow, all who had learned in the school to which the master-weaver belonged.

The wool used is imported from upper Asia through the Punjab and is sold in Lucknow in two varieties, white and black, and prices range from Re. 1 to Rs. 4 per seer. The borders of the long side of *rumáls* are woven separately from the *rumál* and are afterwards sewed on. These borders are woven with wool on a silk warp. In this case the *shálbáf* has to lay in silk as well as wool. He is at no expense for cleaning the wool. It is done by the women of the house. The dyeing is done by professional dyers (Kashmiris) and the charge is according to the color, ranging from Re. 1 to Rs. 3 per seer.

Weaving is done either by fixed monthly wages or by contract. The wages of weavers range from Re. 1-12 to Rs. 3-12 per mensem and not less than two can work a loom. The average is four weavers and the progress made on a web is about ⅔ in. per diem. The contract rates are 2 pies per 1000 *tilis* consumed or at Re. 1 per *patti* in the case of *jámawárs* which are woven in strips subsequently run together.

The following is the account of a *jámawár* or shawl worked in the pine apple pattern :—

				Rs.	As.	P.
3 seers wool,	...	...	...	6	0	0
Rice for dressing wool,	...	...	...	0	2	0
Spinning wool (if not done at home,)	...	...	6	0	0
Dyeing, ...	...	...	...	2	8	0
Paid to weavers at Re. 1 per patti,	...	...	50	0	0
		Total Rs.		64	10	0

This *jámawár* is sold for not less than Rs. 100. The profit is Rs. 35-6. It is 3½ yards long by 1½ yards wide. It is impossible to estimate the profits of shawl weaving when done by contract, unless the number of shawls woven by the contractors and delivered to the master weaver be known and their price. In that case the profit may be safely put down at Rs. 33 per cent. But when a shawl manufacturer has a number of looms working, each loom is worth about Rs. 150 per annum.

Shamafarosh, *vide* **Battisaz.**

Shirfraosh, *vide* **Dudhfarosh.**

Shirinifarosh, *vide* **Halwai.**

Shisha-alatfarosh, *vide* **Bisati.**

Shishesaz —The manufacture of glass or, more correctly speaking, of glass goods, is but in its infancy in Lucknow. It has had a long infancy. It was perhaps more vigorous in nawabí days when English manufactures did not enter the local market to compete with local manufactures. It was in an undeveloped state, for glass itself was not manufactured. Old glass was bought up and remade into new goods. In this stage the industry still continues. Were glass made in Lucknow, there is great local skill available for the execution of really superior work.

There are two manufacturers who do a considerable business. The most extensive is a contractor connected with Husenabad. The other, a far less extensive dealer, has small factories in various parts of the city. I take that at

Mukárimnagar as a sample. It is managed by Rahim Khán. The factory consists of thatched sheds. In one of these is a *bhatta*. This is a mud retort with a warm chamber above. The retort is fired with babul, tamarind or mango wood. The glass used is old and broken glass bought up at 2 as. per seer. Two small boys at Rs. 4 per mensem assist Rahím Khán who is paid Rs. 12 per mensem. The consumption of fuel is about one maund per diem. The outturn of glass goods is about 4 seers per diem and the waste of glass in melting is about 10 per cent.

The goods manufactured here are solid glass, such as branches of chandeliers, and blown glass, such as pickle jars, phials, scent bottles and the like. The goods made are manufactured by attaching to the end of a blow pipe (a brass tube or an old gun barrel) a piece of glass in a soft state. To this other pieces are added and heated in the retort until a sufficient amount of glass to make a given article has adhered together. If the branch of a chandelier be required the glass is elongated and twisted to give it a spiral set or curl and then it is laid on a piece of wood and bent to the pattern required. If a pickle jar or bottle be required it is blown.

The proprietor's expenses and profits on manufacture are given by his manager for one month, say, of thirty days as follows :—

	Rs.	As.	P.		Rs.	As.	P.
Wages of manager, ...	12	0	0	Outturn of 120 seers			
Two assistants, ...	8	0	0	new goods, being			
Fuel 30 mds. at 3 mds.				4 seers per diem,			
per rupee, ...	10	0	0	sold at 11 annas			
132 seers of old glass				per seer, ...	82	8	0
required to produce							
120 seers new goods,	16	8	0	Deduct, ...	46	8	0
Total	46	8	0	Profit	36	0	0

Sirkakash.—Vinegar-maker.—Vinegar is made from *shíra, ras, gur, jáman*, and *dhowan karáhi* : but chiefly from the first named.

Ras, juice of the sugar cane, is too expensive for manufacture of vinegar for the native market. So also is *gur* though in a less degree. The *jáman* fruit is used to make vinegar for medicinal purposes and *attárs* and *araq-kashes* prepare it.

Dhowan karáhi, (washings of pans) is the refuse of the boiled sugar in which *halwais* dip their sweetmeats. The sugar is boiled in a large pan and confections, *jalebis*, &c., dipped in this pan. When the pan is cleaned out the *halwái* puts the refuse aside in a large jar and makes vinegar of it. This he uses to make pickles and chatnis.

When sugar-cane is crushed it gives out the juice called *ras*. This is boiled and *gur* and *ráb* are made. The froth is skimmed off and put aside. The crushed stalks of the cane are laid in a vat (*hauz*) with a small outlet below and the froth is thrown on them with a little water. The substance which comes trickling off is boiled and becomes *shíra*. This is the stuff which is purchased by vinegar-makers and tobacco manufacturers.

The *sirkákash* buries in the ground a large earthen jar (*mathor*) in which he places 1 maund *shíra* and 2 maunds water. Then he closes it up and it remains closed for 5 months except for one day, when the mixture is taken out and strained at the end of about the third month. The average yield is 1¾ maunds per *mathor*, being 1 maund first quality and 30 seers second quality vinegar. The former will sell at 4 paisa the seer and the latter at 2 paisa the seer. This gives 3 Rs. 7 as. per *mathor*, while the cost of *shíra* was about 2 Rs. the maund. But the older vinegar is the higher the price it will fetch, and the second class vinegar of this year, if kept till next year, will double in value : while the first class will increase some 50 per cent. in value.

Each *mathor* will serve twice in a year and affords potentially about 3 Rs. profit. There are *sirkakash* who have as many as 80 or 100 *mathors* always in use for manufacture of vinegar. As the looking after the mathors is not full employment for a *sirkakash* he will often be found to combine with this occupation some other business : for instance, that of a *tálwála* or *gotabáf*, as is often the case in Lucknow.

Sirkifarosh.—Sirki is the upper joint of *sentha*, a reed grass, which is of wild growth, and is cut down and used to make *morhas* and *chiks*. *Sirki* is sold at 8 as. per maund and is made up by the *sirkifarosh* into what are called *joras*. Every one is familiar with these coverings which are thrown over bullock carts for shade in heat and protection from rain. Four of these are made from a maund of *sirki* by one man in one day. His wages are 3 as., and 2 paisa of *bán* will more than suffice to bind the edges of the 4 joras. They sell at 6 as. each. The *sirkifarosh* has thus 11 as. profit on the 4. If he be himself the maker, his profit is 14 as.

Sitarsaz.—It will be convenient under this head to treat of the manufacture of musical instruments in general, as far as I have had opportunity of noting it, in Lucknow.

(1.) Stringed instruments played with the hand and *mizráb* (wire guard for fingers.)

There are only three made in Lucknow, the *sitár*, *bin*, and *tambúra*.

The *sitar* is a variety of guitar. The body is made of a *kaddu* or *lauki*, (gourd) and the *dánd* (handle) is of wood and hollow : but the most expensive *sitár* generally has a body of wood, either *arr* or *tún*, because these woods are not so subject as others to attacks of insects and they are stringless and light. The disc of wood placed on the *tomba* (belly) is called *tabli*. The wood uniting the handle and body is called *gulú* (neck) and this is strengthened by slips of wood called *pattas*. The hollow handle is covered above with a slip of wood called *langot*. The strings are tightened by turning pegs called *khuntis*. These are all of wood.

The frets (*sundaris*) are made of brass or iron and range from 15 to 18 in number. The bridge on the *tomba* over which the strings are carried is called *gorach* and the perforated bridge near the *khuntis* is called *tárgahan*, and is made of ivory or bone. The strings (*tar*) are made either all of brass or steel or of some of each. The number of strings varies from three to seven.

Sitárs are made in Lucknow of three forms 'Madham', 'Pancham', and 'Tarbdár'. The 'Madham' is so called because its first string is the fourth note ('Madham') of the Hindu gamut, and 'Pancham' because its first string is the fifth note. 'Tarbdár' is made with strings producing what may be called a twang.

Sitárs are sold at Rs. 1-4; Rs. 2; Rs. 4; Rs. 5; Rs. 10; Rs. 25 and Rs. 50, and the price varies according to the size, the string compass, and the finish of the instrument. The Rs. 25 and Rs. 50 instruments are called Purbi, because they have bodies made of hollowed wood which is against the custom of the West. The 50 Rs. instrument has also much ornamentation by inlaying, gilding, &c.

The cost of manufacture of the cheapest *sitár* would be about as follows:—

	As.	P.
Wood for *dánd*, &c., ...	6	0
Wire and glue,	0	9
Bone for bridges,	0	3
Sundaris (16)	2	0
Catgut (*tant*) for binding		
Sundries,	0	3
Laui (gourd,)	6	0
Wages of labour,	2	6
	As. 12	3

As this instrument sells for Re. 1-4 the manufacturer has a profit of 7 as. 9 pies. A workman can make a cheap *sitár* in one day.

The cost of manufacture of a Rs. 25 *sitár* is about :—

	As.	P.
Wood for *dánd*, &c.,	1	8
Wire & glue,	0	2
Bone for bridges,	0	1
Sundaris (17),	0	6
Catgut,	0	1
Wages of labour,	2	8
	As. 4	10

This would leave Rs. 5-6 profits to the manufacturer after paying the cost of materials and wages of labor. The labour is a matter of one labourer for 15 days, or more for a less time—*pandarah nafar mazduri*, as natives say, and the manufacturer earns 5 as. 8 pies per diem. Thus the manufacturer who makes both a cheap and a more expensive *sitár* will have, on one Re. 1-4 and one 10 Rs. *sitár*, Rs. 5-13-9 profits. The clippings and cuttings of wood saved in making more expensive instruments are used up in making less expensive and smaller ones : so we may say Rs. 6 instead of Rs. 5-13-9. It will then be found that a *kárkhánadár*, or manufacturer of *sitárs*, makes 6 as. profit on each day's wages paid to each workman.

The *Bín*.—This instrument differs little from the *sitár* in manufacture and in make its essential difference is that it is made with two *tombas*.

The *tambura* is also made in Lucknew. It is like a *sitár* but made without a *pardah*, and it is placed on the shoulder near the ear and played with the fingers close to the ear.

(2.) Stringed instruments played with a bow, (*gaz.*)

Of these only the *sárangi*, *ísrár* and *chikárah* are made in Lucknow.

The *sárangi* is the fiddle of India and is found everywhere. The handle is as broad almost as the body. It is hollow. The body and handle are both of wood. The body is covered with the skin of the *goh*. The names of the parts of the instrument are the same as those of the *sitár*, and the cost of production and profit is about the same. A *sárangi* sells for Rs. 4 and Rs. 5, not more.

The *ísrár* is a kind of compound of the *sitár* and *sárangi* and is played with either bow or finger.

The *chikára* is like the *sárangi* and has seven or eight strings. Three strings are of horse hair, and the rest of brass and *tarbdar*. It sells for Rs. 2.

(3) Drums. The *tabala* or drum is of two kinds—bass (*bam*) and treble (*zir*). Both may be seen with the drummer (*tabalasáz*) who accompanies a dancing woman. They are placed in a *doputtah* which is tied round the waist and the bass is played with the left hand and the treble with the right.

The bass drum is made of an earthen bowl resembling the upper half of an egg and the treble drum is made of a wooden bowl resembling the lower half. *Kumhars* make up the former and sell them at 3 paisa each : *barhais* make the latter and sell them at 4 as. each. The *tabalasáz* purchases these bowls and gives them to such persons as *mashaksazes*, who cover them—the bass at 6 as. and the treble at 8 as.—with prepared goatskin.

(4.) Wind instruments of the style of the fife, &c. Only one of these is made in Lucknow, the *bánsri*. It is made of bambu or of brass and has seven notes. There is not such a demand for these instruments as would encourage a special business in their manufacture.

Sonachandifarosh *vide* Mahajan and Sarraf.

Sujiwala *vide* Chakkiwala.

Sunar.—The gold and silversmiths of India have very simple mechanical appliances and it is wonderful what well finished and delicately executed ornaments a skilful *sunar* can turn out with his comparatively rude tools. His workshop is usually but a small room and the ground is his bench. His tools consist of a few anvils *(nihái)*, some hammers *(hathauri)*, a perforated plate *(janta)* for wire-drawing, a pair of pincers *(zambúr)*, a pair of tongs *(chimti)*, a pair of scissors, a blowpipe *(phunkani)*, some *thappas* (brass punches and dies for stamping patterns on gold and silver), and scales and weights. To these add the *angetha*, crucible *(ghariya)* and some moulds *(sanchas)* and a gold and silversmith's workshop is furnished.

There are many vendors of made up jewelry in Lucknow, but of these nothing will be said under this head for their profits are quite separate from those of manufacturing goldsmiths who are alone treated of in this note.

Gold and silver ornaments are of four classes and manufacturers' charges are regulated accordingly :—

Silver Ornaments.

Sádah	...	...	1	paisa per rupee of silver.
Chitái	...	...	2	,, ,,
Murassa or *jaráo*		...	2	annas ,,
Jáldár	...	...	4	,, ,,

Gold Ornaments.

Sádah	...	...	1	anna per tolah.
Chitái	...	...	2	,, ,,
Murassa or *jaráo*		...	8	,, ,,
Jáldár	...	...	1	rupee ,,

These are the prices charged by manufacturers or mastersmiths who employ workmen.

The term *sádah* includes all plain work in which there is no ornamentation such as plain gold or silver *kharas* for hands or feet. *Chitái* includes all work in which there are cut or engraved designs of flowers, letters, inscriptions, &c. *Murassa* and *Jaráo* include all work involving the setting of stones and raised and joined work. *Jáldár* work is of various classes, European goods, filagree, etc.

Besides this there is a large business done by *sunars* in cities in the manufacture of silver and silver-gilt vessels, &c., such as *thális, tashtaris, chimbals, khassdáns, ughóldáns, changels, suráhís, gulábpashes,* &c., for the Indian market, and teapots, sugarbowls, tumblers, &c., for the English market.

Where manufacture of ornaments or vessels involves enamelling and gilding these processes are not performed by the gold or silversmith, but by other artizans (*vide* **Minasaz, Mulammasaz**).

A mastersmith who makes up ornaments, generally pays his workmen by the month at from three rupees to five rupees each, according to the skill and efficiency of the workman, but sometimes he pays by task rates. For instance, a journeyman goldsmith of the first class will get 3 as., per diem for turning out four mashas of gold or one rupee of silver. As the master-goldsmith gives a trifle of *chabena* daily to each workman, it will be seen that a first-class workman whether at Rs. 5 per mensem or at 3 as., per diem, is about equally paid. Three first-class workmen will turn out a tolah of worked gold (12 mashas) in a day or three rupees weight of silver. They will in either case get 9 annas (three annas each) wages. The master goldsmith will, however, charge one rupee in either case for making up, and will thus have a profit of 7 as. on the tolah of gold or three rupees of silver. It is obvious that a master goldsmith who does not employ first-class workmen but manufactures plain goods will not enjoy such a high rate of profit per rupee or tolah weight of work turned out, but inasmuch as his plainer work is more rapidly executed, he may by the greater outturn he can show make daily profits equal to the superior manufacturer. Thus, let us take the second-class. A master-smith employs second-class workmen and does second-class work. His workmen will receive Rs. 4 per mensem or 2 as. per diem each. One workman will turn out eight mashas of gold in a day. Thus two workmen will earn 10 as. 8 p. for their master but will receive only 4 as. This leaves only four pies difference in the daily profits of the first-class and second-class manufacturer; but the latter has had to turn out a greater weight of worked goods to come up so close to the former.

Sunars who make only *sádah* (plain) goods seldom employ journeymen, but they and the members of their family work. Even the females of some *sunár* families in Lucknow work in gold and silver with considerable skill.

The manufacture of vessels differs but little from that of ornaments. They are usually made of silver and very seldom of gold, and the charges for manufacture are never less than 1 anna and do not exceed 4 as. per rupee.

There is no doubt that manufacturers of gold and silver goods add considerably to their profits by adulterating the metal in which they work. Custom allows them to represent a slight loss of weight in manufacture and under cover of this they take a further profit. They also store up the scrapings of their shops and sell them to *nyáriyas* (*q. v.,*). From all these sources another 2 as. may be added to the 9 as. profits per tolah of gold or 1 anna per three rupees weight of silver. Gold affords greater opportunity for adulteration than silver. This calculation will give a first-class master gold and silversmith who employs three journeymen a profit of from Rs. 228 to Rs. 250 per annum.

The Persian word *zargar* is sometimes used in lists of traders for gold-smith instead of *sunár* : and the word *sádakár* is also used. *Zargar* is a broad term equal to *sunár* : *sádakár* is a maker of plain goods, light rings, &c., but the term is sometimes used to denote a Hindu goldsmith who has turned Muhammadan.

A *sádakár* who is purely what the word denotes generally works alone in a small shop and makes up silver and gold armlets and rings for the native market. He can turn out a score and-a-half perfectly plain articles per diem and will receive 8 as. per score. He can turn out a better class of goods with slight ornamentation, flower-engraving, &c., (*sohankári*) at the rate of a score in four days and he receives Rs. 2 per soore.

T.

Tabalasaz, *vide* **Sitarsaz.**

Talwala.—This word in its broad sense of fuel-vendor would include the charcoal vendor and *kandafarosh* as well as vendors of fire-wood, but it will be here used in the last, which is its restricted sense. The dealer in fire-wood (*hema sokhtani*) is also called *lakrihára* in opposition to the *lakriwála* who is a timber merchant.

There are many persons in Lucknow who trade as importers of fire-wood. They buy up groves and odd trees, and jangals of *dhák* and other *khúdrú* trees, and cut them down and import the wood. The chief means of import is by boat but much fuel is imported by road from the south-east. The purchaser of groves and jangals estimates by *kut* (mental calculation) the approximate outturn of the trees (standing or fallen) which he proposes to purchase and tenders to the zamindars about Rs. 2 per 100 maunds for *dhák* and other trees of wild growth, and Rs. 4 to Rs. 5 per 100 maunds mango wood. Less is tendered for dhák, etc. because the labour and expense of cutting is greater than in the case of mango trees. The mango wood which the fuel merchant takes from a grove is only the refuse wood which is deemed unfit for building or manufacturing purposes. The wood cutters who fell trees receive 4 as. per diem or Rs. 7-8 per mensem each and cut as much as 100 maunds in 4 days. The charge for carriage to boats depends on distance, but as a rule it does not pay to buy at more than 25 kos from boats. The charge for carriage by boat from Muhamdi jangals is Rs. 10 per 100 maunds. About 800 maunds on an average come in a boat, and suppose that a month expires in cutting and despatching this quantity, the wages of a responsible servant must be added, say Rs. 15. Thus, if we suppose five 2-bullock carts to carry 100 maunds 25 kos in four days at 4 as. per bullock per diem, and half fare for each return journey, the cost to the importer of 800 maunds mango wood delivered at a ghát in Lucknow is Rs. 180. The present wholesale price is Rs. 30 per 100 maunds. Thus the importer makes a profit of Rs. 60. This is a profit of about Rs. 33⅓ per cent. on his outlay. This profit is not excessive for in all fuel dealing the rate of profit must be high because the element of insurance against risk is an important factor.

The fire-wood thus imported is sold by the importer at the ghát by a special weight of 48 seers to the maund. All calculations hitherto have been in this maund. The *tálwálá*, properly so called, comes to the ghát and buys by the 100 maunds, and the cost of conveying to his *theki* or fuel yard lies on him. The charge ranges according to distance from Re. 1-4 to Rs. 2-8 per 100 maunds, and there are carriers who contract for the delivery. A *tálwálá* who lives at the furthest part of the city from a ghát thus gets 4800 seers for Rs. 32-8. He sells at the lambari maund, 3 maunds or 120 seers for the rupee. He thus makes Rs. 7-8 profit minus the wages of a permanent servant who chops the wood into small pieces. 120 seers is a very small estimate of daily sales for a *theki*, but take even that and deduct 4 as. for wages of the wood cutters who chops the fuel and profit will remain to the *tálwálá* Rs. 7-4 on 100 maunds or

22⅓ per cent. This is a very low estimate. In 1879 during the cold weather importers sold fire-wood wholesale at the gháts for Rs. 20 the 100 maunds, and *tálwálás* stored at that price and had their stock round until Kuar when they sold retail at 2 maunds the rupee.

Parchunwálás who buy from *tálwálás* at 3 maunds the rupee sell by the seer at 1½ seer the paisa. This gives them 4 as. per rupee profit.

Tambakuwala.—There are various classes of tobacco dealers. There are first wholesale purchasers of the dried leaf from cultivators. These import and sell the dried leaf, buying at 48 seers to the maund and selling at 40 seers to the maund, or they make up the leaf with *shíra* for sale in the prepared state. There are others who buy the dried leaf from importers and manufacture and vend the drug in a prepared state, and there are shopkeepers of an humbler class who buy up manufactured tobacco and retail it.

It is clear that the importer of leaf who sells tobacco-leaf makes at least 20 per cent. profit. He makes more in reality by storing but that may be allowed as a more than ample set off against octroi duty.

The leaf is made up either *sóda* or *khamíra*. In the case of *sáda tambáku* the dried leaf is first pounded and then mixed with half as much again as its own weight of *shíra*. It is then pounded again. Wages are paid each time of pounding at the rate of 3 as. 3 pies per maund of tobacco first pounding and half that for second pounding. The cheaper kind of leaf is used up in this way. The account for a maund of leaf would be :—

				Rs.	As.	P.
Tobacco leaf 40 seers,	...	...	...	4	0	0
Shíra 60 seers,	...	...	...	3	12	0
Pounding 1st time, ...	...	...	...	0	3	3
Pounding 2nd time, ...	...	...	...	0	1	9
		Total Rs.	...	8	1	0

This preparation (100 seers) sells at 8 seers per rupee, for Rs. 12-8. The profit is therefore Rs. 4-7 or over 55 per cent. The tobacco when prepared is really over 100 seers because it is damped and *sajji* is often added, but this increase in weight may be thrown in to the tobacconist's good to cover all miscellaneous charges.

Khamíra tambáku is prepared as before with the addition of spices and scent. The best tobacco leaf is used :—

					Rs.	As.	P.
Leaf 1 maund,	...	...	...	...	10	0	0
Shíra 1½ maund,	...	...	...	...	3	12	0
Two poundings,	...	...	...	...	0	5	0
Khamíra 1¼ seer,	...	...	...	...	0	2	6
Mishk,	...	...	...	...	1	0	0
Spices,	...	...	...	...	0	4	0
			Total Rs.	...	15	7	6

The yield is at least 2 maunds 21½ seers, but practically very much more, owing to the moisture communicated in manufacture. *Khamíra* tobacco is kept in store so that the perfume mixed with it may rise and spread with the leaven. The 'tops,' or upper part of the heap, sell cheapest, at about 3 as. per seer and this is about half the *táo*. The last few seers, 'tails', sell at 8 as. the seer. The rest sells at 4 to 5 as. per seer. It is very fair to take the whole at 4 as. the seer. The price thus realized is Rs. 25-6. The profit is over Rs. 66 per cent.

From the foregoing note it will be seen how enormous must be the profits of a tobacconist who buys leaf from cultivators and manufactures it himself for retail. He must make cent. per cent. at least.

So much for *kashídani tambáku*. There remains *khurdani tambáku*, i. e., tobacco which is for eating purposes. This is steeped in *geru* (red ochre) by cultivators and then dried. It undergoes no further change in the tobacco vendor's hands, but it dries more between the time the cultivator passes it to the wholesale purchaser and the time when the latter sells it to the retailer. The loss is about a panseri in the maund of 40 seers. Thus the storer who buys from the cultivator 48 seers at Rs. 12 and keeps the leaf till it further dries, may be said to buy 42 seers at Rs. 12. He sells at 8 as. the seer. He thus makes Rs. 9 on an outlay of Rs. 12 or Rs. 75 per cent.

Tamboli.—This is the name of the caste which is devoted to the cultivation and vend of *pán*. *Tambol* or *pán* is a succulent creeper the leaf of which is heart-shaped, and from this resemblance the heart at cards has come to be called pán * It is planted on an elevated slope where there is shade: and a heavy moist soil is preferable. The *barai* ploughs and digs the earth deep and encloses it with stakes and *tattar*. The top is covered with *tattar*. Long shallow trenches are dug, and the plant laid in layers. From each knot rises a shoot which climbs up a stake securely driven into the earth at its base. Planting takes place in February and the leaves begin to reach their fulness in June. The plantation is called *bhit*, *bári*, or *pánwári*, and the cultivator *barai*.

The profit of cultivation is certain for the demand for the leaf is unvarying. Although in a dry year the crop is liable to injury, yet the cultivation being under all circumstances artificial and. crop the forced, there is not any danger of an absolute failure of produce.

---

* The four suits are *pán* (hearts), *ínt* (diamond), *hukm* (spades). and *chiriya* (clubs). The cards are *ekka* (ace), *duggi* (deuce), *tiggi* (three), *chauka* (four), *panja* (five), *chhikka* (six), *sattha* (seven), *attha* (eight), *nahla* (nine), *dahla* (ten), *ghulám* (knave), *bíbía* (queen) and *bádsháh* (king). The ace is the highest card of each suit. Three persons only play and the two of diamonds (*ínt ki duggi*) is discarded from the pack. There thus remain fifty one cards. Seventeen are dealt to each player. A trump card is not turned up, for spades (*hukm*) are always trumps and the holder of the ace of spades leads. There is no partnership, each player being for himself. The play and deal pass to the right. To deal the cards is *tás bhántna* ; to play a card is *patta phenkna*; and to play the winning card in a trick is *sar karna*. *Tás*, it will be seen, is a pack of cards and *patta* is one card. *Khilál* is the correct term for defeat cards and is used thus : *kis ke upar khilal hua*, i. e. who has lost ?

The rent paidfor the ground occupied by a *bhit* in Oudh is usually charged by the zamindar at so much per *antar* or line of plants ; 2 as. to 4 as. according to length of *bhit*. In some districts this rule is not adhered to, *e. g.* in Naugawan, in Zillah Cawnpore, the charge is Rs. 12-8 per biswa. The biswa will yield 318 *dhólis*, and the average price is 6 *dhólis* per rupee. Then it may be taken that a biswa of pán will yield in one year, Rs. 53. The labor is all hand labor of the *barai* and his family. The only expenses are the erection of *tattar*, &c. This is calculated at the outside at Rs. 20 per *bhit* and thus the profit of a biswa of pán will be Rs. 33 per annum.

The leaves are plucked every fifth day and made up in bundles of 200 each, called *dhólis*. The average purchase price at place of cultivation is 6 *dhólis* per rupee. Beoparis bring pán to Lucknow from all districts, but chiefly from Patná and Rai Bareli. They sell their *dhólis* unopened at either of two places. One is Qila Jalálábad, outside Municipal limits. The beopari who sells here escapes payment of octroi. From these beoparis the tambolis of Lucknow purchase by *dholi* and the beopari sells at such a price that after paying all expenses he shall have one dholi in six as profit. The whole of the sales at Qila Jalálábad take place through the Chaudhri of Tambolis who takes from the beopari one *dholi* in six as his *haqq*. Thus a beopari who brings 72 *dholis* has 12 *dholis* as profit and the Chaudhri has 2. The other place at which beoparis sell is Victoriaganj-Dareba. Beoparis who bring pán to this place have to pay octroi : but they arrange their prices as as to have their profit as in the previous instance and the Chaudhri also takes the *haqq árhat* as in the other market.

Tambolis who purchase at either place will sell either retail or at a quasi wholesale rate. In the latter case they take one dholi in five as their profit and if they sell by the leaf their profit is much more. The leaf made up with *katha, chuna, supári* and *ilachi* is called *bíráh* or *gilauri*. There are four varieties of leaf imported *kapuri, kaker, bangla, begami, desawari,* and *kalkatiya*. At the present time two dholis of kapuri pán cost 10 as. 8 pies. This is 400 leaves and 1½ leaves go to one *gilauri*. To make these up the tamboli needs :—

			As.	P.
Katha,	one	chittak,	... 0 0	3
Chuna,	½	do.	... 0 0	1
Supari,	4	do.	... 0 1	6
Ilaichi kalan,			... 0 0	3
Add two dholis of pán,			... 0 10	8
			———	
			... 0 12	9

This gives 300 *gilauris* which sell at 4 per paisa for Rs. 1-2-9. This gives to the tamboli 3 as. per *dholi* profit purely on retail business.

It remains to note the process of whitening pan which renders it more valuable. Whitened pan sells at a fancy price. The leaves are laid in layers in a basket made of *patáwar* and sprinkled with earth and kept damp. In twelve days green leaves become white—*angúri rang*. Pan will keep for three months buried in the earth in large crates and then are storers of pan in Nurbári in Lucknow City whose sole business is to store pán and re-export to distant places where the season offers advantages, *e.g.*, to Alwar, Ajmír, Rewári, Delhi, and the Panjab generally. Desawari and Begamipan alone are used for store and export.

Tardabkaiya, *vide* **Gotakinarifrosh.**

Tari farosh.—*Tári*, or, as it is vulgarly called, 'toddy,' is of two kinds, *tári* proper, which is the juice of the palmyra tree, and *sendhi*, the juice of the wild date tree.

Tári proper is extracted from a cut made in the tree and trickles into an earthen pot suspended below the cut. The fasl is Chait and Asarh. Sita Ram of Aminabad has at present the lease of 36 trees at Garhi Chinauti, six kos from the city. He pays 8 as. per tree for the season to the zamindar. He has two servants on the spot to cut the trees and gather the juice. He receives daily a consignment of 4 *mons* (an earthen vessel which holds 20 seers). He retains four carriers at 1½ as. each per diem. Towards the end of the season the yield will fall off to 2 *mons* per diem. The whole season is 3½ months. It will, therefore, be proper to calculate for 2½ months at full yield and one month at half yield to approximate the entire season:—

	Rs. As. P.		Rs. As. P.
2½ months.		*Yield.*	
Two servants at trees,	20 0 0	360 *mons* of 20 seers	
Four carriers, ...	28 2 0	each, sold at 2 paisa per	
1 month,		seer of 3 pau tári to 1	
Two servants at trees,	8 0 0	pau of water,	300 0 0
Two carriers, ...	5 0 0		
Rent of trees, ...	18 0 0		
Fee of shop at 12 as.			
per diem, ...	78 12 0	Deduct	158 8 0
Tosal,	158 12 0	Total,	141 8 0

Thus the profit which he makes is, roughly speaking, about double the fees which he pays for the license to sell.

I regret that I have not an account of a known lease of *khajúr* trees and yield of *sendhi*; but if a case arose the account could be framed on the lines of the foregoing. The *khajúr* is cut in the middle of Asarh and the yield continues to the middle of Magh.

Tarkash, *vide* **Gotakinari farosh.**

Tat pattiwala:—*Tát* is woven by Kahars in Lucknow and the standard *patti* is 9 inches wide and 22 or 24 *háths* long. The average weight is $3\frac{1}{4}$ seers. A Kahar buys *san* at $3\frac{3}{4}$ seers for 5 as., cleans it and twists it into *sutli* with an instrument called *phéri* or *pukli*. This is two sticks crossed with an upright rising from the place where they meet. In 2 days $3\frac{1}{4}$ seers *sutli* are prepared from the $3\frac{3}{4}$ seers *san*. The rest is waste. The *sutli* is then woven at a loom called *tána* in the same way as a dari; a whole *patti* is woven in one day. The weaver sells it for 9 as. His profit is therefore 4 as. The shopkeeper who purchases at 9 as. sells as a rule at 12 as.

Teli.—Three classes of oil are made in Lucknow, if they be classed by process of manufacture. The first class includes *alsi* (linseed), *sarson* (mustard), *dána postah* or *khashkhásh* (poppy seeds), *túyah* (black mustard), *mahua, gola náryal* (cocoanut), *til* (sesamum), *láhí* (eruca sativa,) *tukhm-i-kusum* (safflower), *gehuán* (a wheat grass yielding grain), and *nímkauri* (berry of the *ním* tree). These all are crushed and oil pressed from them in an ordinary *kolhu*. *Réndi ká tel* (castor oil) is a class of itself. It is made either with an iron machine, purchased in Calcutta, or by *bhurjis*, as will be hereafter described. The third class is medicinal oils, *badám* (almond), and *káhu*.

Of the first class those most extensively manufactured are *alsi* and *sarson*. Take the former as a specimen case; and, passing by the *kolhu* worked by hand, which of itself can never be made so paying a machine as to lay the proprietor open to taxation, consider the case of an ordinary *kolhu* worked by bullock power. The *kolhu* consists of a thick upright block (*kolhu* proper) fixed in the ground, with a hollow in the top to receive the seed, and a hole below through which the oil trickles; a revolving pestle-like piece of wood, called *ját*, which crushes the seed; a long pole coming from the *ját* to the bullock yoke (*jua*) and an attached seat below the *ját* re-: volving with it, on which the *teli* driving the bullock sits, and the pressure of his weight helps the *ját* to crush the seed. This seat is called a *kátar*. When the *teli* leaves, he places a stone on this to keep up the pressure. The bullock is hoodwinked to prevent its becoming dizzy in its continuous circuit. The amount of seed thrown into a *kolhu* at one time and pressed out is called a *ghán*. A *kolhu* holds at least 3 seers, but as much sometimes as four. Let the *ghán* be taken as low as three seers. Two *ghán*s of linseed are crushed in a day and, as *alsi* is now $12\frac{1}{2}$ seers the rupee, we may say that in a day nad a half $12\frac{1}{2}$ seers will be pressed, and the yield is never less than 2 seers of oil to 5 seers of seed. That is, 5 seers of oil will be produced in $1\frac{1}{2}$ days. There will be left 7 seers of refuse seeds. This is called *khali*, and is sold by the teli at 26 seers the rupee. The bullock is fed on *khali* (one seer) and *bhúsa* 5 seers per diem, and *chunni* $\frac{3}{4}$ seer. *Bhúsa* is now 2 maunds per rupee and *ckunni* is $1\frac{1}{4}$ seer in the anna. The wholesale price of linseed oil is $3\frac{3}{4}$ seers the rupee. The profit, therefore, of an oil mill worked by a bullock is a few pies over 10 as. in a day and a half, or in three days Re. 1-4.

There is in Lucknow but one proprietor of patent machinery of English manufacture for pressing castor oil. A set of plant consists of two machines, a seed crusher and an oil presser. The seeds are first broken in the former, and then winnowed by female hand labour with a *sirki súp*. The kernels are folded in canvas bags and placed in the oil pressing machine. The husks (*bhusi*) are used to burn in iron troughs beside the pressing machine to heat the seeds and expedite the fall of the oil. Sometimes these husks are sold to *bhurjis* who use this refuse to fire their ovens. There are two sets of machinery in the only mill of this kind in Lucknow. An estimate of the monthly outturn of one set of machinery follows :—

	Rs.	As.	P.
2 workmen at the crushing machine, ...	8	0	0
8 females to winnow at 1½ as. each per diem,	22	8	0
1 boy to fill canvas bags, ...	2	0	0
2 men at the oil pressing machine, ...	10	0	0
1 manager, ...	5	0	0
2 servants to purchase and store seed, ...	8	0	0
Fuel, ...	25	0	0
Canvas for bags, ...	10	0	0
Miscellaneous expenses, ...	2	0	0
Total Rs. ...	92	8	0

The quantity of seeds crushed in one day is as much as 15 maunds and the oil yielded is 5 maunds. The husks of the seeds are either burnt in the factory as fuel, in which case wood is not bought, or sold to *bhurjis* who use them to fire their *bhár*. The present price of castor seeds is 13 seers the rupee and the oil sells wholesale for Rs. 10-12 per maund. The potential profit is therefore Rs. 135-8 per month on one set of machinery.

The *bhurji* makes castor oil in a totally different way. He first crushes the seeds with a *musal* and separates the husks from the kernels of the seeds. He then boils the kernels, and when the water cools down, the oil floats on the surface and is skimmed off. The oil is sometimes separated from the water by straining in a cloth.

The third class is medicinal oils. These are made usually with a *kolhu*, but when required in small quantities, they are made by rubbing the drug of which the oil is needed between the hands.

Tezab bananewala, *vide* **Nyariya.**

Thani, *vide* **Arhat-galla.**

Thathera, *vide* **Zaruf birinji-farosh.**

Topiwala.—This is the maker of the ordinary skull cap, generally made of some light material, muslin or the like, and simply embroidered, which is worn by nearly every native of the East, Hindu or Mahommedan, either as a sole covering for the head or under the *dopattah* or *àmámmah*. But this trader generally combines with this the manufacture and sale, on a more or less extensive scale, as his means allow, of cloth, velvet, and silk *topis*.

There are three classes of *topiwálas*, some of whom have been taxed under Act II, 1878 : the manufacturer and wholesale vendor of the pairs of semicircular pieces of embroidered stuff not made up, which are required to make *topis* : the wholesale vendor of made up *topis* : and the retail vendor of made up *topis*. The retailer of *topis* not made up is not a case for taxation. Though all these three classes vend very expensive goods as opportunity offers, yet it will suffice to review the manufacture of the cheapest and least profitable kind of *topi* in order to give an insight into their business.

The cloth used for the ordinary *topi* is bought by the web, twenty yards for Rs. 7-8, and each yard suffices to cut out sixteen *topis*. Thus a web will give 320 *topis*. This is a universal rule. I have before me a pair of semicircular pieces of embroidery (not made up as a *topi* yet), which the manufacturer sells at Rs. 1-6-6 the score. That is the whole 320 will sell for Rs. 17-8. The cost of production is :—

	Rs.	As.	P.
Web of 20 yards, ...	7	8	0
Stamping patterns, per web, ...	0	4	0
Embroidery, (4 as. per score *topis*,)	4	0	0
Thread for do., (2 *polas* 8 *lachchas*,) at 6½ as. per tola, ...	1	5	0
Silk netting of the hearts of flowers in embroidery, @ 1 anna per 20 *topi*, including silk, ...	1	0	0
Dhobi, for washing and stiffening, at 4 as. per 100 *topis*, ...	0	12	10
Total Rs.	14	8	6

This leaves a profit of Rs. 2-15-6.

There is now the case of the vendors of made up *topis*. I have a sample case before me. These are sewn and bound ready for wear :—

	Rs.	As.	P.
Web of 20 yards, ...	7	8	0
Stamping pattern, per web, ...	0	4	0
Embroidery (4 as. per score,)	4	0	0
Binding (*paisa fí chár topi,*)	1	4	0
Thread, as above, ...	0	15	8
Sewing, (*pánch paisa ji korí*), ...	1	4	0
Washing and stiffening (*damrí topi pichha*), ...	1	4	0
Total Rs.	16	7	8

These *topis* sell wholesale at Re. 1-4 per score, or the 320 for Rs. 20. Profit of wholesale vend is Rs. 3-8-4.

These *topis* the retailer sells at from 5 paisa to 6 paisa each, as his customer may bargain. Say he sells all at 5 paisa each. His profit will be 5 Rs. on 320 *topis*.

The foregoing is an approximate estimate of the profits of trade in the cheapest style of *topi* put into the market in Lucknow itself. The illustration will only partially illustrate the trade of exporting manufacturers such as Ali Bakhsh of Faringhi Mahal.

U.

Uttusaz, *vide* **Gotakinarifarosh.**

W.

Waraqsaz.—Gold beater.—In Lucknow gold and silver leaf are made in large quantities for use in plating. The gold and silver are flattened and cut into small pieces of approximately equal weight so as to have 150 sheets to a *gaddi*. If the silver be not quite clear the *waraqsáz* places up to a tolah of it in a funnel-like copper vessel called *chonglá* and adds *shora*, salt, and *schága*. He heats this vessel in a fire, blowing up the fire with a blowpipe. This clears the silver of all foreign matter. The next process is to place each piece of metal on a *jhilli*, and then lay them one over the other and enclose them to the number of 150 in an envelope made of sheep skin. This *gaddi* as it is called is then pounded with a hammer. The pounding is done by laborers who receive wages at fixed rate. These wages are the only expenses of the silver beater except the annual renewing of stock of *jhillis*. The gold beater is at a further charge, viz:—wages paid to the *dáwálikash* who draws the gold into wire preparatory to cutting it into pieces.

There are three kinds of gold and silver leaf made, thick for *mulamma*, thinner for use with medicines, and still thinner for wrapping *pán*. The *jhilli* used to place between the pieces of metal is a thin leather membrane, fine as tissue paper, made from deer skin.

The following account shows the intrinsic value of each leaf and cost of production and profit to the gold-beater :—

	Mashas to the gaddi.	Wages of laborer.	Total cost.	Selling price.	Profit on a gaddi.
SILVER.		Rs. As. P.	Rs. As. P.	Rs. As. P. (per gaddi)	Rs. As. P
1st quality, ...	12 mashas,	0 4 0	1 6 0	2 4 0	0 14 0
2nd do. ...	9 ,,	0 6 0	1 3 6	2 0 0	0 12 6
GOLD.					
1st quality, ...	27 ,,	1 4 0	48 8 0	56 4 0	7 12 0
2nd do. ...	9 ,,	1 4 0	17 0 0	18 12 0	1 12 0

Y.

Yakkawala.—A *yakkawálá* who takes a *yakka* out of town will travel 10 kós per diem and will charge 12 as. per diem. Two persons will be accommodated in the vehicle. A *yakkawálá* considers it a loss to take passengers out of town ; hence it may be concluded that a *yakka* in town is pretty sure to bring the owners something over 12 as. per diem. The expenses per diem of keeping a *yakka* are $4\frac{1}{2}$ as., *i. e.*, $1\frac{1}{2}$ as. grass, $1\frac{1}{2}$ gram, $1\frac{1}{4}$ as. driver's wages. Thus one *yakka* will not give the owners Rs. 200 net annual earnings, unless he drives it himself. Then the earnings just pass Rs. 200. Otherwise the income will be about Rs. 165 per annum. Three *yakkas* will support Rs. 10 tax.

Z.

Zangarsaz.—The manufacture of *zangár* (acetate of copper) is carried on by the *sirkakash*, manufacturer of vinegar. He buys up copper filings and chips from copper-vessel-makers at about 13 as. the seer. He takes unrefined vinegar worth about Re. 1-12 per maund and distils it by means of a *dol jantar*. The process is this. A large vessel is placed on the fire and vinegar poured into it. A smaller earthen vessel with a very wide mouth is placed inside. It is empty. The large vessel is closed air-tight and the vinegar boiled. The *araq* as it is called, distilled vinegar, passes into the smaller vessel. This *araq* is used to pour on the copper shavings. About one seer of these is placed in a pot of (crockery of some kind) and enough *araq* to cover the shavings is poured on them and stirred up. The pot is closed by night and left open in the sun by day. The *araq* is poured off after 24 hours into another vessel and water added. It is left standing until the water evaporates and the *zangár* remains as a deposit. The copper shavings which were left in the pot when the *araq* was poured off are again used as before with more *araq* and some fresh shavings. Thus the process goes on for the whole round of the cold weather. The manufacture ceases in the hot weather and rains.

A maund of vinegar yields about 25 seers of *araq*, and this is about the proportion which is calculated to go to a seer of copper filings or shavings. Two maunds of wood (costing about 6 as. in the cold weather) are needed to boil up the maund of sirka. The outturn of *zangar* is $1\frac{1}{2}$ seers, and the average price is Rs. 3-4 per seer. Thus the expenditure is Rs. 2-15, the price realized Rs. 4-1, and the profit Re. 1-2.

A deposit of *zangár* is also made in one of the processes of the nyáriyá's business (*vide sub verb.*)

Zardoz.—The gold embroidery of Lucknow is much famed and commands a large market. This branch of industry took its rise under the native court and became so extended as to rival the products of Dehli. The demand was at first only for goods for the native market, saddle cloths, pillow covers, *masnad takiyas, pardahs,* elephant housings, bed covers, *pankahs, topis,* shoes, *angarkhas,* and other articles of clothing : but there is now a large European market for slippers, table covers and other goods. One of the special demands of the native market is for *patkas* to carry on Muharram processions.

The process of manufacture is simple but interesting. A piece of coarse canvas or *nainsukh,* or *márkin,* is sewn to the four sides of a frame, like a Berlin wool work frame, capable of adjustment by pegs fixed in holes in the sides. This frame is called *kárchob* and this base of inferior cloth is called *astar.* On the *astar* is tacked the velvet, silk, crape, sarcenet, or other ground on which the gold embroidery is to be worked out, and the pattern is traced on the material by a *masawwir* who uses a brush or pencil made of squirrel's hair and a white paste of *sandal* or *chandan.*

Flowers, etc., *bél* and *búta,* are worked with thread and then worked over with silk. The whole material is then weighed and the gold embroidery is begun. This embroidery is all done with *salma* and *sitára* which will be described hereafter. On completion the work is again weighed and the whole weight of the gold (or silver, for the silver embroidery is done in the same way) is ascertained by deducting the weight already noted. The gold embroiderers are paid at rates varying according to skill of the workman from 10 as. to Re. 1-8 per tolah of precious metal (*mál*) used. The master *zardoz* makes a total of whole cost and adds to it 4 as. per rupee (minimum rate ever charged) for profit.

Thus the following is the account of a pair of slippers now before me purchased for the Melbourne Exhibition :—

		Rs.	As.	P.
Astar, ...		0	2	0
Makhmal, ...		2	0	0
Cotton and silk thread, ...		0	8	0
Likhá (wages of painter,)		0	8	0
Wages of thread sewers 4 as. per die..., 2 laborers, 5 days,		2	8	0
Mál, (*salma-sitára* 8 tolahs at Rs. 2·2 per tolah, ...		17	0	0
Wages of embroiderers at 12 as. per tolah,... ...		6	0	0
	Total Rs.	28	10	0
	Adds 4 as. per Re. for profit,	7	2	0
	Selling price,	35	12	0

That the foregoing must be correct, I have no doubt as the greatest *zardos* of Lucknow has assured me that 4 as. per rupee is minimum rate of profit.

What are *salma* and *sitára* ?

The former term covers *salma* proper, *landani, dapka saima, aflait, gokhru ki bogali.* These are all made of fine gold or silver wire made to curl so as to make a spiral wire. The thread may be close or slightly free in its curl. In the former way are made up all *salma, dapka salma* and *aflait,* and in the latter way are made *landani* and *gokhru ki bogali.* All these again are made of round wire or flat wire. Of the former are made *salma* and *landani,* and of the latter *dapka salma, aflait,* and *gokhru ki bogali.* The wire used in manufacture of all is the wire which is delivered round by the *tárkash* or flattened by the *tárdabkaiya, (vide* **Gotawala**). These are given by gotawálas and zardozes to *workmen* who make up *salma,* &c., chiefly three-classes of goods, whether gold or silver (*sunahra* or *rupahla*) (1), 1 masha of metal to 8 yards, in which case the pay is 10 per tolah : (2) 1 masha to 4 yards, in which case the wages are Rs. 4 per 100 tolahs : (3) 1 masha to the yard, and in this case wages are Rs. 3 per 100 tolas. The gold *Salmá* which is of the first-class, one masha to the yard, sells for Rs. 2-4 per tolah.

Sálma is made up chiefly by Muhammadan women living in pardah and it is difficult to find one willing to show the machine with which it is made or explain the process of manufacture. It is said that there are two machines used, differing in construction. I have seen but one. On a bench some 15 inches high, resembling a four-legged stool, before which the operator sits, there is a long, fine needle of spring steel, the point of which is toward the worker. This needle has the point passed through a hole in a small wooden upright and the other end, which is covered with a knob of wax, is passed through a hole in another upright and fixed in the axle of a lathe. This lathe is turned by a wheel which is on the bench at the worker's right. To the left is a reel of gold or silver wire on a perpendicular pin. The end of the wire is brought to the steel needle and twisted round it until it gets a grip. Then the wheel is turned with the right hand. The needle revolves and draws the wire to itself. The wire is guided with the left hand and the revolution of the needle gives the wire a spiral set or curl as it draws it on and winds it on itself. The *sálma*, as the needle fills falls, over the point into the operator's lap.

The prices of *salma* etc. per tolah are at present :—

Gold.

Salma,	... Rs.	1-10	to	2-4	
Landani,	... ,,	1-12	,,	2-6	
Dupka salma,	,,	1-12	,,	2-6	
Aflait,	... ,,	1-12	,,	2-4	
Gokharú ki bogali		1-12	,,	2-4	

Silver.

Rs. 1-4 6 to Rs. 1-6-6

The price of *góltár* is now Rs. 1-12 per tolah for gold, and Rs. 1-8 per tolah for silver ; and of *dapkatár* Rs. 2-14 for gold, and Re. 1-9 for silver. It will thus be seen that the vendor of *salma* has a large margin of profit.

Included in *sitára* are *sitára, chamki, terha tár, kalabatún,* and *battan :* which are all made up in factories. *Battan* is exceedingly fine gold wire, selling at Rs. 1 13 to Rs. 2-2 per tolah. This is wound round silk thread to make *kalabatún* which sells at 12 as. to Rs. 2-4 according to the deftness and closeness of the winding, as it totally conceals the silk, or leaves it partly exposed. Silver *kalabatún* sells at 12 as. to Re. 1-8 per tolah. *Terhatár* is thick silver or gold wire flattened out and worked into scolloped tape. It sells at from Re. 1 to Rs. 2 per tolah if gold and for not more than Re. 1-6 if silver. *Sitáras* are small round pieces of silver or gold with a hole in the middle and are supposed to resemble stars. *Chamkis* are similar but thicker. They sell alike at from Rs. 1-12 to Re. 2-2 per tolah if gold, and for Rs. 1-4 per tolah if silver.

In all *sunahli salma-sitará* the gold is only enough to give color and the average proportion of gold to silver is 8 máshas in $62\frac{1}{2}$ tolahs. Gold is now $20\frac{1}{2}$ Rs. per tolah.

A calculation of the average case (worked out similarly to the case worked out under gotáwála) shows that the profit on manufacture of all goods coming under the head of *salma-sitára* is on the trade prices $7\frac{1}{2}$ per cent.

Zargar, *vide* Sunar.

Zaruf birinji-o-missi-farosh —The manufacture of brass and copper vessels is a most extensive business in Lucknow and affords employment to a very large number of moulders, casters, turners, copper-smiths, and polishers. With those who are merely labourers there is no concern here as they are not cases for taxation. Manufacturers are, however, generally cases for taxation and many of them manufacture both brass and copper vessels. I shall, however, for the sake of convenience give a separate note on each.

Brass vessels.—The manufacturer of brass vessels is called indifferently Thathera, Kasera, and Bhariya, though these words have obviously had different meanings originally. He manufactures either from new metal imported in sheets or from a compound of brass and other metals.

The chief articles made from brass imported in sheets are *tháli*s and *kháss-dáns*. A maund of this metal is 46 seers and costs Rs. 38. It is delivered to an artisan. He makes, let us suppose, only *khássdáns*. He will cut 34½ seers weight of these out of the sheets delivered to him and 11½ seers will remain of *katran* or cuttings. The artisan receives 8 as. per nawábi seer for his workmanship and all costs he incurs in manufacture. The employer sells these goods at Re. 1-8 per seer and the 11½ seers of cuttings he disposes of at 13 as. per nawábi seer to manufacturers of bell-metal and *bharat*. It will thus be seen that for an outlay of Rs. 53 the wholesale manufacturer realizes Rs. 59-14 or 13 per cent.

Copper vessels.—The name of these manufactured in Lucknow may be said to be Legion, but those most extensively made are *patélis*, *rkábis*, *lotas*, *pándáns*, *dégs* and *dégchis*. *Patelis* are to be found in every Muhammadan house and will serve as a sample case of all these vessels for they are all alike made of copper imported in sheets (*chádar*). A maund of copper is 46 seers and costs Rs. 43-2. Thirty-four and a half seers weight of *patelis* will be made from this weight of metal, and the artisan who makes these will receive Rs. 5-4 to cover wages of labour and all other expenses. The made up goods are sold by the manufacturing dealers at Re. 1-4 per seer. The 11½ seers which remain from the maund of metal delivered to the artisan consist of clippings and filings (*katran* and *chunas*, in proportion of 3 to 1). The former are kept for making up small articles such as ladles. The filings are sold to the *zangár-sáz* at Re 1 per nawábi seer. Thus on an outlay of Rs. 48-6 the wholesale manufacturer realize Rs. 53-11. His profits are a long way over 10½ per cent.

Mixed metals.—The first of these to notice is *phúl*, a mixture of copper with *ránga* in the proportion of 4 to 1. These are melted together and the objects made from the mixture are either *kút*, that is, beaten out with an iron hammer, or *bedahn*, that is, cast in a mould. Of the former the *ghuryál* or gong is an example, and of the latter the *batwa katóra*, *ábkhora*, etc. All articles made of *phúl* are sold at an uniform rate of Re. 1-8 per lambari seer. A nawábi maund of the copper used in this alloy costs Rs. 40-4; and 10 seers of *ránga* cost Rs. 14-6. The wages of the artisan are Rs. 15 per nawábi maund of metal. On an outlay of Rs. 73-6 the manufacturer realizes Rs. 82-10-6. Profit is over 12⅝ per cent. Another alloy is of old copper and zinc in equal parts. This is *kánsa*. Of this are made *lutiyas*, *batwis*, etc. It is not necessary to go into details, but in this case the profits are almost Rs. 14 per cent.

The foregoing cases illustrate the profits of those who buy metal in the local market and manufacture for the wholesale supply of retailers and exporters. If a manufacturer import metal he has of course somewhat larger profits. For instance, the manufacturer of copper goods who imports the metal from Calcutta makes up to Rs. 15 per cent. instead of the Rs. 10½ per cent. which he would make if he bought metal in Lucknow. The reason is that the rise in price between Calcutta and Lucknow (owing to profits made by importers, not to carriage merely) is in the proportion of about 19 to 22.

The next class to the manufacturers are retailers of brass and copper vessels. It is curious that the rule is that the retailer charges a larger profit on a small article than on a large one. The retailer will charge 2 as. per seer profit on a small brass *ábkhora* while he will charge 1½ as. per seer profit on a gigantic *deg*. *Patelis*, *batwis*, and *lotas* are the articles most widely in demand. On these the retailer charges a profit of one anna per seer.

There is a large class of dealers called beoparis, who buy up goods whole-sale from manufacturers both in Lucknow and elsewhere and supply these goods on trust to retailing shop-keepers to sell at a price not less than a mini-mum fixed by a beopari. In this case the retail vendors sell at the lowest pos-sible price they can afford so as to realize for themselves at least ½ anna per rupee over the price which they have to give to the beopari. If the goods are not sold within a month after date of delivery, the beopari charges interest at 1 per cent. per mensem.

Copper vessels are not imported into Lucknow but are very extensively exported. Brass vessels are imported, chiefly specialities. The articles imported are *istris* and *kanchani tháhs* from Calcutta; *lotas*, *katoras* and *batwis* from Mirzapur; *parát*, *toknas*, *handas*, *taulis*, and *gagras* from Farrukhabad; *lotas*, *pándáns*, *tháhs* and *katoras* from Cawnpore; *lotas* and other goods from Maharaj-ganj and Newalganj.

Zaruf gili-farosh, *vide* Kumhar.

Zerpaiwala, *vide* Jutawala.

GLOSSARY

OF

INDIAN TERMS OCCURRING IN PART III.

A.

Abí, a colour—pale blue.

A'bkár, distiller of country spirits.

A'bkhora, a drinking vessel.

Achár, pickles.

Achárwálá, maker or vendor of pickles, preserves, &c.

Adad, a unit, one of anything : *fi-adad*, apiece.

Addá, stand where porters, carriers, &c., congregate.

Addá-gári, livery stables, carriage-stand.

Addedár, owner of a dolí-stand.

Addhí, half a damrí.

Addhí, half a web of cloth.

Addí, the sides of the uppers of shoes.

Adrak, ginger.

Afiún-farosh, opium-vendor.

Aflait, a preparation of gold and silver wire used in *zardozí*.

Agárí, the best threads of a cocoon of silk.

Agraí, a brown-leather colour, shade of cocoanut fibre.

Agraí-bádámí, a lighter shade of do.

Agraí-khashkhashí, shade of dried poppyheads.

Agraí-mahúá, a brownish yellow or yellowish brown.

Ahír, a caste devoted to cow-keeping and milk vending.

A'ína, looking-glass, mirror.

A'inak, eye-glass, spectacles.

A'inaksáz, optician, manufacturer of eye-glasses.

A'ínasáz, manufacturer of looking-glasses.

Ainthá, an instrument used in twisting strands of rope.

A'l, a dye-stuff extracted from a tree (Morinda citrifolia).

Algání, a strand of rope stretched in a rope-walk to be twisted into rope.

Almás, diamonds.

Almás-tarásh, diamond-cutter, lapidary.

Alsí, flax, linseed,

Amba-haldí, a plant (Curcuma zedoaria) used in dyeing It is *jadwár* (v. p. 21.)

Ammámah, pagrí as worn by Muhammadans.

Amrúd, guava.

Anánás, pine-apple.

Anár, pomegranate; mudshell used in making fire works.

Angarkhá, a long calico frock-coat.

Angiya, a tight-fitting bodice worn by Indian women to support the breasts. It is also called *cholí*.

Angúrí-rang, pale green (of whitened pán.)

Angúthí, ring for finger or toe.

Anjali, a seer of grain received by the village carpenter from each cultivator's *khalíyán*.

Ankurá, a lever-like appliance for keeping a diamond to the lapidary's lathe.

Antar, a line, a row.

A'nwalá, the fruit of the *Phyllanthus emblica*.

Anwat, a ring with bells attached worn on the great toe.

A'rad, flour.

A'rad-farosh, flour vendor.

A'ráish, artificial flowers and other things made of paper, tinsel, &c.

A'ráishwálá, maker of the foregoing.

A'rámpaí, a kind of shoe worn by begams.

Araq, essence of flowers and fruits.

Araq-kash, extractor of foregoing.

Argarah, livery stable.

Arhar, a species of pulse (Cytisus cajan.)

A'rhat, commission agency.

A'rhat-galla, grain-broker.

Arhatiyá, broker, commission agent.

Arwalí, a kind of paper resembling parchment.

Asámí, a tenant; (*technically*) a debtor to one who lends augáhí and rozáhí.

A s ás, household furniture.

A shtánk, eight-sided, octagonal.

A smáni, sky-blue.

Astar, lining, plaster: also (*technically*.) the cheap fabric laid under velvet to give it strength in gold embroidery.

A'tá, flour.

A'tá-farosh, flour vendor.

A'tashbáz, firework-maker.

Athárahwáṇ, of shoes, no 18, or 'eighteens,' i. e., eighteen finger breadths long.

Athiyá, do. No 8. or ' eights'.

Athwás, (of precious stones) cut with eight corners (as viewed from above.)

Atlas, satin.

Attár, drug-vendor, but properly a perfumer.

Augáhi, a system of money lending.

Augí, embroidered front of the uppers or too-piece of a shoe.

B.

Babúl, a tree,—the Mimosa Arabica.

Bachakána, of, or for, children; children's size (of clothing).

Bádám, an almond.

Bádámcha, almond-shaped. (*technically*) a shape in which precious stones are cut for pendants and earrings.

Bádámí, almond-coloured.

Bádlá, flattened gold or silver wire or thread, used in weaving lace.

Bahaṇgí, a pole with baskets at each end carried slung over the shoulder.

Bahar, a peculiar flaw in a pearl.

Bahí, an account book.

Baijaní, purple.

Bálgír, an attendant on horses.

Bálisht, a span.

Ballí, a long, thick pole, usually the stem of a sákhú tree from which the branches have been lopped off, used in scaffolding, &c.

Ballíwálá, a vendor and letter-out of poles.

Bam, bass in music.

Bambú, the pipe stem with which a Hindú smokes Chándú, as opposed to the nigálí, which Muhammadans use.

Bán, coarse twine made of múnj.

Bának, the raw silk of Lower Bengal.

Báná, the woof in weaving.

Bandí a skein (of silk.)

Bandish, form in which precious stones are cut.

Bán-farosh, a vendor of twine and rope.

Baṇglá, a variety of pán imported from Bengál, whence the name.

Bansáz, owner of a rope-walk, maker of twine and rope.

Báṇsphoṛ, a worker in bambú ; *literally*, bambú splitter.

Bánsrí, a flute, or fife ; a shepherd's pipe.

Báṇswálá, a dealer in bambus.

Bagam, sappan wood.

Bárahwáṇ, size of shoes, No. 12, 'twelves', being twelve finger breadths in length.

Baraí, cultivator of pán.

Baran, the quality or 'water' of a diamond as determind by its colour.

Bardásht, purveying ; *bardásht uṭhánewálá*, a person who supplies food, &c, by contract daily, or to order, to the houses of Nawábs and others.

Baṛer. a rafter, or beam of a house.

Baṛhaí, a carpenter.

Baṛhal, jack fruit.

Barí, a substance used as a polishing medium, in grinding lenses, &c.

Bárí, a wattled enclosure in which pán is cultivated.

Bárík, fine ; *bárík bán*, fine twine.

Barinj, rice.

Báṛiya, knife-grinder, razor setter.

Barmá, a gimlet worked with a bow.

Barmí, the axle of a lathe.

Barranákas, the rejected parings of betel nut.

Basantí, pale yellow, lemon colour.

Baṭṭá, a stone used for crushing spices.

Batáshá, a kind of sweetmeat.

Batáshewálá, a maker of the foregoing.

Baṭṭá, fore charge of interest on credit sales and discount received for cash payments.

Baṭṭan. a preparation of gold and silver lace used in zardozí (v. p. 196.)

Baṭṭe-khátá, account of battá. (q. v.)

Battísáz, chandler.

Batwá, a metal pot.

Bázár, a market.

Bázárgasht, a wanderer in a bázár.

Bazzáz, a cloth merchant, draper, hosier, &c.

Bedáha, cast in a mould(of vessels made of mixed metal) as opposed to kúṭ (beaten out.)

Bedbáf, a cane-worker, a weaver of cane work.

Begamí, a variety of pán.

Begrí, a lapidary.

Behná, a cotton-vendor.

Bel, a running pattern in embroidery ; *bel búta*, flowers and stripes worked on cloth.

Bel, a fruit (Aegle marmalos.)

Belá, two threads of the silk warp of gold lace, by which the width is reckoned by gotáwálás.

Berá, a raft, logs of timber or bambus chained together and floated down a river.

Berábandi, the system of floating timber and bambús in chained rafts.

Besan, gram flour.

Bhadsár, grain storing (corrupted for *bhandsál*)

Bhang, (Cannabis sativus.) the hemp plant.

Bhang-farosh, a vendor of bhang,

Bhapká, a still.

Bhár, Bhárá, a grain parcher's oven or kiln.

Bharat, an alloy or amalgam of copper and lead.

Bhariya, a metal-caster, a brazier, foundryman, &c.

Bhanrsár, vide bhadsár.

Bhartú, solid (of bambús and reeds.)

Bhattá, a furnace, retort, kiln.

Bhít, a wattled enclosure for growing pan.

Bhurjí, a grain-parcher.

Bhúsá, chaff, chopped straw.

Bhúsáwálá, dealer in do.

Bhúsí, husk of pulse.

Bhúsíwálá, dealer in do.

Bichhauná, a drugget.

Bichhiyá, or *bichhúí*, a toe-ring worn by women.

Bidar, damascene-work.

Bidarsíz, damascene-worker.

Bidhiyá, a perforator of precious stones.

Bíghá, a land-measure, ⅝ of an acre, if of standard measure.

Bihí, quince.

Bihishtí, water-carrier.

Bilkí, (of a diamond in the rough) almond shaped.

Bín, a stringed musical instrument.

Bírá, pán made up for eating.

Bisátí, a vendor of miscellaneous dry goods, needles, thread, glass, and—what not.

Biskut, Anglice, biscuit.

Biskutwálá, a biscuit-baker.

Biyáj, interest on money.

Bod, pile of a carpet.

Borah, a sack, in the case of grain usually holding 2½ maunds.

Buqcha, head load.

Burinj, brass.

Bút, Anglice, boot.

Bútá, flowers worked on cloth.

Bútsáz, bootmaker.

Buz, a kid or goat.

Buz-qassáb, goat-butcher

C.

Chádar, a sheet of any fabric worn as a shawl or wrapper, a sheet of metal.

Chakkí, a mill stone.

Chhallá, thick ring for finger.

Chhallí, thin ring for finger.

Chamkí, a spangle.

Champaí, a golden yellow colour.

Chalna, a sieve.

Chaná, gram.

Chándí, silver.

Chandiyá, country iron, used to make griddles, &c.

Chándní, a cover, wrapper, floor cloth of coarse calico.

Chandú, a preparation of opium.

Chandúwálá, a vendor of do, on whose premises it is usually smoked.

Changel, a flower pot, (properly *changer*.)

Changerdán, a flower pot.

Chánwal, rice.

Chánwalwálá, rice-dealer.

Cháo, a kind of bambu.

Chaprá, shellac.

Charbí, fat, grease, tallow.

Charkhá, a spinning wheel.

Charkhazan, a cotton spinner (usually a female.)

Charkhí, a spinning wheel.

Charsa, leather, hide.

Charsa-farosh, hide-dealer.

Charhauwán, a kind of shoe.

Chaudahwán, (of shoes) no 14, 'fourteens,' *i. e.*, fourteen finger breadths in length.

Chaudhrí, a headman.

Chaugazí, a boat of four yards in width.

Chauthaíyá, a boat of certain dimensions drawing little water.

Chhippar, a thatch covering.

Chhaparband, a thatcher.

Chhápekhána, a printing-press.

Chhar, a pole, flagstaff.

Chhárí, earthen pan used to hold ashes.

Chhatrí, an umbrella, a frame tied to a bamboo for a pigeon-perch.

Chheni, a short iron chisel or wedge used in opening boxes & cutting iron.

Chhípí, a calico printer, and maker of dies for calico printing.

Chikárá, a musical instrument.

Chittá, a slip on which an account is kept.

Chitáí, matting, a pattern in gold & silver work.

Chiterah, an engraver on metal.

Chikwá, a butcher, fell-monger.

Chikní ḍalí, betel nut.

Chikanwálá, a dealer in embroidered work *(Chikan.)* done on muslin with needle and thread.

Chhílan, scrapings of skins and hides, and of metal vessels during manufacture.

Chíṭá, a ball of *madak*.

Chhiṭánk, a chittak, one sixteenth of a seer; *literally*, six *tanks*.

Chiúṛá, parched rice.

Chob, wood, a mace.

Choba, a peculiar flaw in a pearl giving it a wooden appearance.

Chokar, bran.

Chokídár, a watchman.

Chonglá, a copper funnel used by gold beaters to refine metal before beating it out.

Chuchí, a *(korí)* weaver's bobbin.

Chuhárah, dates.

Chúna Kánp-farosh, a vendor of lime, a lime-burner.

Chúnas, clippings and filings of copper.

Chúnní, the husks of pulse which fall from the dal when the grain is crushed on a *dharetí*.

Chúrí, a bangle for the wrist, made of glass or lac.

Churihár, a maker or vendor of bangles.

Chuṭkí, gota crimped for fancy trimmings.

D.

Dáb, the heaviest and richest form of gold lace, similar to that used for officers' uniforms.

Daftarí, a bookbinder, a stationer.

Dal, thickness, shell of a bambu.

Dál, split pulse.

Dál-farosh, vendor of foregoing.

Dálhard, (v. p. 21.)

Dallál, broker, dragoman, commission agent, guide.

Damrí, a coin, value 20 cowries.

Dána, a bead, a grain.

Dána-postah, poppy-seeds.

Dánd, the handle of a fiddle.

Dandá, bar iron.

Dándiyá, a weighman.

Dánk, silver foil.

Danwás, a kind of bambu.

Dapka Salma, salma (q. v.) made of flattened wire.

Daṛká tár, flattened gold or silver wire or thread.

Darí, a cotton carpet or rug.

Darí-báf, a weaver of the foregoing.

Daryáí, a silk fabric used for bindings and facings.

Daryáí-báf, a weaver of the foregoing.

Darzí, a tailor.

Dasáwar, an exporter.

Dasmariya, the largest size of river-boat, built with ten cross planks.

Dastah, a stick on which a silk-reeler holds his reel when winding off the silk.

Dastárband, a person who folds pagrís on a dummy.

Dastarkhwán, a table cloth.

Dast-farosh, dealer in second-hand goods, hawker.

Dawálikish, a wire drawer employed by gold beaters.

Dáwát, the bowl of a pipe.

Deg, a metal pot, or caldron.

Degcha, a smaller do.

Degwálá, a lender out of pots.

Derhkhamí, (of the joint of a pipe stem) shaped like an S.

Deorhá, 50 per cent.

Desáwarí, a variety of pan.

Desí, made, produced, or grown in the plains of India, as opposed to English, foreign, or hill produce.

Dháliyá, a metal caster, a pewterer.

Dhálnewálá, do. do.

Dhání, a shade of green, the colour of growing rice.

Dhánuk, crimped gota.

Dharetí, prop. *Daletí*, a mill stone used to break pulse.

Dharkár, (prop. *dhirkár*) a worker in bambu.

Dharkí, a bobbin.

Dhaunkaní, a blacksmith's bellows.

Dhelá, a coin equal to 80 cowries in value.

Dhima, the ball of twine used by a chhapparband in making chiks.

Dhiriya, an instrument used to twist twine, wool, and the like.

Dhobí, washerman, laundryman.

Dhoídár, carrier.

Dhotar, a kind of coarse cloth.

Dhotí, a coarse cloth worn by men round the loins and also as a sole garment by korí women.

Dhowan Karáhí, the syrup left in a confectioner's pán and washed out and laid by to make vinegar.

Dhunailá, a clouded crystal used in making lenses for spectacles.

Dhuniyá, cotton-carder.

Díwár, sides of uppers of shoes.

Distah, the staff on which a silk-winder places his reel when winding off silk.

Dofaslí, (of fields) yielding two crops.

Dol, a bucket made of leather or iron.

Doljantar, a contrivance used for distilling vinegar in the manufacture of acetate of copper.

Dopalká, involving two processes (of the manufacture of counterfeit precious stones.)

Dopattah, a cloth tied round the head by men or used as a wrapper by women.

Dor-kankawwewálá, a vendor of kites and kite-cord.

Do-rukhí, (of betel nuts) cut with two faces.

Doshálá, a double shawl.

Dosútí, a cotten fabric woven in two colours.

Dosútí-báf, a weaver of the foregoing.

Dúdhiyá afíún, opium not passed through the Government godowns, so called because it is more juicy (milky) than the standard article.

Dúdhiyá ábí níl, a light blue, milk and water colour.

Dúdh madár, sap or juice of *Asclepias gigantea*, used in the manufacture of catgut.

Dúdhwálá, dairyman.

Dulaí, a sheet or wrapper made of two breadths of stuff.

Dungiya, the ordinary country boat, a skiff made of the hollowed trunk of a tree.

E.

Ek-bárá, once distilled.

Erí, padded heel of a shoe.

F.

Fákhta, grey, dove colour.

Fánús, a glass shade to keep a candle alight in the wind, also a lantern.

Farashí, a large huqqa, smoked with a snake-like stem.

Fard, a single sheet of cloth, a unit of anything.

Faqír, a beggar.

Fauládí, of steel: *fauládí qalam*, an engraver's pencil, an etching or graving tool.

Fí, is the Arabic preposition 'in,' but it is used idiomatically in Urdu like *per* in English—*v. g., paisa fí rupiya*, one paisa per rupee, and also like 'a,' as in *fí adad*, or *fí fard*, a piece.

Fihrist radífwár, the index to a ledger.

Fíroza, a turquoise,

Fírozaí, turquoise blue.

G.

Gadariyá, name of a caste devoted to sheep-farming.

Gaddí, a retail liquor-shop.

Gaddí, a bale of goods, or of cotton.

Gaddídár, a retailer of liquors.

Gadhewálá, a donkey-owner who is a carrier.

Gadra táwa, a kind of iron used to make griddles for native use.

Gagrá, a large brass pot.

Gahak, mortgage, pawn.

Galledár, a drover, sheep and goat dealer.

Gamla, an earthen pot, flower pot.

Gandá, four units.

Gandhak, sulphur.

Gandhí, a perfumer.

Gadedár, (of a pipe stem) wound with silk in a particular style.

Ganj, a market, generally a private property.

Gánjha, hemp-plant (Cannabis sativa).

Gánth, mortgage, pledge, (prop. a bundle, because of the system of pawn-broking by *chittas* (vide mahájan.)

Gáo-qassáh, beef-butcher.

Garaj, a flaw of a peculiar kind in pearls.

Gargará, a wooden huqqa-stem.

Gargarewálá, a maker of the foregoing.

Gárhá, a coarse kind of cloth, used to sew up to make ceiling cloths, floor cloths, chándnís, &c.

Gárí, a cart.

Gáríwán, a cart-driver.

Garm, warm, used of plating (*mulamma*) by overlaying, opposed to *thandá mulamma*, electro-plating.

Gáyál kháta, the heading under which a merchant or banker writes off losses.

Gaz, a yard. The standard Indian gaz is the iláhí gaz of the Emperor Akbar, 33 inches.

Gehuán, a wheat grass yielding an oilseed.

Gendá, a marigold.

Gendaí, marigold colour.

Gerú, red ochre,

Ghair-kamíladár, of retail butchers as opposed to slaughterman.

Ghalla-farosh, grain-vendor.

Ghán, the quanity of oilseeds which are thrown into an oil mill at one time.

Gharâ, an earthen water-pot.

Gharísár, a watchmaker.

Ghariyá, a crucible.

Ghariyál, a gong of bell-metal.

Ghellí, a kind of shoe.

Ghí, clarified butter.

Ghíwálá, a dealer in the foregoing.

Ghoriya, a clasp, which holds a diamond brought to the lathe.

Ghosi, a caste devoted to dairy-keeping and buffalo-breeding.

Ghoyían, an esculent root (Arum colocasia).

Ghuná, weevil-eaten, used of bambus and grain.

Ghúngí, a blind (*lit.* dumb) cocoanut, that is, without kernel or milk, used for making huqqas.

Ghúra, the refuse taken from a caldron in distilling.

Gilásí, (of cotton ropes made by newár-báfs) made partly of old and partly of new thread, as opposed to *khális*.

Gilauri, pán prepared to be eaten.

Gilkhan-afroz, a grain parcher.

Girda, round (of a lahsaniya, cat's eye).

Girmit, a wire used to clean the stem of a chándú pipe.

Girw, pawn, pledge, mortgage.

Girwí, do., do.

Gojaí, mixed crop of wheat and barley.

Goh, an iguana.

Gokhrú, vide Zardoz, p. 197.

Gokhrú kí bogalí, vide zardoz, p. 197.

Gola, a pole classed with *ballís.*

Gola, a ball of meat (cooked and sold by a kabáb-farosh)

Golí, a ball or pill.

Gol tár, round gold or silver wire or thread as opposed to *dapká,* flattened.

Gomáshta, a head accountant or shopman.

Gon, a sack holding 3 nawábí maunds of salt.

Gorach, the bridge for the strings of a fiddle.

Goshwára, a form in which diamonds, &c., are cut for pendants and earrings.

Goshwárá, an abstract of an account showing the net result of a series of transactions.

Gotá, gold or silver lace.

Gotá-báf, a weaver of the foregoing.

Gotakinarí-farosh, a vendor of the same.

Guchchí, a string or skein of beads.

Gúdar, rags and other tatters and fragments and old goods in general.

Gudarí bázár, a bazár tenanted by ragmen.

Gudariya, a ragman.

Gujarí, a wrist ornament, bracelet, made of base metal

Guláb, a rose, rose-water.

Gulábí, rose-colour.

Guláb-pásh, a bottle or casket used for sprinkling rose water.

Gulbadan, a kind of silk fabric.

Gul-farosh, a rose-dealer who supplies perfumers.

Gulnár, pomegranate, a shade of scarlet.

Gulú, the neck of a fiddle.

Gunya, a tower of a boat.

Gur, molasses, unrefined sugar.

Gur-farosh, a vendor of the foregoing.

Gurwálá, a dealer in do.

H.

Hakím, a native medical practitioner.

Hakkák, a lapidary, seal-engraver.

Haldí, turmeric.

Hallálí, (of hides) taken from slaughtered animals, as opposed to *murdárí,* stripped from animals that have died.

Halwáí, a confectioner.

Handá, a small metal pot, generally of brass.

Hándí, a small earthen pot.

Hansalí, a necklace.

Hansráj, a variety of rice.

Haqq, a due or right—*haqq dallálí,* a broker's dues; *haqq árhat* commission.

Hár, a nut (myrobalan.)

Hár dená, the process of rubbing in a paste of starch & boiled rice into the strands of kite-cord.

Hársingár, the weeping nyctanthes.

Hátah, a courtyard, a cattle-yard; any enclosure.

Háth, a hand, a cubit length.

Hathá, a weaver's batten.

Hathaurí, a hammer.

Háthí-chingár, the aloe plant.

Hauz, a tank, a vat.

Hírá, a diamond.

Hisáb, an account; *hisáb-fahmí,* a running account.

Huchkí, a reel for kite-cord.

Hundí, a bill of exchange, draft.

Hundiáwan, the heading of account in a banker's book under which are entered receipts & payments on bills of exchange : commission on bills of change.

Huqqa, a smoking pipe.

Huqqewálá, a maker of pipes.

I.

Igárahwán, of shoes, No. 11, 'elevens' i. e., eleven finger breadths in length.

Iláichí, cardamum.

Iláqeband, a maker of petticoat strings & the like.

Imlí, a tamarind tree.

Insí, stuff mixed with syrup of opium in making it up for smoking.

Íntwálá, a brick-dealer, brick-burner.

Isfanjiá, the sponger at a printing-press.

Isrár, a musical instrument played with a bow.

Istiqmálí, husked rice.

Istrí, a smoothing-iron.

Itr, a perfumed oil.

Itrdán, a casket for holding scent bottles.

Itr-farosh, a vendor of perfumes.

J.

Jabdí, a cotton fabric.

Jai-kháta, a book in which a trader notes his daily profits.

Jajmán, a client, a customer; properly, an adherent or 'parishioner' of a Hindu priest.

Jáldár, filagree & other European patterns in gold.

Jalebí, a sweetmeat, resembling an involuted piece of soft sugar stick.

Jalebídár, curled (of a pipe-stem-joint.)

Jálídár, open-woven cane work.

Jama, the debit side of an account.

Jáman, a tree and its fruit (a plum) the bark is used in dyeing.

Jamawár a weft shawl or wrapper of pashm.

Jámdání, a fabric into which flowers are woven.

Jánamáz, a praying carpet.

Jántá, a large millstone worked by two persons.

Janta, a machine, a windlass used in wire-drawing.

Jantra, same as preceding.

Jaráo, gold or silver work involving setting ; stone-setting in gold or silver.

Jarhan, a winter rice.

Jariyá, a setter of precious stones.

Jasta, zinc.

Jású, the ingredients mixed with opium-syrup to make *madak*.

Ját, the pestle of an oil-mill.

Jauharí, a dealer in precious stones.

Jawáhirát kháta, account of sales and purchases of precious stones.

Jázam. a cloth used as a carpet-cover.

Jhandí, a flag, a flagstaff.

Jhánjh, cymbals.

Jhár, a chandelier, a lustre.

Jhárí, front of shoes embroidered in imitation of silver lace.

Jhillí, gold beater's leaf.

Jilasán, a disc, used on a lathe, to polish precious stones.

Jilasáz, polisher of precious metals and stones.

Jildband, book-binder.

Joga, foreign matter extracted from opium when preparing the syrup to make chandú, madak, &c.

Joláhá, a weaver.

Jorá sirkí, a double mat of reed grass used to cover laden carts.

Júá, a yoke.

Juriya, a kori weaver.

Jútá-farosh, shoe-vendor.

Juz, one sheet of a book, eight pages.

K.

Kabáb-farosh, a vendor of cooked balls of meat and cutlets.

Kabariyá, a caste devoted chiefly to market gardening and tobacco growing and vending.

Kachahrí, public offices.

Kachár, the worst or roughest and cheapest thread in a cocoon of silk.

Kacherá, a maker of glass chúrís, a worker in glass.

Kaddú, a pumpkin.

Kafsh, a shoe worn by Maulavis.

Kafshdoz, a maker of the foregoing.

Káhí, green inclining to blue.

Káhú, seed of a vegetable (Lactuca sativa) used to extract a medicinal oil.

Kaker, a variety of pán leaf.

Kakraundá, a tree (probably that yielding the berry called karaundá) from the wood of which are made the bobbins (tílis) used by shawl-weavers.

Kakrezá, a colour approaching purple.

Kalábatún, gold or silver thread used by *zardozes*.

Kalaunjí, a small pyramidal seed used as a spice and as a medicine ; also tied round the necks of women to induce easy childbirth.

Kálbhut, an instrument used to twist together the strands of a rope.

Kalkatiya, a variety of tobacco and of pán.

Kalwár, name of a caste generally employed in distilling and liquor-traffic, but frequently grain dealers and money lenders.

Kamání, a bow used to move a gimlet or auger.

Kamar, the third class of pearl.

Kambal, a blanket.

Kambal-farosh, a blanket dealer, wool-monger.

Kámdání, embroidery with gold and silver thread on crape or muslin.

Kamílá, a dye prepared from a tree (Rottlera tinctoria.)

Kamílá, a slaughterman.

Kamíládár, a butcher who employs slaughtermen, i. e., wholesale butcher or master-slaughterman.

Kamlí, a small blanket.

Kamrang, (of colours) light or faint shade.

Kanchaní-thálí, a brass vessel made in Calcutta.

Kandá, cowdung cakes, used as fuel.

Kandá, the third rate part of rice (*vide* cháwalwálá p. 80.)

Kundelowá, a variety of bambu.

Kandewálá, a dealer in *kandá* (q. v.)

Kandila, a standard bar of pure silver, weight 62½ tolah, length one cubit.

Kandilasáz, an artisan who draws a kandilá into wire and who applies the gold to the silver kandilá to make *sunahra tár*.

Kanghí-sáz, a comb maker.

Kanjaí, a deep lilac colour.

Kanjar, a caste which deals in jungle-produce.

Káns, a fibrous grass (Saccharum spontaneum.)

Kanwal, an ornamented candle shade of glass, silk, or talc.

Kaprá, cloth fabrics in general.

Kapúrí, a variety of pán.

Karáhí a large metal pan, used in boiling sugar-cane-juice, making preserves, sweetmeats, and cooking in general, and in processes of calico printing and soap boiling.

Karáhíwálá, an owner of such pans who lets them out on hire.

Karánchí, a tumbril, a cart used to convey iron or timber.

Karchhá, a ladle.

Kárchob, embroidery on a frame; an embroiderer:

Kárkhána, a manufactory; a factory; a workshop.

Kárkhánadár, an employer of labour at a factory; a master-tradesman.

Kasarát, miscellaneous profits of trade.

Kaserah, a brazier and pewterer.

Kasgar, a class of potter employed in making suráhís, chillams &c.,

Kashídání, (of tobacco) for smoking—to be smoked.

Kashíd-dár, a distiller, still-owner.

Kasís, sulphate of iron:

Kásní, a faint purple.

Kataiyá, a cutter of precious stones received in the mass, who makes smaller pieces of the lump for delivery to a lapidary.

Kátar, the seat on which a telí sits to drive the bullock turning an oil-mill.

Katarní, scissors.

Kathá, catechu.

Kathrah, a wooden kneading trough.

Katorá, a brass plate or dish.

Katran, clippings, cuttings.

Keorá, an odoriferous plant (Pandanus odoratissimus.)

Khaiyát, a tailor.

Khajúr, wild date tree.

Kháki, dry earth colour.

Kháki fákhta, an earthy grey.

Kháki gahrá, deep shade of kháki.

Kháki dúdhiyá, a faint brownish-grey.

Khál, a skin; the bellows used by a qalaígar (tinman.)

Khalí, the refuse seeds left when oil has been extracted in an oilmill, used as cattle fodder.

Khalí, a framework reel used in silk winding.

Khális, (of cotton-thread ropes) made wholly of new thread.

Khaliyán, a threshing-floor, a barn.

Khamdár, curved or bent.

Khamír, barm, leaven.

Khamíra, (of tobacco and bread) raised with barm, leavened.　　　[masses from kilns.]

Khangar, semi-vitrified bricks extracted in confused

Khar, or *Khará*, in the rough (of precious stones other than diamonds.)

Khará, an ornament for the wrist or ankle.

Khará, of good quality, pure.

Khárá, a basket of open texture used to carry bhúsá and cowdung cakes.

Kharach, expense. *Kharch-khátá*, account of business expenses.

Kharádí, a turner. *Kharádí-dánt*, an ivory-worker.

Khariyá mattí, chalk.

Khárwa, a coarse red cotton fabric.

Khássdán, a metal casket for keeping pán.

Khatái, vegetable acid, mineral acid, dried mango-stones and tamarind pods used in cooking.

Khatík, a caste devoted to fowl-breeding.

Khímadoz, tent-maker, felt-manufacturer.

Kherkí, emerald or ruby less than one ratí in weight, and bored to make a bead.

Khet, a field: a place yielding any precious stone in abundance: a separate area within which money is lent by augáhí, and for which a separate account is kept. (v. p. 144.)

Khíl, parched grain, inflated so as to appear like froth.

Khilat-poshák, wedding garments let out for the occasion.

Khoá, inspissated milk.

Khogírdoz, saddler (ál'orientale.)

Khoyá, the chrysalis of the silk worm used in native medicine as an aphrodisiac and as a reinvigorator.

Khúbrang, (of colour), bright, deep, brilliant.

Khudrang, (of leather, &c.) of natural colour, un-dyed.

Khudrú, of wild growth.

Khurda-farosh, a retailer, a petty dealer.

Khurdaní, (of tobacco) to be eaten.

Khurí, the heel of a shoe or boot.

Khurjá, a variety of indigo.

Khurpí, a scraper, used in leather dressing.

Khushbú-sáz, a perfumer.

Khwáncha farosh, a trayman, a wandering vendor of sweetmeats who carries them about on a tray.

Kíl, a nail, an iron spike.

Kímukht, shagreen—leather made from horse, mule, and donkey skins.

Kímukht-sáz, a maker of shagreen.

Kíráná, spices, &c.

Kiráya-khwáh, a letter out of goods on hire.

Kirkin, shagreen (vide *kímukht*.) This word seems to be a corruption of *kharkin*, as it is made from donkey-skins.

Kirkin-sáz, a maker of *kirkin*.

Kirmdánd, cochineal.

Kishmish, raisins.

Kishtí, a boat, a shuttle.

Kishtíwálá, a boat owner.

Kitáb-farosh, a bookseller.

Kochkí, a shade of purple.

Koelá, charcoal.

Kokaí, a deep purple.

Kolhú, an oil-mill.

Korághát, in the rough state (of diamonds.)

Korí, a caste devoted to weaving.

Kos, a measure of distance, varying with locality: but generally about two miles.

Kothícháh, thirty rows of curved bricks designed for well construction.

Kuchará, thin tips of sirkí used to make brooms.

Kuhnídár, jointed like the elbow.

Kumhár, a potter.

Kundan, refined and soft gold used in setting.

Kundan-sáz, a maker of *kundan*.

Kuntiyán, pieces of chopped sugar stick.

Kuppá, a leather jar or bottle.

Kurand, corundum stone.

Kurtá, a short coat worn by men.

Kurtí, do. worn by women.

Kusum, safflower, bastard saffron.

Kút, valuation.

Kút, (of metal alloy and vessels made of alloy) beaten out, welded with a hammer.

Kutbí, a *ghát* of diamond (v. p. 119.)

L.

Lachchhá, a skein of thread, 20 go to a pola, or packet.

Lachchhí, a standard length of gold or silver thread (*bádla*) ready for weaving lace.

Lachkí, a kind of gold or silver lace trimming.

Laddú, a sweetmeat, ball-shaped, made of sugar, cocoanut and cream.

Lagán, rent; (*technically,*) the money falling due within a khet, or area on which money is lent by augáhí (v. p. 114.)

Lagan, a copper kneading trough.

Lahar, a peculiar flaw in a pearl.

Láhí, an oilseed (Eruca sativa.)

Lahngá, a petticoat.

Lahsaniyá, a precious stone, cat's eyes.

Laí, rice parched with sugar.

Lákh, lac.

Lakherá, a worker in lákh.

Lakríhárá, a dealer in firewood.

Lakríwálá, a vendor of building timber; timber-merchant.

Lal, a ruby.

Lál, red colour.

Lálrí, an inferior ruby.

Lambardár, a headman of a village; headman of a corporate body of dealers (vide *Arhat-ghalla*, p. 59.)

Landaní, a preparation of gold or silver wire used in gold embroidery.

Langar, the roll of hemp twine used by chhapparbands in weaving chiks. The word seems to have originally signified the weight which hangs at the end of the twine to steady it.

Langot, the strip of wood which covers the hollow handle of a sitár.

Lapetan, a weaver's beam.

Laukí, a gourd.

Laung, cloves.

Lekh, a floating or running account.

Lekhá, a ledger.

Liautí, a framework reel used in silk winding.

Liháf, a quilt, counterpane.

Likhái, wages of the person who traces patterns for embroidery.

Lochdár, springy, bending.

Lohchun, iron-filings.

Lodh, bark of Symplocos racemosa.

Luhiyá, an ironmonger.

Luk, patent leather, varnish.

Lukdár, covered with varnish so as to become like patent leather.

Luksáz, a maker of patent leather and varnish.

M.

Madak, a preparation of opium used in smoking.

Madakwálá, a vendor of the foregoing.

Maháwar, red colour obtained from the lac insect (Coccus lacca.)

Mahín sán, the second circular disc used in cutting precious stones.

Máhi táwa, a frying pan.

Máhrú, the chillam used in smoking *madak*.

Mahtábí, a rocket.

Mahúá, a tree (Bassia latifolia) which gives flowers and fruit. The flowers are used to make liquor and the fruit is eaten: the kernel being used to make oil (*gullú.*)

Maidá, flour.

Maidá-farosh, flour vendor.

Majírá, cymbals of brass.

Majún, an aphrodisiac made of several ingredients, among which is bháng.

Makán, a house: *makán kháta*, an account of proceeds of houses bought for demolition.

Makhmal, velvet: *rúmí makhmal* is a kind imported from Káshání (hence also called *káshání*,) ; it is of various colours, green and red, but yellow is the favorite colour, and is used in making *kafsh.*

Makoi, Sarsaparilla.

Maktúl, (prop. *maftúl*), silk made up in thread for sewing.

Mal, the substance used as a triturating medium in grinding pebbles and crystal for glasses.

Mál, goods, stock : *mál khata,* stock book.

Malhní, a boat 66 feet keel, either *chaugazí* or *tigazí* according to width of beam.

Málí, gardener.

Mál-khata, stock book.

Malláh, a boatman.

Malmal, Indian muslin.

Mandí, a market. They say of Lucknow in Saádat Ali's time that the city consisted of *báwan mandí, tirpan bazár.* A mandí is a market in which, as a rule, only one class of shopkeepers have permanent shops, *e. g.* Chobmandí, Lakarmandí. A bázár is a market to which beopárís come, vend their goods and depart, *e. g.,* Báolí bázár, where weavers and vendors of country cotton fabrics come twice a week, sell their webs, and go away. To trace the names of the original 52 mandís and 53 bázárs of Lucknow, would be to write the history of Lucknow City.

Mani, an emerald or ruby over a rati in weight, bored to wear as a bead.

Manihár, a maker or vendor of bangles.

Mánik, a ruby over one rati in weight.

Manjhá, middle piece of a *kathiya* bambu.

Mánjhí, a steersman or pilot of a boat.

Manjít, a drug used as a dye (Rubia majistha).

Mardána, of or belonging to men.

Márkín, unbleached calico.

Másh, a pulse, a vetch (Phaseolus max).

Máshá, a weight of 8 ratís.

Mashak, a goatskin dressed and sewed up for carrying water.

Mashalchí, a torch bearer.

Máshí, a very dark green.

Masnad takiyá, (also called *gáotakiya*), a large bolster for the back.

Masúr, a kind of pulse (Ervum hirsutum).

Mát, a dye vat.

Matar, pease.

Mathaila, a *bandish* of precious stones (v. p. 120).

Mathor, a large earthen jar.

Matká, a smaller make of the same.

Maulví, Muhammadan priest or teacher.

Máwá, a paste or starch; the base of all perfumes (*sandal ítar).*

Mesha, sheepskin.

Mewa-farosh, fruiterer.

Mína, enamel.

Mína-sáz, enameller.

Mishk, musk, gathered in a bag at the navel of the musk deer.

Misqal, an instrument used to polish metal.

Mizráb, wire guard for the fingers used in playing the *sitár,* *bín,* and other instruments.

Mochí, a shoemaker.

Mon, an earthen pot which holds 20 seers.

Moṇdhá, a stool made of senthá or bambu.

Moth, a kind of pulse, lentil, or vetch.

Motí, a pearl.

Motiyábind, a disease of the eyes : a lense made for persons to wear who are afflicted with the disease.

Muhar, a seal.

Muhar-kan, a seal engraver.

Muhra, a rubber used in making panní and by chhípís.

Mukheri, a Muhammadan (usually Ghosí) who deals in ghí.

Mulamma, plating with gold and silver.

Mulamma-sáz, a gold or silver plater.

Mundí, a wild vegetable (Sphœranthus Indicus).

Múṇg, a pulse, black grain (Phaseolus mungo.)

Múṇgá, coral.

Múṇgiyá, green colour such as is seen in the pod of the pulse called *múṇg.*

Muním, (properly *muníb gomáshta*) an accountant, who is also managing agent.

Múṇj, a grass yielding a fibre for rope and mat making (Saccharum munjúm).

Muqarrarí, fixed, unvarying, (of prices, weights, proportions of ingredients or materials, &c.)

Murabba, a preserve of fruit.

Murabba-níl, an English preparation of indigo blue.

Murassakár, setter of precious stones.

Murdárí, (of hides) stripped from an animal that has died, not been killed by bleeding.

Murgí-andewálá, poulterer and egg-dealer.

Musawwir, painter, designer.

N.

Nafa, profit.

Náfarmání, violet colour.

Nafr, Nafrí, a unit, an individual, a head, e. g., *mazdúrí ek roz das nafrí,* ten men employed one day.

Nag, a gem, counterfeit precious stone.

Nagnasáz, a maker of the foregoing.

Naichá, a huqqá stem or pipe.

Naicheband, a maker of the foregoing.

Náiká, a mistress of a brothel, a *ságin* who has *nauchís.*

Nainsukh, a cotton fabric.

Najja, carpenter.

Nakwá, the sprout of pulse (from its resemblance to the clitoris.)

Nal, drain pipes made by potters.

Nal, horse-shoe.

Nalband, farrier: horse-shoe-smith.

Nám, credit side of account.

Namak, salt; *khárí namak*, the saline substance used by leather dressers.

Nánbáí, baker.

Nánd, an earthern pot.

Nándá, do.

Nandolá, a very large earthen tub.

Nár, a joláhá's shuttle.

Náránjí, orange colour.

Narí, a joláhá's bobbin.

Narkul, (properly, *narkut*) a reed, (Arundo tibialis).

Náryal, a cocoanut, *náryal khushk* (or *gunga*) the blind cocoanut used for making huqqa bowls: *náryal tar*, the fresh cocoanut which yields a kernel and milk.

Náspál, the rind of an unripe pomegranate, used in dyeing.

Náspáti, (properly, *náshpáti*), a pear.

Nauratan, technically, the nine conventional precious stones of the East.

Nauratangír, an armlet, set with the foregoing.

Naushádir, salammoniac.

Nauwán, (of shoes,) No. 9, 'nines,' *i. e.*, nine finger breadths in length.

Nawábi, of, or belonging to, or dating from native rule as opposed to *sirkárí*, meaning English.

Neauchí, a young woman bound to a *sáqin*, and not openly trading for herself.

Nebú, lemon.

Newár, girthing, or girth-web.

Newárbáf, a weaver of the foregoing.

Nigáhdár, (of a lense) convex.

Nigálí, the stem of a chandú pipe; a bambú staff used to hold reels in winding off silk.

Niháí, an anvil.

Nihanni, an instrument used to pare the nails.

Níl, indigo.

Nílá, indigo-blue.

Nílá-ábí, a light blue.

Nílá-dudhiyá-ábí, (also called *firozaí*) a turquoise blue.

Nílak, sheep skin dressed and dyed blue.

Nílam, a sapphire.

Nílá-surmaí, blue colour almost black.

Nílkanthí, a neutral tinted crystal used in making lenses for spectacles.

Nimchikni, an inferior kind of betel nut.

Nímkaurí, berry of the ním tree.

Nirakh, a price prevailing in a bázár.

Nishásta, wheat starch.

Nyáryá, a gold refiner, a gold washer.

O.

Okhalí, an open wooden dish used as a morter in which to crush pulse.

Opní, final smooth polish given to precious stones.

P.

Pachchí, setting a precious stone after the English style.

Pachhelá, an armlet.

Pachmel, unassorted.

Páe áma, trousers, drawers, (vulg. Eng. pánjáms.)

Patrí, a cloth worn round the head by Hindús, as opposed to *ammámah* worn by Mussulmáns. The distinction is now rapidly disappearing.

Pahal, a facet of a precious stone.

Pairí karná, to shear sheep.

Paiwand, a patch.

Paiwar, the first colour extracted from *kusam*.

Palang-posh, a counterpane.

Palledár, a porter, burden bearer.

Pálkí, a palanquin, for four bearers: opposed to *do'í* carried by two.

Pá'kí-gárí, the cab of India.

Pán, leaf of the *Piper-betel*.

Pándán, a box for holding pán.

Pandarahwán, (of shoes) No. 15, or 'fifteens' *i. e.*, fifteen finger breadths in length.

Pán-farosh, a vendor of betel leaf.

Panjah, the toe-piece of shoes.

Panj-shákhá, a chandelier of five lights.

Pankharí, a facet of a precious stone.

Panná, emerald.

Panní, tin foil, brass foil, leather coated with foil.

Panní-sáz, a maker of the foregoing.

Pánsár, treddles of a loom.

Pansarí, a dealer in *kiráná*. (q. v.)

Panserí, a weight of five seers.

Panth, a corporate body, deriving a joint income subsequently divided, the chairman (called *lambardár*,) being the manager.

Panwá, a tiny looking glass worn by children suspended from the neck.

Pánwárí, a wattled enclosure used for pán-cultivation.

Papuya, papaw tree and its fruit (Carica papaya.)

Pará, quicksilver.

Parab, a diamond cut with a horizontal facet above and below.

Parát, a large brass tray.

Parchhattí, a narrow strip of thatch laid along the top of mud walls in the rains to prevent the rain washing them away.

Parchunwálá, a vendor of grain, flour, ghi, salt and oil, and also firewood.

Párí, a lump or cake in which *gur* is made up.

Pashmína, woollen goods imported from Kashmír and the Panjáb.

Pataŋg, sappan wood.

Patáwar, thatching grass.

Patílí, a metal vessel, used in cooking ; holds about 2 seers.

Patsán, the disc used to cut diamonds.

Pattá, a slip of bambu or aught else ; an ornament for the ears.

Pattí, a standard length and width in which tát (coarse bemp canvas) is woven.

Pattí, hoop-iron.

Paṭṭiya, do.

Paṭwá, a maker of petticoat strings, braid, tape, &c.

Páu, ¼ of a seer.

Pauná, the second quality of rice when it is husked.

Páyá, the least valuable class of pearl.

Pizeb, an anklet with bells attached.

Pechkash, a press-man.

Perá, a sweetmeat.

Peshwáz, the upper dress worn by a dancing woman, often worth over Rs. 1000.

Pethá, a kind of gourd.

Pharyá, a vendor of grain within limits of a gunj.

Pharyáh, bordered sheet (generally blue) worn by Kachí and Murao women.

Pherí, the instrument with which a kahár makes *sutlí*.

Pheríwálá, a wandering dealer, hawker, pedlar.

Phirauná, an instrument used for twisting catgut.

Phiṭkirí, alum.

Phúl, a kind of bell metal.

Phuleli, a small leather phial for holding perfumes and medicines.

Phúl-gulábi, a rose colour.

Phuŋkaní, a blow pipe.

Phutkar, retail-selling, broken lots.

Piází, colour of inner part of an onion.

Piází-gulábí, a similar colour but tinged with red.

Píchhe, used like *per* in English, e. g., *min píchhe do rupiyá*, two rupees per maund.

Píli miṭṭí, a cretaceous earth found in river-beds, used to make crucibles.

Pípal, Indian fig tree (Ficus religiosa.)

Piráchiyr, a dealer in remnants and old clothes.

Pisanárí, a woman who gets her livelihood by grinding flour.

Pistaí, the colour of raw pistachio nuts.

Piṭárá, a large basket made of múnj, bambu, or cane

Podína, mint.

Polú, a bundle or packet of cotton thread, containing 20 lachchhis or hanks.

Pola, hollow.

Polkí, a *bandish* of diamonds, (v. p. 119.)

Pot, glass beads.

Pukhráj, topaz.

Puklí, the instrument with which a kahár makes sutlí.

Pula, a wisp of thatching grass, as much as a reaper can grasp in one handful.

Puzáwewálá, a brick-burner.

Q.

Qalaígar, tinman.

Qálib, a dummy used to tie pagris on.

Qálín, a cotton drugget.

Qá'ínbáf, a weaver of the foregoing.

Qand-siyáh-furosh, vendor of gur.

Qarába, a large glass flagon used in India for perfumes, Ganges water, &c., and in Persia for wine.

Qassáb, a butcher.

Qímat, price : *pukhtá qímat*, a fixed or arbitrary price: *ajzi qímat* (of books,) price according to number of sheets.

Qiwám, syrup.

Qulfí, a metal joint for a huqqah stem.

Qulfigar, maker of do'.

R.

Ráb, juice of sugarcane inspissated and boiled.

Rachchá, a leaf of heddles.

Rafúgar, a darner, one who mends holes in shawls and daris.

Ragraisán, the first disc on which precious stones are cut.

Rákh, ashes.

Raṇḍí, a woman, a prostitute.

Rángá, pewter.

Rangaiyá charsá, a leather dyer.

Rangbhurá, a pewterer.

Rangrez, a dyer.

Rangsáz, a painter.

Ránpí, a scraper used in leather dressing.

Ras, juice of the sugarcane.

Rasrí, twine, rope.

Rassibat, rope-maker.

Rati, a berry (the Abrus precatorius); a weight.

Razáí, a padded quilt.

Ráwá, pellets of precious metal which the niyáryá refines.

Ráwá, the pulverized inner husk of wheat.

Reg, dust, sand.

Reg aur kámún, the pulverized husks of rice.

Reṇḍí, castor-oil plant.

Resham, silk.

Resham-farosh, silk vendor.

Rihn, mortgage.

Rikábí, a plate (generally of metal.)

Rírí, a kind of mango.

Rogan siyáh-farosh, oil vendor.

Roghan zird-farosh, ghí vendor.

Rora, fine fragments of brick.

Rozahí, a system of money lending (v: p. 144:)

Roznámchí, a daybook, diary.

Rudegar, catgut-maker.

Rúífarosh, cotton vendor.

Rúíz, the man who applies the ink-roller in a press.

Rúmál, a pocket handkerchief, small shawl, (*literally*, face wiper.)

Rund-kharbúza, papaw.

Rupahlá, made of silver.

Ruqa, a note of hand; a memo: an I. O. U.

S.

Sábun, soap.

Sabun furosh, soap-boiler, soap-vendor.

Sabz, Sabzí, green.

Sádih, plain, unornamented.

Sádah, (of tobacco) opposed to khamírá (leavened.)

Sádekár, a gold and silver smith.

Safed, white, of silver, as opposed to *surkh* (gilt, or of gold.)

Saifa, a book-binder's knife.

Saiqalgar, an armourer.

Sají, an alkaline earth; impure carbonate of soda.

Sikkí, a bark used in dyeing: any astringent bark.

Salemsháhí, a kind of shoe.

Salma, spiral, curled, or coiled gold wire.

Salma-sitárewálá, a dealer in salma and spangles.

Salúká, a short vest with sleeves.

San, hemp, tow, oakum.

Sánchá, a mould.

Sangul, silk from the western frontier.

Singtarásh, a stone-cutter, sculptor.

Sáqin, a female who vends *charas*.

Sárangí, a kind of fiddle.

Saresh, glue.

Sareshsáz, glue-manufacturer.

Sarráf, a money-changer, pawnbroker, vendor of made-up jewellery.

Saro, a form of diamond when cut.

Sarson, mustard plant and seed.

Sathwrá, the tips of the san-plant (Crotolaria juncea) used to make spills.　　[breadths in length.

Satiya, (of shoes,) no. 7, 'sevens,' *i. e.* seven finger

Saunf, aniseed.

Sausní, a bluish shade of lilac.

Sáwán, a grain sprinkled on horse and donkey skins in tanning.

Seb, an apple.

Semal, a tree (Bombax heptaphyllum) yielding cotton; the cotton itself. Natives fondly, but somewhat suggestively, call a smooth, fat woman *semal ki gaddí.*

Seṇdhí, juice of the khajúr, wild date palm.

Senthá, reed grass (Saccharum sara.)

Shaftálú, a peach.

Shágird, an apprentice.

Shákh, a piece (of coral.)

Shálbáf, a shawl weaver.

Shalam, a turnip.

Shamadán, a candlestick.

Shatranjí, a drugget.

Shewálá, a temple devoted to the worship of Shíva. (met. a charcoal kiln.)

Shikanja, a bookbinder's press.

Shíra, the refuse which remains after extracting ráb from sugarcane.

Shír-farosh, milk-vendor.

Shíríní-farosh, vendor of sweetmeats.

Shísha-álát-jarosh, vendor of glass-wares.

Shíshesáz, glass blower.

Shorá, saltpetre.

Shorá qilmí, saltpetre, a kind of, used in fireworks.

Shutari, the colour of camel's hair.

Síkh, a spit.

Síkh, iron in rods.

Sil, a stone used with a slab (*batţá*) for grinding spices and drugs.

Sípí, a shell.

Sirácha, a kind of bambu.

Sira suráhídár, the first class of pearl.

Sir boha, a kind of bambu.

Sirká, vinegar.

Sirkákash, vinegar manufacturer.

Sitkár, Government.

Sarkárí, of, or relating to, or ordained by, Government, English as opposed to *nawabí* (vide verb.)

Sirkí, the tips or upper joints of *senthá* (reed grass.)

Sitár, a kind of fiddle or guitar.

Sitára, a glittering piece of gold, a gold spangle used in embroidery.

Siyáh, black.

Siyáh-bhúrá, brown bordering on black.

Sohágá, borax.

Sohanfárí, filing; ornamental work in gold and silver.

Soná chándí-farosh, dealer in bullion.

Sozankárí, needlework.

Sújá, the bobkbinder's needle.

Sújí, flour.

Sújiwálá, flour vendor.

Suljedár, bent at an obtuse angle (of qulfis.)

Sun thrú, gold or gilt, as opposed to *rupahlá*.

Sunár, a goldsmith.

Sundrí, a fret of a musical instrument.

Súp, a sieve made of *sirkí*.

Supárí, betel-nut.

Surábí, an earthen water bottle.

Sutlí, twine.

T.

Tabala, a drum.

Tabalasáz, a drum maker, a drum beater.

Tablí, the wood over the belly of a sitár, the sounding board.

Tah, a layer.

Tahrí, the bobbin used by a *daríbáf*.

Taká, two paisa.

Takht, a platform.

Talí, dregs.

Talí-nil, dregs of an indigo vat.

Tambákú, tobacco.

Tambákúwálá, tobacconist.

Tambol, pán, betel leaf.

Tamboli, a vendor of betel leaf.

Tambúrá, a tambourine.

Tánk, a weight equal to 24 ratís among Jauharís, but according to some 30 ratís. The word seems to have come from China, but is the basis of Indian weights (cf. *chhaták*, a chittak).

Tanna, the warp.

Tannáí, warping.

Tántiyá, a catgut maker.

Tinzeb, a fine cotton fabric, muslin (lit. body-adorning).

Táo, a batch, or, one might say, ' a go' of anything.

Tár, wire, silver or gold thread.

Tar, (of cocoanuts and fruits), fresh.

Tatuk, a beum, a pole.

Tardbktiya, an artificer who flattens gold thread preparatory to its being woven into gota.

Tárgahan, the perforted bridge through which are carried the strings of a fiddle.

Tárí, toddy, juice of the palmyra.

Tari, refuse, or dregs.

Tárífarosh, vendor of toddy.

Taríf, the valuation, appraisement, good quality of anything, a formula expressing it.

Tariya, an ornament worn on the arm.

Tárkash, a wire drawer, a reeler of wire.

Tashtarí, an earthen or metal pán or plate.

Tasma, a leather strap or thong, one used with a wooden bow to work a gimlet or auger.

Tathiya, a kind of indigo.

Tátiyá, a raft, a chained bundle of bambus, a screen.

Tátpattíwálá, a maker of strips of coarse hemp canvas or sackcloth.

Tattar, a wattle, a screen made of grass.

Tattí, (corrupt, for *tátí*), a matted shutter.

Tattú, pony.

Taul, weight.

Taulái, wages or fees paid to a weighman.

Taulí, a metal vessel.

Taura, a *banaish* of precious stones, (v. p. 120).

Túziya, an emblematic representation of a tomb carried in the Muharram processions.

Telí, an oil presser.

Terahwán, (of shoes), No. 13, 'thirteens, *i. e.*, thirteen finger-breadths in length.

Terhá tár, gold or silver wire flattened out and made in a scalloped pattern, used in zardozí.

Tesú, flowers of the pálas tree.

Tezáb, aquafortis.

Thak, a bambu spike used to shove the quid of chándú into the pipe-bowl.

Thandá, cold, (technically) eléctro-platiug, *thandá mulamma*.

Tháni, a cornfactor.

Tháp, local market weight.

Thappá, a die, a stamp.

Thatherá, a brazier, coppersmith.

Theki, a fuel yard, bambu yard.

Thelgári, a handcart.

Thok, a wholesale consignment.

Tigazi, a kind of boat, 3 yards width of beam.

Tihái, a payment of grain to a village carpenter.

Tikiyá, a wad, a cake of charcoal dust and lime.

Tikoní, triangular.

Til, sesame, an oil seed.

Tilakrí, a facet of a precious stone.

Tilakrídár, cut with many facets above but one level or horizontal facet below.

Tilí, a shawlweaver's bobbin.

Tipái, a three-legged stool, a bench at which an artificer works.

Tiraunthí, a machine used to twist ropes.

Tokna, a brass vessel.

Toah, a weight, one-sixteenth of a seer.

Tomba, a gourd used to make musical instruments.

Tukhm-i-kusum, safflower-seed.

Tun, a tree (Celdrela tuna) yielding an excellent timber.

Tútiyá, tutty, sulphate of copper, blue vitriol.

Túyrh, black mustard, an oil seed.

U.

Udá, brown.

Udakár, marking of outlines in brown colour in preliminary process of calico-printing.

Ughádán, a spittoon.

Ultíchín, a pattern of silk binding on pipe stems.

Ungalí, a finger breadth.

Unnábí, colour of purple grape.

Urd, a black pulse.

Usárá, gamboge.

Uttú, stamping of gold and silver lace so as to impress a pattern by raising and depressing the material.

Uttúsáz, stamper of gold and silver lace.

W.

Waráq, a leaf, gold and silver leaf.

Waraq-sáz, a maker of gold and silver leaf.

Wasíqa, a pension or trust, especially a political pension administered by the British Government as trustee of a defunct native ruler.

Wasíqadár, a pensioner.

Waslí, a paste-board used in book-binding, mill board.

Wazankash, a weighman.

Wiláyatí, English, Afghán, Kábulí.

Y.

Yakka, Yikka, (also *ekka* and *ikka*,) a one-horse conveyance used by natives.

Yikkawálá, an owner or driver of a *yikka*.

Yáqút, a ruby.

Z.

Záfrání, a shade of yellow, saffron colour.

Zambúr, a pair of pincers.

Zamín, *technically*, sandal *itr*, the basis on which are made all other perfumes.

Zamurrad, an emerald.

Zamurradí, emerald green.

Zanána, of and for women, or worn by women.

Zanána jorá, a suit of female clothing.

Zangár, acetate of copper.

Zangár-sáz, a manufacturer of verdigris, acetate of copper.

Zard, yellow

Zard surkhí máil, yellow inclining to red.

Zardoz, a maker of gold and silver embroidery on silk and velvet.

Zargar, a goldsmith.

Zarúf, pl. of *zarf*, a vessel.

Zaruf-birinjí, (properly, *burinji*,) brass-vessels.

Zarúf-gilí, earthenware.

Zarúf-missí, copper vessels.

Zerpáí, a kind of slipper or shoe.

Zerpáí-wálá, a maker of the foregoing.

Zewar, ornaments.

Zír, the treble in music.

For EU product safety concerns, contact us at Calle de José Abascal, 56–1°,
28003 Madrid, Spain or eugpsr@cambridge.org.

www.ingramcontent.com/pod-product-compliance
Ingram Content Group UK Ltd.
Pitfield, Milton Keynes, MK11 3LW, UK
UKHW012200180425
457623UK00020B/310